First as a teacher, then as a pastor, ~~Bob has bro~~ able skills to the task of preparing a "teachable" ~~book that brings~~ together the how and why of prayer. Each chapter chronicles his life experiences and turned them into lessons that will enrich your prayer life. Having used his previous book in an adult Sunday school class, I look forward to the weekly lessons that focus on a single word or concept written to bolster the reader's personal prayer life. This book will engage the reader in the Christian disciplines of study, meditation and prayer.

Dan Mangelsdorf
Bob's friend from across the street
Superintendent of Schools, retired
Gilpin County and Telluride, Colorado

This book was written by one who has a long-time experience of talking with and listening to God. He has made numerous career changes, but always with a determination to share the good news of salvation and only after he became convinced that the Lord would be his strength. He understands that God is Love and that especially when God leads him to accept new challenges he must daily talk to God in prayer and seek strength and guidance from God's inspired word. We recommend his book for anyone who desires to walk with Jesus in Christian love and service.

John Deterding
Pastor Emeritus of St. Lorenz Lutheran Church
Frankenmuth, Michigan USA

KEEP ME AND KEEP ALL *Life's Journey with Prayer* is a must "use" not only "read" for all Christians. While Bob describes his life's journey guided by prayer, this book also becomes a devotional and a personal reflection of the reader's prayer relationship to God. Bob's journey is a great example of how God sends, man responds, and God blesses. After reading each chapter with themes like

"Doubting," "Confidence," "Helplessness," "Growing," Bob asks the question, "What example in my life is similar and how do I now respond?" Bob's purpose in sharing his wisdom and experiences is to encourage the reader's prayer life.

Having served with Bob and Alice in Michigan, Hong Kong and Indonesia, wonderful personal memories returned as I read the book. As friend and co-worker, I can say from personal experience that Bob definitely "walks the talk." It's his prayer that you will as well.

Darrell Van Luchene D.Litt.
Coordinator Emeriti of Pelita Harapan Schools
Lippo Karawaci, Indonesia

In this book, Bob Smith provides a wonderful description of ways in which a Christian can and should develop his prayer life. Prayer is the vehicle that keeps us connected with God.

Rev. Jim Weber
German Pastor
St. Lorenz Lutheran Church
Frankenmuth, Michigan

This little book contributes significantly and practically to one's understanding of prayer. Having been a prayer partner of Bob for several years I know of his commitment to and his appreciation of the value of a regular, prayerful conversation with God. Insightful and instructive, the book captures Bob's devotion to his prayer life and challenges its readers to enrich and enhance their own conversations with our Lord and Savior.

Dr. Harlan Lyso
Retired Headmaster
Seoul Foreign School
Seoul, Korea

It was a privilege to be asked by Pastor Bob Smith to read proof on his book of the art and joy of praying. His detailed and well explained message on how to live a prayerful life brought a smile to my heart, a prayer to my lips, and a greater understanding of my journey here on earth while preparing for life hereafter. A major lesson learned from these writings is... 'Being prayerful is being peaceful!'

Gretchen A. Rau
Frankenmuth News Writer
Frankenmuth, Michigan
Retired

With this updated edition of his helpful and inspirational book, Pastor Smith shares new stories from his ministry to demonstrate how an active, intentional prayer life continues to provide him with strength and wisdom to meet ministry challenges. We can all learn something from reading this book."

Rev. Mark Brandt
Administrative Pastor
St. Lorenz Lutheran Church
Frankenmuth, Michigan

# KEEP ME AND KEEP ALL

*Life's Journey with Prayer*

## Robert W. Smith

### Illustrations

### By

### Wilis Sumargo & Harold Eckert

# Dedication

To my wife, Alice, who fits the words of this poem so well.


"Love without a Net"
By
Roy Croft

I love you, not only for what you are
But for what I am when I am with you.

I love you, not only for what
You have made of yourself
But for what you are making of me.

I love you for the part of me
That you bring out; I love you
For putting your hand into my heaped-up heart
And passing over all the foolish, weak things
That you can't help dimly seeing there,
And for drawing out into the light
All the beautiful belongings
That no one else had looked
Quite far enough to find.

I love you because you are helping me to make
Of the lumber of my life, not a tavern
But a temple; out of works of my every day,
Not a reproach but a song.


Also to our sons, Kurtis and Eric; our daughters in love, Teresa and Susie; our eight grandchildren; Sophia, Jeffrey, Naomi, Timothy, Ellesha, Scott, Kennedy, and Christina.

# CONTENTS

**Section I**
**PRAYER THOUGHTS..... 25**

**Chapter**                                                 **Page**

## Section II
### PRAYER QUESTIONS..... 237

## Section III
## PRAYER INSIGHTS..... 297

# Acknowledgments

This book would not have been completed without the unselfish assistance of so many of my friends and my faithful wife, Alice, who prayed with me and for me. Curtis Lowen, Sue Van Luchene, Dennis Denow, Sinta Lucia, Monica Belcourt volunteered many hours toward making it appear that my command of the English language is considerably better than it actually is for the previous printing of parts of this book. I am grateful to those who read all or part of the manuscript and provided valuable suggestions for this second edition: Gretchen Rau, Jim Weber, Christopher Gioe, Karen Rummel and my wife Alice. Wilis Sumargo contributed the original artwork. Harold Eckert sketched the cover and two additional illustrations. Dan Mangelsdorf and others offered personal support and encouragement for this rewriting and printing. Thank you, most of all, to our Lord Jesus, for answering my prayer that I might bring this second book into a reality.

# Foreword

**B**ob Smith. It is a simple name. Bob Smith, the man I call my husband, is not a simple man. He would disagree, but then he is not me. I feel very blessed to be called Mrs. Bob Smith. During our marriage of forty-five years, we have lived and worked in four states and on five continents, resulting in a kaleidoscope of adventures, people and places. Dear friends, relatives, colleagues and students from all over the world continue to touch our lives through shared experiences, phone calls, correspondence and connections on the Internet.

The Greek philosopher Socrates advised each individual to "Know thyself". Throughout his adult life, Bob attempted to know himself better as a Christian man of God. I witnessed my husband evolve from a typical young college student into an outstanding educator and administrator who eventually earned two advanced degrees and several honors. He has also been a parish pastor, chaplain, university lecturer, public speaker and writer. Since Bob is my husband, I can testify to his Christian faith and lifestyle. His disciplined daily life, his passion, excitement and confidence are infectious, a rich blessing to his family, the Christian church, and the communities where he has lived and worked.

Driven by his quest to share his signature strengths, Christian beliefs, and enduring values with his children and grandchildren, Bob decided to become an author. I agree with the Rev. Rick Warren's statement, "Life-changing books are written by changed lives." For many readers, Bob Smith's first book was a life-changing book.

*Keep Me from Evil, Harm and Fear* (2004) was published while we lived in Indonesia. It was a compilation of autobiography, thoughts on prayer, and a challenge to implement a more active personal prayer life. This little book took on a life of its own and many people wanted to have a copy. The second edition (2005) was a translation of the book into Bahasa Indonesian. That year, Universitas Pelita Harapan, the university where Bob worked, gave a copy of the book to each of its one thousand graduates. Still more people asked for copies.

Following his retirement, Bob felt compelled to update, rename and restructure the book. Keep Me and Keep All -*Life's Journey with Prayer* is the result of that endeavor.

Now, go ahead, join him in his journey. My prayer for you, as he leads you along the path of his *Life's Journey with Prayer*, is that you, too, will be forever transformed through his inspiring words. To God be the glory!

Alice E. Smith

# INTRODUCTION

W hen I was nine years old, I received this wall decoration for a
Christmas present from Immanuel Lutheran Sunday School,
Rock Island, Illinois. Each letter of the words in the prayer glowed
in the dark.

> Bless, Savior dear
> Be always near.
> Keep me (and keep all)
> From evil, harm, and fear.
> Amen

I hung the prayer on the wall across from the foot of my bed.
By doing this, I could read it every night before I went to sleep.
When I first received it, the words "and keep all" were not included.
I don't remember when I actually changed the original. The Holy
Spirit reminded me that what was good for me may also be good
for others, so one night I added "and keep all." Speaking this prayer
became a nightly ritual and was the starting point of a lifetime
journey with prayer for me. Over sixty years later I continue to
include these words in my daily prayers.

If I could change any one aspect of my life, it would be to pray
more often. Now, it is my prayer that especially my grandchildren
will catch the spirit of what these pages are all about. I want them
to have firsthand knowledge of the power of God and to know that
Christ is alive and active today. Writing it down is the best way I

know of giving it to them. You are invited to look over their shoulder as they read their grandfather's book on prayer. May the insights gained be remembered and applied to your own spiritual maturity for a lifetime of prayer.

Part of this book on prayer was first compiled for Seoul Foreign School (SFS) students to guide their studies while at Jesus Abbey in the T'aebaek Mountains of South Korea during SFS Discovery Week of 1997. Prayer has been the motivation behind Jesus Abbey since its beginning in 1965. It was "to be a house dedicated primarily to intercessory prayer for individual needs...for revival in the church, for the nation of Korea...for world peace and world evangelism." Prayer is a frequent theme in Scripture. For the permanent residents of Jesus Abbey it has become a lifestyle. About 10,000 guests visit Jesus Abbey each year. It has been a pleasure for me to be part of this community of prayer warriors who were led by Father Archer Torrey III.

We may express our belief that God can answer prayer. Yet there is a big gap between what we say and what we do. Let us follow the path beyond the status quo, break through the barriers of doubt, and into a new level of being on fire with prayer. Let us be driven to our knees, into prayer closets, as well as into group prayer.

I have discovered that average Christians want to improve their conversations with God. Because so many Christians - new and old alike - know so little about prayer, my wish is to share some simple basic truths and answer some vital questions about the art of praying.

Section One in my book is the story of how prayer has enriched my relationship with God. He gave me strength, hope and encouragement to overcome my fears as I was exposed to different experiences along my journey of life. This book is my spiritual autobiography about the discipline of prayer. I have selected fifty-two key words that have cultivated my life of prayer. These words are trucks to carry my thoughts about prayer to you. They could guide a reader's prayer life for an entire year. One chapter could be used for each week. I also included several questions in the "Personal Reflection Time." They are to stimulate thoughts on how you might apply this chapter to your own life. I purposely did not include a written prayer. I want you, the reader, to create and carry on your own conversation with God.

Section Two contains fifty-two questions I have personally been asked about prayer. To each one I present my answer, a passage that I believe applies from Scripture, tips I have compiled from other experts over the years, and space for you to write your own answer. They could be combined with the fifty-two devotional words from Section One.

Section Three offers questions for you to use to examine your own prayer life. Hopefully you will develop a vision for your life's journey with prayer and how you will achieve it. Forming a vision is well within the capabilities of any average person.

Too many of us need to slow the pace of our lives and adjust our priorities so that communication with God can become our top priority. I want to challenge each of you to set a new vision for your life with prayer.

The writing of this book has helped me to learn more about how to pray. It has also taught me there is so much more that I don't know. May this book inspire, teach, and coach you to spend more time plugging into God's hotline of power through prayer.

In His Service,
Bob
Dad
Grandpa
Uncle Bob
Mr. Bob
Mr. Smith
Coach
Pastor
Chaplain
Rev. Bob Smith
Rev. Robert W. Smith

Section I

# PRAYER THOUGHTS

Some go to prayer, not to ascertain the will of God,
but to ask Him to do that which they have fully set their minds.

# 1

# Jesus

*After He had dismissed them, He went up on a mountainside by Himself to pray. Later that night, He was there alone* (Matthew 14:23).

E ven though we sat in front of our television on the opposite side of the world on September 11, 2001, in Lippo Karawaci, a suburb of Jakarta, Indonesia, my wife and I saw the second plane hit the World Trade Center building. Etched into our minds are pictures no one could ever expect or imagine: a jet liner plowing into a skyscraper. There were clouds of smoke and fire billowing into the sky. Millions of tons of concrete collapsed like a house of cards and turned into dust and rubble. American citizens ran through the streets of New York City in terror. Firemen, policemen and others were coated in ash and soot. It seemed like a movie, but it wasn't; it was real life.

I'm sure that many passengers in the four jets that crashed on that day were terrified in those last few minutes. It was one of those "I-can't-believe-this-is-happening-to-me" experiences. There were, no doubt, screams of fright and despair. I wonder how many were calling on God in prayer. Perhaps nearly all were.

I wonder how many of the victims knew how to pray to God. I once heard that the true test of a Christian is how they act when

No man is greater than his prayer life. *Leonard Ravenhill*

something unexpected happens. Those who have a close relationship with the Lord before surprises will be ready to turn to Him in emergencies. They will be prepared. Sincere Christians will have identified with the same request made by the disciples, "Lord, teach us to pray." Jesus, of course, is our best model to follow for knowing how and when to pray. He often went to quiet places to communicate with His Father. In fact, He built his entire life and ministry on prayer. The Bible tells us Jesus prayed:

> **When He was busy.** Jesus got up "a great while" before daybreak to pray (Mark 1:35). He knew that time with the Father should come before time with people.
> **When He was tired.** Once after a full day of work Jesus asked His disciples to go to the other side of the sea. Then He sent the people away and went up on a mountain to pray (Matt. 14:23). At a time when we might have said we were too tired to pray, Jesus prayed.
> **When He had decisions to make.** Before He chose His apostles, Jesus spent the whole night in prayer (Luke 6:12).
> **When He prepared to start his new ministry.** After His baptism Jesus was led by the Spirit into the wilderness to spend forty days fasting and praying (Luke 4:1-2).
> **When He faced the cross.** Jesus prayed for three hours in Gethsemane before He went to His trial and crucifixion (Matt. 26). A long time of prayer can prepare us for facing trials and sacrificial service.

Prayer has power. "What is the source of that power", you might ask, "so I can tap into it?" A person walks into a dark room, flips a light switch, and presto - the room is bathed in light! Is the person who is flipping the switch the power source of that light? People say there is power in prayer. Does this mean that our prayer words, by themselves, can make things happen? There is power in prayer because God, for Jesus' sake, promises to hear and answer the fervent prayers of a righteous person, a person made righteous by Jesus Christ's death and resurrection.

If Jesus needed to pray, how can we do less?

Following Jesus' example will help us to keep the power turned on. He not only set an example, but He also told His disciples what to pray. In Luke 11:2 He said to them, *"When you pray, say: 'Our Father... (Luke 11:1-4),'"* and proceeded to give them the Lord's Prayer.

Let me remind you of what Matt. 6:7 says, too. *"And when you pray, do not keep on babbling like pagans, for they think they will be heard because of their many words."*

The power of prayer is available only through the Word of God and the work of the Holy Spirit. For just as putting water into an automobile's gas tank cannot propel it, so also watered down man-made plans and goals cannot fuel us. We need first and foremost the power of God's living Word for us to reach our peak potential.

Let's be honest. Why is it, that we are not more active in sincere prayer? Christians struggle with periods of stagnant prayer. The dullness may be due to sin in our life – in that case we need to repent and pray. Business, discouraged by grief, no answers, and out of the habit, are common excuses. I also believe prayerlessness exists simply because we do not believe that it will make a difference. If we actually believed that prayer would make a change in our lives, in our families, in our marriages, schools, and the churches, then we would pray regularly, urgently and persistently. Join me in asking God to lead us to be prayer warriors in His mighty army of servants, moving ahead to conquer giants of fear and evil, boldly proclaiming His love and forgiveness.

Jesus used prayer to its full potential. My continuing prayer is: "Lord, teach me to use prayer to its potential in my life."

### Personal Reflection Time

1.  When have you had an "I-can't-believe-this-is-happening-to-me" experience in your life?

2.  How do you model Jesus' prayer life?

3.  What do you do to overcome times of prayerlessness?

Do not make prayer a monologue -- make it a conversation.

## 2

# Learning

*He said to them, 'When you pray, say: 'Our Father,...'*
*(Luke 11:1-4).*

The seed was planted when he was a boy of 8 or 9 living in Rock Island, Illinois. He would run across the street to visit the Manglesdorf family, who had three boys, Bob, Ken and Dan. It was great to enter their home. This little boy knew there was something special about them. Their family was filled with love. He found out it was the love of Jesus Christ that permeated the Manglesdorf family. In many ways they treated him as part of their family, except he didn't kiss Marie, the mother, 'good-bye' when they went out to play, as Danny did. There were the times when he knocked on the door and a big tall man, Herman Manglesdorf, the father, would come to open it. With his good sense of humor he would ask, "Who are you?" The lad would quickly respond, "I'm the little boy from across the street." He would point in the direction of his home. That was the cue to enter the house. From then on a good time was had by all.

The little guy came from across the street from a loving family of six. Mom and Dad and three children named Albert, Mary, and Kathryn. Later the little boy came along as an afterthought. He believed he had the greatest childhood of all. However, at this

A child of God can see more on his knees than a philosopher on his tiptoes.

point in his parents' lives, attending church was not a priority on Sunday mornings. His parents did go on special occasions, but not regularly. Nevertheless, they did believe it was important for him to go to Sunday school. It was not the highlight of his week. The Sunday morning ritual was to receive ten cents from his mother for the bus to Sunday school, five or ten cents for the Sunday school offering and ten cents to return by public transportation. He would go a block and a half down to Seventh Avenue to the bus stop. Sometimes when it finally came he would purposely take two steps back and refuse to get on the bus. Then he would go home and tell his mother that there was no bus. He knew it wasn't honest, but there were two reasons why he didn't want to go. One was to keep the money that was given to him for transportation and the offering. His mother would forget to ask for it back. He would use it later for special treats.

The other reason was even sadder. He deeply disliked the Sunday school class. His classmates were very knowledgeable about who Jesus was and knew other common stories of the Bible, because during the week they attended the Christian day school that was connected to the church. Because they understood so much, he was laughed at when the teacher asked him, "Who was Mary? Who was Joseph? Who was Jesus?" He had no clue. As a result, the rest of the class quietly chuckled at his answers. The only bright spot was that the Manglesdorf family would usually give him a ride home in their black Ford car.

One summer Danny and his parents made a special effort to invite the little neighbor kid to their church's weekday parochial school. He refused after asking about their sports program. It was non-existent. Playing sports was his number one priority in life, so he resisted with vigor. The "little boy from across the street" was to learn later in life that victories in sports were not as important as the victory that Christ won for him on the cross. If by now you haven't figured it out, that little boy was me, Robert (Bob) Wayne Smith.

I began playing softball the summer after my third grade at Longfellow Grade School. Every time our school's fifth and sixth grade softball team had a game at Lincoln Park, I was there to

God's promises are always broader than our prayers.

watch. During one game, the team was short one player and I was asked to fill-in. Of course, I was placed in right field. Throughout the game I hoped that the ball wouldn't be hit in my direction. My teammates probably thought the same. "Let's hope they don't hit it to Bobby Smith; he's sure to make an error." That was stage number one of my baseball career. I was fearful of making a mistake.

Stage two began the next year. Since I had filled in for one game the year before, I was allowed to play on the team again, even though I wasn't old enough. Now I knew that I would get a few balls hit my way in center field. This time I thought, "I hope I don't make too many errors." I had a little less fear of making a fool of myself.

As I advanced in my baseball playing days, I went through two more stages. I enjoyed playing and knew I could be successful. This third stage was positive, but still I wasn't at my peak performance. It was not until I played as a catcher that I realized how much I wanted to play baseball. I wanted to catch and hit both on high school and college teams. In my mind I challenged them, "Just try to keep me off the field!" I looked forward to every opportunity with passion. As I look back, I realize that my problem was that I didn't go through these stages fast enough as an athlete. I missed out being a better athlete in all my playing of baseball, basketball, and football, because I didn't have enough confidence in my ability. God had given me the tools to use, but I didn't reach my potential as soon as was hoped.

Now how do these athletic experiences relate to my prayer life? I think there have been similar stages in learning to pray with power. At stage one, I was taught that I could pray by my Sunday school teacher in about third grade. I was given the prayer referred to in the introduction of this book as a Christmas present. I made sure to attend when Christmas came to receive the present of the year. Once it was a plaque that glowed at night and could be hung on a wall. It said this prayer:

The Lord's Prayer may be committed to memory quickly,
but it is slowly learned by heart. *Frederick Denison Maurice*

Bless, Savior dear
Be always near.
Keep me (and keep all)
From evil, harm, and fear.
Amen

At that time, I was a very poor reader and was not sure what the words meant and to whom I was praying. All I knew was that the Sunday school teacher said it was good to pray. So I did it.

I needed to learn to follow Jesus' example. He not only was a model but He also told His disciples what to pray. In Luke 11:2 He said to them, *"When you pray, say: 'Our Father... (Luke 11:1-4),'"* and proceeded to give them the Lord's Prayer.

Oswald Hoffmann once said this: "The Lord's Prayer is the beginning of prayer, not the end. It is for people who want to learn how to pray... The first gesture has to be a hand reached out to God, as to a father. The hand is not a fist; it is open, ready to receive."

I don't know about you but I've learned many years ago to keep my hand open and be a lifetime learner when it comes to prayer.

### Personal Reflection Time

1. Who taught you how to pray?

2. What was the first prayer you learned?

3. What is the latest thing you have learned about prayer?

Speech distinguishes men from animals, but speech rising into prayer distinguishes the children of God from the children of this world.

# 3

# Growing

*Before they call I will answer; while they are still speaking
I will hear* (Isaiah 65:24).

By high school I was praying a little more, especially when I had a crisis situation. Stage two had arrived. I was progressing in my prayer life. A youth Bible class teacher suggested that we begin each day with prayer. I respected him, so I tried to do it, but usually I forgot. During my adolescent years I received a prayer book as a gift, called <u>Teenagers Pray</u>. It was on my shelf, but very seldom read. However, the summer before college I was convinced I should use it. To teach myself to pray in the morning, I put the prayer book on the one pair of shoes I consistently wore. The deal I made with myself was to pray before I put on my shoes. It worked!

Stage three began and continued as I studied God's Word and became surrounded by other strong praying Christians. Sports no longer were my number one priority in life; it was my relationship with Jesus. I now knew He was my personal Lord and Savior, God's Son. Therefore, I watched and listened to my mentors who supported and encouraged me. Yes, I wanted to be a man of prayer, while providing for a wife and sons, teaching school, directing youth programs, coaching sports, shepherding a congregation, and administering a Christian day school. There were quality times of prayer

Devotion to God and devotion to prayer are one and the same thing.

and then there were just prayer times, because it seemed to be the thing to do. There is no doubt in my mind that God has blessed my life with answers to my prayers despite my feeble efforts. But I remained in stage three, playing on God's team, learning to pray.

One day in Nigeria, I prayed one of my shortest prayers. I cried, "Help!" This was when our car caught fire in the city of Kano after we had taken another missionary to the airport. We were in the middle of the busiest intersection in this huge city right at 12:00 noon. Hundreds of Nigerians were on lunch break. Our car stopped running and I had my head down turning the key when my wife said, "I think the car is on fire." When I looked up I discovered she was right. *"Yikes!"* Smoke was coming out from under the hood. I told my wife to steer the car from her passenger's seat, and I would push it to the side of the road.

Finally after fumbling around, I opened the hood and found a small fire. Since I'm not a mechanic or fireman, I thought maybe the best thing to do was to run. By this time we were the center attraction for what seemed like the whole city. One very smart young man went over to a dirt pile, picked some up, returned and threw it on the right place. It was put out. With the excitement gone, everyone started to walk away. At that moment I silently bowed my head and said a prayer, "Help!" I didn't have a clue what I was going to do next in this strange city where I did not know the language. Immediately, a Nigerian man said, "Do you need help?" It was in English. My affirmative answer came back quickly. He said, "I'll be right back." He walked to a parked taxi and borrowed some tools. Within ten minutes he had us back on the road. God provided an answer to my prayer before I could pray it specifically.

There are innumerable stories of how great God is at answering prayers as we have traveled and lived around the world. Yet it was not until our move to Korea that I think I moved into stage four. When I was at that stage in my athletic career, I felt I was reaching my peak performance. Although there is always room for improvement, this is how I presently feel about my prayer life. It has been a combination of experiences that has influenced me. The list starts with a prayer chapel, and continues with Bible study, Jesus Abbey, Moms

Prayer is not conquering God's reluctance, but laying hold of His willingness.

In Touch, reading many prayer books, a Promise Keepers account-ability group, prayer partners, Habitat for Humanity, Missionaries of Charity India trips, a Papua trip, the Afghanistan experience, and the list goes on. All have helped to lift me to stage four. The most important responsibility I have as a Christian pastor is to pray for my family, parishioners, students, friends, world leaders, the spread of the Gospel message, workers for the harvest, and personal concerns. It is not a problem, but a privilege. There is no way I can help this world more than to spend time in prayer.

Sadly, many Christians pray, but they really don't expect an answer. I heard this story from Adrian Rogers. A Sunday school teacher who had her children write letters to a missionary they had been praying for. The teacher explained that missionary was very busy and wouldn't have time to send a reply to every child, so they should not expect to hear back from him. One little girl wrote this letter: "Dear Mr. Smith, I am praying for you. But I really don't expect an answer." Are you like that? You pray, but you aren't really expecting an answer?

God answers all prayers and every prayer of His true children who truly pray. God is waiting to be put to the test by His people in prayer.

- He invites and commands us to carry on a loving conversation with Him.
- Failure to pray is just plain foolish.
- Failure to pray is an insult to almighty God.
- Failure to pray is a sin.
- Failure to pray is a tragedy.
- Proper prayer is a source of power that is untapped by most Christians.
- Proper prayer can meet every need in our lives.
- Proper prayer can be done by each one of us.
- Proper prayer is also a privilege and an opportunity.
- Proper prayer is a blessing.
- Proper prayer can be a priority in your life.
- You can be taught how to pray properly.

To be little with God is to be little for God.

- Decide now to grow in understanding how to pray.

## Personal Reflection Time

1. There were five frogs on a log – 3 decided to jump off – How many were left? [Five, the three that decided, never did do it.]

2. How would you apply this illustration to prayer?

3. Do you expect an answer to your prayers?

The devil has to work hard for all he gets in the home of a praying mother or father.

# 4

# Doubting

*But when you ask, you must believe and not doubt, because the one who doubts is like a wave of the sea, blown and tossed by the wind. That person should not expect to receive anything from the Lord. Such a person is double-minded and unstable in all they do* (James 1:6-8).

Coach Stan Patrick said, "Smith, I hope someday you become a coach, so you will realize how difficult it is to put a team together." It was the week before the first game of our basketball season at Belvidere High School, Belvidere, Illinois. In no way did he want me to miss practice time on the court. I had just asked if he would permit me, a junior player, to be absent a couple of practices that Friday and Saturday. I wanted to go to a Christian retreat for all Lutheran high school youth in the area. I'm glad I chose to go. It was a life-changing experience.

The theme of the weekend was: "Here am I. Send me!" It came from the verse Isaiah 6:8. *Then I heard the voice of the Lord saying, "Whom shall I send? And who will go for us?" And I said, "Here am I. Send me!"*

- Isaiah saw the Lord in all His MAJESTY. He saw the King of Kings! "Holy! Holy! Holy!"

We lie to God in prayer if we do not rely upon Him after prayer.

- Isaiah saw the Lord's MERCY. "Woe is me! I am a sinner!" He was overwhelmed by his sin.
- Isaiah saw the Lord's MISSION. "Here am I. Send me." He responded to the call for someone to go.

The more I understood Isaiah's vision, the more I heard a call and saw a vision being directed to me. As I looked around I saw and knew many others with far more talents and abilities than I had. I was just an ordinary guy with an ordinary name of Bob Smith. I think God looked over the crowd to find a young man weak enough to do His work. *"His strength is made perfect in our weakness..."* (2 Corinthians 12:9).

By the end of the weekend I saw the vision of a mighty God asking me to become a full-time partner in some unknown way. I proceeded to pray that the Lord would use me for His work. In my mind I was waving my hand like a windshield wiper so God could find me. "Here am I, Bob Smith, send me!" Little did I know how far I would be sent. Yet, it was a beginning of a lifelong journey around the world. This was a prayer that continues to be answered today. I saw the vision. I kept the vision and tried to obey the vision since experiencing that special weekend.

Before attending the conference there were those who asked what my plans were after high school. My response was "I'm not sure." I really didn't know what I wanted to do. From that point on when people asked what I was going to be, there was no doubt. I told them I was going to be a pastor. However, the closer I came to those college days the more I "chickened out." I was afraid to even try since, at that time, the Lutheran church required pre-seminary and seminary students to learn Latin, German, Greek, and Hebrew. I was having trouble speaking English and had failed my first year of Latin in high school. It was good that the church had other avenues to serve. I decided to become a Lutheran School teacher instead.

Over the years there was never too much doubt that I was led by the Holy Spirit to serve as a teacher and pastor. I've learned that doubt means being double-minded or saying yes and no at the same time. Doubt can be both positive and negative. However,

Cold prayers, like cold suitors, never make much headway.

doubting can hold God at arm's length. Doubt does happen but it should never be so great that it could cause you to abandon your faith.

Faith and trust are the foundation of prayer. "Have faith in God." "Trust in the Lord." They are the keys to a strong prayer life. I believe doubt comes from undernourished faith and trust. How then is a believer to grow and trust the promises of God?

The first thing John the Baptist did when he or his disciples were in doubt was to send two disciples straight to Jesus to talk to Him. The conversation they had with Him pointed them to the facts of Jesus' actions on earth. Christianity is grounded in the fact of God's entrance into human history in the person of Christ. Christ's entrance into the human sphere is open to examination by non-Christian and Christian alike, and the doubter will find compelling evidence in support of Christ's claims. We have solid reasons for making a total commitment to Him. His entrance is verifiable by way of His resurrection. Remember, He showed Himself alive after His passion by many infallible proofs (Acts 1:3) - eye witness proof.

When in doubt go to God in prayer. The greater the challenge the greater the trust needed. Ask Him to fill you up with His Holy Spirit. He will give you the mighty power that comes from heaven. He will fill your soul up to the point that there will be no way to doubt God.

The center of faith and trust is God. Faith and trust perfected, is prayer perfected. Faith and trust is not a belief that God <u>can</u> bless, that He <u>will</u> bless, but that He <u>does</u> bless, here and now. Trust always operates in the present tense. What prayer needs at all times, is abiding and abundant faith and trust.

**Without a doubt show others that Jesus is the answer to all:**

- He is the solution for every problem,
- He is the escape for every temptation,
- He is the comfort for every sorrow,
- He is the victory for every battle,
- He is the wisdom for every decision,

Morning prayer leads to evening prayer.

- He is the hope for every tomorrow,
- He is the one to go to in prayer.

### Personal Reflection Time

1. Have you answered the call of God to serve? If so, when was it?

2. How do you overcome doubt in your prayer life?

3. I dare you to doubt your doubts!

Praying hands are dearest in the sight of God above,
for in their sweet and earnest clasp are reverence and love.

Our ability to stay with God in the prayer closet,
is the measure of our ability to stay with God when we are outside of it.

# 5

# Closet

*But when you pray, go into your room, close the door and pray to your Father, who is unseen. Then your Father, who sees what is done in secret, will reward you (Matthew 6:6).*

To be the manager of the Concordia College Canteen in St. Paul, Minnesota was a special privilege. It was an answer to my prayer. The Lord knew I needed the money to help pay college costs. This was a major challenge, because I had to put myself through without any financial support. However, this position did more for me than give me money; it encouraged my growth in prayer.

After I closed the canteen at night I found myself alone in the larger administration building. Down the hallway under a staircase was a very small prayer chapel. It became my regular habit to stop in and spend some time kneeling in prayer. Here was the secret place where I communicated to my God the struggles of surviving as a college student. Here the Lord and I carried on a conversation about my needs and desires.

Money always seemed to be on my prayer list, especially when I transferred to Concordia Teachers College in River Forest, Illinois. There were always tuition costs, books, and room and food bills coming due. Finally, during my third year I couldn't stall the accounting office any longer. They insisted that I come up with the money the first Monday in May. God brought several situations together before

The prayer closet is the best school for Christian workers.

that date to provide the answer to my money problems. I was paid by the YMCA where I was working on Saturday nights from 6:00 to 12:00. Also, Concordia College paid me for working on their gym crew on special occasions. Finally on Sunday afternoon my parents brought a special Catholic friend of our family to visit me. Her name was Etta Lamb. During the visit she told me to close my eyes and open my hands. She placed four fifty-dollar bills into my hands. It was a great blessing to see God at work. After paying off my college debt I discovered about one dollar and fifty cents was left. Cheers!

One common desire for a young man was to find a wonderful young Christian girl who would eventually be his lifetime bride. Now this wasn't always at the top of my prayer list, but I thought about it in my prayer closet. Surely the Lord was preparing someone for me, but who could she be? No one seemed to "click" during the early college years. Finally, after an intern-teaching experience in Frankenmuth, Michigan, I returned to Concordia for my senior year. Mike Bauer, the "Joe College" type, was another senior friend who was also scouting the same field. He and I made a pact with one another. We decided we would take a different girl out every weekend. Also, we concluded it wasn't good to take a date to a movie. A movie did not give us enough time to get to know the person. So we had two objectives: find a girl and do something creative. Being in the Chicago area provided the variety of activities: car shows, sporting events, flower shows and plays. There was always something to do. To find girls that would go out with us was the challenging part. We continued on our adventure from September into March. Then after one Saturday night I went to Mike and told him I could no longer keep this up. I had to take last week's date out again. She was a beautiful young lady whom I had met three years previously but did not have sense enough to date her earlier. A year and a half later on August 7, 1965 Alice Evangeline Kratt became the Lord's answer to being my lifetime partner. God knew that I needed a farmer's daughter from Minnesota just like her. Alice had the Christian faith, background, talents, gifts, interests, beauty and personality to meet the challenges of the years to come. I can never praise Him enough for this answer to prayer. Not only was

The prayer closets of God's people are where the roots of the church grow.

she a great choice, but also, Alice brought the prayerful support of Christian parents. I am especially confident that God heard the hours of prayer concerns conveyed to His throne by Clara Kratt, Alice's mother, our faithful prayer partner for so many years.

Clara was an outstanding example of a lady who used her prayer closet faithfully. She lived out her 101 years witnessing and praying for others. The Rev. Eugene Chase, her pastor, told us this story at her funeral: When he walked into her room at the senior home to give communion the last time, he attempted to shut the door. She said, "No, keep the door open. I want the resident across the hall to hear your message. I've been praying for her." I will not forget finding among her things the student and teacher manuals she had used as a teacher for 50 years of Sunday school classes. Reading God's word and praying was a way of life for Clara Kratt.

A story comes from Africa about an entire village of people who became believers. They were told to learn to pray individually in their own privacy. Since they had no closet doors to close, they each selected their own location in the jungle near their village. As they daily walked back and forth on their own footpath, the grass disappeared. Eventually others could recognize whether or not a person was spending time in prayer. It became a habit when they saw another's footpath fill with grass to say to that individual: "Grass is growing on your path." It was a gentle reminder. They wanted that person to be spending time in conversation with God.

### Personal Reflection Time

1. Where is your prayer closet?

2. Give an example of how God has answered a prayer you repeatedly prayed over and over for a long period of time.

3. May I gently leave you with a challenge? **Don't let the grass grow on your path to prayer.**

Prayer is the language of a man burdened with a sense of need. *E.M. Bounds*

# 6

# Confidence

*Let us then approach the throne of grace with confidence, so that we may receive mercy and find grace to help us in our time of need* (Hebrews 4:16).

"Where are you from?" It is a very common question when you are in a different culture. We have always answered, "Frankenmuth, Michigan". As a married couple we lived there for 14 years. I personally had two more years of teaching there when I was single. Both of our sons, Kurtis and Eric, were born while living there. The impact on us by the people and the church history can't be overstated. God often used friends as answers to our prayers for help. It was there, I matured as a responsible Christian and my prayer life moved forward. There were many incidents where only God could have been involved to make things happen as they did. People who provided support when it was needed were; Grandma Rose Herzog, Pastor John Deterding, Principal Walter Bleke, St. Lorenz teachers, an insurance salesman, the city mayor, local businessmen and women, and many more. We were helped just when the struggles were the greatest as we jumped in and out of their lives as we came back to Frankenmuth from overseas. God's timing has always been perfect. He knew our wants and desires before we had a chance to bring them to His throne. When I go around a room full of people we know in Frankenmuth, I can remind each one how

No operator assistance is necessary. God can be dialed direct.

they were used by God as a blessing to us. The foundation for the rest of our lives was set in this place. Below are three examples which I would like to share that brought me more confidence in prayer.

I remember Louie Armbrecht, an 8th grade teacher at St. Lorenz and one of my mentors, giving a talk on prayer to our Parent Teachers' League in about 1965. He went through all parts of life and kept repeating, "Have you prayed about it?" "Have you prayed about it?" Several years later, just before he died of leukemia, I asked him after a Bible class held in the basement of our home, "What would you have done differently in your life, if you could live it over?" He answered, "I would pray more." Here was a man who prayed honestly and consistently, but still knew he could have prayed more. I'll never forget his words. "I would pray more." I didn't want to make the same mistake.

*Again, I tell you that if two of you on earth agree about any-thing you ask for, it will be done for you by my Father in heaven. For where two or three come together in my name, there am I with them* (Matthew 18:19-20).

The exact year is hard to remember but sometime in the 1970's a weekly men's prayer and Bible study group was started. Wally Bronner, Ray Bauer, Herb Kueffner, Lawrence Loesel and I were some of the initiators. We met at each other's homes for a con-tinental breakfast. It was a high privilege for a young man like me to be mentored by these faithful men of God. Little did we realize how God would help this group to grow. Today, St. Lorenz Men's Bible breakfast held in the church basement can have as many as 70 to 80 and even more men in attendance. It is faithfully taught by Pastor Mark Brandt. God's Word gave us direction for praying and keeping each other accountable to being the Christian men we were meant to be.

One night in October 1978 Alice and I finished reading a book. We had taken turns reading aloud each night before we fell asleep. That night, we didn't realize our prayer would become a signifi-cant turning point in our lives. The name of the book was GOD'S SMUGGLER. It was about Brother Andrew and his experiences of

The saint who advances on his knees never retreats. *Jim Elliot* taking Bibles into the Iron Curtain countries. His book basically inspired us to pray together:

"Lord, we love it very much here in Frankenmuth, but we need some new goals in serving you. They could be right here, but we want you to know we are willing to serve you anywhere in the universe. In Jesus name we pray. Amen."

During the following Christmas holidays we received a letter from Bill Driskill. He was a close friend from days at Concordia College, who was then serving as an educational missionary at Hong Kong International School (HKIS), a Christian school owned and operated by the Lutheran Church Missouri Synod. His letter reminded us of our prayer. It led to a call to serve as an educational missionary. My position was to be Elementary Sportsmaster. Were we up to the challenge of living in another culture? Were we sure we wanted to leave God's comfortable Frankenmuth? The next summer we were on our way to opening new doors on the other side of the world. The answer to that October prayer came quicker than we expected. Because of answered prayer we had the confidence that God would be with us.

Confidence is more than thinking you can. It knows you can do something. Confidence is a belief and an attitude. An attitude can be worked on. Who controls your attitude? With the help of the Holy Spirit, you do. You control how you react to the situation around you and remember; confidence develops from having positive experiences given to us by God. Therefore we went to Hong Kong with confidence. We knew God would be with us on the other side of the world. Also we had a team of positive people praying for us on both sides of the world. The more difficult the times, the more positive a person must be. We saw the obstacles as an opportunity to improve. We quickly learned to live in the present tense, free from the failures of the past and the difficulties of the future. God was in control. He was the driver and we were along for the ride.

While living in another culture we took our lumps and kept on going. My family refused to give up. This does not mean being over-

The trouble with our praying is, we just do it as a means of last resort. *Will Rogers*

confident and not needing assistance. Often there were times of helplessness. We could only turn to God to provide. I think that is exactly where God wanted us to be. We found that worry looks at God through the circumstances but prayer looks at the circumstances through God. We were and are never separated from the love of God. Confidence is balanced with true humility. I am not in this life alone.

### Personal Reflection Time

1. What would you have done differently in your life, if you could live it over?

2. Since you are a child of God, what level of confidence do you have in Him? …. In yourself? Limited – Insufficient – Proficient – Superior

3. Are there any key prayers that were turning points in your life?

As you go to the Lord in prayer, pray for others, but don't forget yourself.

# 7

# Remain

*If you remain in me and my words remain in you, ask whatever you wish, and it will be done for you* (John 15:7).

The reception at the airport was magnificent. We were an exhausted couple guiding two young boys down the ramp, but our tired spirits quickly rose to new levels. A welcoming crowd of more than fifty people waved signs and colorful flowers to greet us! This unforgettable memory is an example of how God provides at times when we least expect it.

Over the next three years west did meet east and often with tension broken by laughter. Learning to eat with chopsticks, riding double decker buses, typhoons, coaching and playing Little League Baseball, Cub Scouts and Beavers programs, teaching, and traveling carried challenges filled with memories. The Lord kept us mindful of who we were and why we were there. It was to share His love with those lives we touched.

The second year we were in Hong Kong I was asked to lead the adult education program for Church of All Nations (CAN). After struggling with the invitation and not wanting to accept it, I prayerfully consented. I knew I was going to need God's direction and help for this task. The result influenced my life for years to come. I prayed for guidance as to what topics to study and

One prays for miracles and works for results. *St. Augustine*

who should teach them. It was good timing to talk about "The Church in China." The doors had just opened in 1979 after thirty years of silence to outsiders to come into China. The stories were plentiful. I decided to bring in "China Watchers" to CAN Sunday morning "Mission Life Hour." These were Christian experts living in Hong Kong who knew what was happening in the mainland Chinese churches. Ten different watchers were invited to come ten weeks in a row and share their understanding. At the end of the series we were probably the fifty most informed people in the world on the topic of the "Church in China." It was similar to hearing the "Second Book of Acts." How did the church grow from approximately a half million to over thirty million in thirty years? These Christians survived persecution and the church grew through prayer. Repeatedly, we heard stories of how God answered prayers. A year later we followed this up with five more sessions. Since that time I have shared this fantastic story around the world in speaking engagements to whoever would listen. God helped me to meet the challenge of the CAN Mission Life Hour that I thought should be in the hands of another person. I admit I have underestimated the impact of the church in China story on my personal prayer life.

It was at this time I first heard about missionary Hudson Taylor. He was a British Protestant Christian missionary to China, and founder of the China Inland Mission (CIM) (now OMF - Overseas Mission Fellowship International). He lived from 1832 to 1905. Taylor spent 51 years in China. The society that he began was responsible for bringing over 800 missionaries to the country. CIM began 125 schools and this directly resulted in over 18,000 Christian conversions. They also established more than 300 stations of work with more than 500 local helpers in all eighteen provinces.

Taylor was known for his sensitivity to Chinese culture and zeal for evangelism. He adopted wearing native Chinese clothing even though this was rare among missionaries of that time. Under his leadership, the CIM was singularly non-denominational in practice and accepted members from all Protestant groups, including indi-

The best theology is the fruit of kneeology.

viduals from the working class and single women as well as multi-national recruits. Primarily because of the CIM's campaign against the Opium trade, Taylor has been referred to as one of the most significant Europeans to visit China in the 19th Century. Historian Ruth Tucker summarizes the theme of his life:

> "No other missionary in the nineteen centuries since the Apostle Paul has had a wider vision and has carried out a more systematized plan of evangelizing a broad geographical area than Hudson Taylor."

At one period Hudson Taylor's morale became very low in China. He began to question himself and he thought he was dogged with failure. He had constant conflict and failure instead of victory. How could he preach with sincerity to others when it was not in his own experience? His life was on an emotional roller coaster ride between joy over being a saved sinner and sad over his sinning and failures. He was strong and yet weak. He prayed for faith but it seemed not to come. How could his barren branch become a portion of the fruitful stem? This is when he encountered the scripture where Jesus calls Himself the vine and believers the branch. Hudson Taylor finally understood that One life reigns throughout the whole vine and branch to bear fruit. It was and is Christ's life; not his faith but God's faithfulness that would make him significant. He was to abide, remain, and stay connected to Jesus. Hudson Taylor was to trust Him for the power to bear fruit.

It was not striving to have faith, or to increase our faith but a looking to the Faithful One for time and for eternity. Jesus has promised never to leave us and to remain in us and never to fail us.

Think through the vine and branch one more time. Read John 15:1-8 in its entirety. We do not have to make ourselves branches; the Lord Jesus tells us we are branches. We are part of Him. We are just to believe it. We are bonded to Him. It is resting in Jesus now, and letting Him do the work through us – which makes all the difference! Hudson Taylor realized if you are clinging to Christ, the vine, you are guaranteed to bear His fruit.

You must GO forward on your knees. *J. Hudson Taylor*

This can be a new found peace. Troubles do not have to worry you anymore. You come to realize your total dependence is upon His strength. STOP AND REST AND RELAX RIGHT NOW.

Read again John 15:7 *If you remain in me and my words remain in you, ask whatever you wish, and it will be done for you.*

Wow! What a promise this is for your prayer life.

### Personal Reflection Time

1. What lives of famous world missionaries have you studied? If you are interested, these are a few you could start with: William Carey – Adoniram Judson – Karl Gutzlaff – David Livingstone – William Townsend - Jonathan Goforth – Ralph Winter – Ravi Zacharias – Wilhelm Loehe – Billy Graham

2. How do you intend to apply John 15:7 to your prayer life?

3. How does your prayer life provide you peace?

Prayer will become effective when we stop using it as a substitute for obedience.
*A. W. Tozer*

8

# Answer

*And I will do whatever you ask in my name, so that the Father may be glorified in the Son. You may ask me for anything in my name, and I will do it* (John 14:13-14).

Some people called it "Rock Fever." This meant to stay on the island of Hong Kong too long. Our family wanted to prevent this by going somewhere outside of Hong Kong after being there two and a half years. We made arrangements to go to the island of Boracy in the Philippines. We went in the days before it became famous to the rest of the world, during Christmas holidays of 1981. This is where God provided our most memorable family vacation. Two incidents that affected my prayer life took place on that island paradise. The first was at a church service where the local people asked me to preach. After I provided a New Year's message the person in charge shared a personal blessing that was received during the past year. Then the lady turned and gave the mike to me to do the same. I communicated my blessing and quickly gave the microphone to my wife. This continued throughout the entire congregation of about eighty people in attendance. These people didn't have much materially, but there was great thankfulness that permeated the bamboo church shelter. It was a powerful example for me to remember to always count my blessings.

Count it a blessing when God delays the answer to your prayer
in order to enlarge your capacity to receive.

As midnight approached we were talking to Roger, the owner of the resort where we were staying. As soon as it was twelve o'clock, Roger quickly disappeared. He gathered his family and went with them into a time of prayer. It was an example for me to follow for each New Year's Eve since then.

During the previous October of 1981 it was time to inform David Rittman, the HKIS Headmaster, whether we would be returning the following year to teach at the international school. I asked David if I could have another month to decide. I figured I had three positive choices: 1) Continue to stay in Hong Kong and teach there, as many colleagues hoped we would. 2) Go back to the USA and teach in a Lutheran School system as done previously. 3) Go back to a seminary for pastoral training. The third option was still buried in the back of my mind. During the next three weeks, we prayed as a family something like this:

*"Lord, this is a very important decision to make. We want to know, without any doubt, **YOUR** will for our lives. Please send us a **BOLT OF LIGHTNING** so we can be absolutely sure of what **You** want us to do. In Jesus name we pray."*

This idea, a bolt of lightning, was repeated often in our prayers during the first two weeks of October. Then it happened! Suddenly I received a letter from the United States. My knees shook when I read and reread it. It was my bolt of lightning from God. Reverend Luther Werth had never written a letter to me before. In it he told me that he had been thinking of me and thought that now was the time for me to become a pastor. The interesting point to this is that the letter was written in August, before I even thought about the future. Mysteriously, it did not arrive until the middle of October. This was the prod I wanted and needed to go back to school to become a pastor. My wife offered encouragement and the boys agreed. They were up to the challenge more than I was. This was another answer to prayer coming at just the right time.

For years as a coach I have believed in the principle that success motivates. This answer to prayer became an incentive for praying.

God doesn't use an answering machine; He takes each call personally.

Also I believe the reason God gave me a bolt of lightning, the letter, was to impress on me that I could be absolutely sure He wanted me to be a pastor. I would face difficult and rigorous times. Looking back at that answer helped me to get through those challenging times.

To get unquestioned answers to my prayers was not only important as to the satisfying of my desires, but was also evidence of my abiding in Christ. The mere act of my praying was no test of God's relationship to me. But to pray and receive clear answers, not just once or twice, but daily, is the sure test that by His grace I have a connection to Jesus Christ my Savior and Lord.

Faith teaches it is God's will to answer prayer. How well assured the answer to prayer is, when that answer will glorify God the Father! John tells us: *"so that the Father may be glorified..."* And Jesus Christ is eager to glorify His Father in heaven.

I am reminded of a woodpecker story often told by Johnathan Goforth, missionary to China from 1888 to 1934. A certain woodpecker flew up to the top of a high pine tree and gave three hard pecks on the side of the tree as woodpeckers do. At the instant of the third peck a bolt of lightning struck the tree leaving on the ground a pile of splinters. The woodpecker had quickly flown to a nearby tree where it clung in terror and amazement at what had taken place. It all remained quiet and the woodpecker said to itself: "Well, well, well! Who would have imagined that just three pecks of my beak could have such power as that!"

My talents, abilities, successes all are to praise God. Also to Him be the glory for every answer to prayer.

What men usually ask of God when they pray is that two and two not make four.

56

## Personal Reflection Time

1. What is your tradition at midnight on New Year's Eve?

2. Can you think of a time when an answered prayer has motivated you to pray again?

3. Skeptics question that God really answers prayer. People need to share their answers to prayer. God receives glory in this way. Think of an answered prayer that you could share with others.

If there is one thing I think the Church needs to learn,
it is that God means prayer to have an answer. *Andrew Murray*

I believe in prayer. It's the best way we have to draw strength from heaven.
*Josephine Baker*

## 9

# Scripture

*If anyone turns a deaf ear to my instruction, even their prayers are detestable* (Proverbs 28:9).

A visit to the Holy Land of Israel was one of our once-in-a-lifetime experiences that the Lord allowed our family to experience while traveling home from Hong Kong. After walking in the ancient footsteps of Jesus, people asked me what the trip did for my spiritual life. My answer was, "Being there helped me to accept the humanity of Christ." Yes, Jesus was a real man. Walking Michael, our local tourist guide, said that Jesus stood here or Jesus walked down this path. I thought, "Why was it not here or there? It must have been somewhere in the area." Jesus became an actual genuine human being to me.

We also spent two days with another man named Zarmir. We hired him to drive us south and north of Jerusalem. One day we went swimming in the Sea of Galilee. Here I found out why Jesus walked on top of the water. It is because the bottom is so rocky! At least the part was where we went swimming. On the day we left Israel Zarmir took us to the airport. I asked him this question, "What would you like me to tell Americans when I have a chance to

Prayer gives a man the opportunity of getting to know a gentleman he hardly ever meets.
I do not mean his maker, but himself. *William Inge*

preach?" His response was this, "Tell them to know the Bible. They come here to Israel and don't know the stories."

It has been important for me to follow the suggestions and examples of these two men. Walking Michael taught me the importance of memorizing scripture. He quoted verses as we walked around inside and outside of old Jerusalem. (In appendix "A" of this book are the passages I have memorized concerning prayer. I put them in an ABC order to make it easier to remember them.)

God has commanded us to memorize His word:

*He declared, These commandments that I give you today are to be on your hearts* (Deut.6:6).

*Then He taught me, and He said to me, "Take hold of my words with all your heart; keep my commands, and you will live* (Prov. 4:4).

*I have hidden your word in my heart that I might not sin against you* (Ps. 119:11)

Of all of the methods of learning, none has been more rewarding nor more difficult for me than memorizing verses. They have become so valuable to me personally when trying to get through difficult situations. More than one night I've fallen asleep trying to say them. I have been able to remind myself of God's promises. On many occasions I have had the opportunity to share them with others. They seemed to have appreciated God's message to them. Too often memory work has been thought of as an end in itself. The importance of a memory verse learned by heart has been the ability to apply it to my life and others.

Years later I was teaching a Christian ethics class at Valley Lutheran High School. Picking up on the suggestion of Zarmir I decided to ask ten questions on a quiz the first day of class with the seniors. I don't recall all of the questions. They were something like: "How can a person make good decisions for his life?" "How can a

The Word of God represents all the possibilities of God as at the disposal of true prayer.
*A. T. Pierson*

person become wise?" "How can a person have good relationships with other people?" "How can a person have a conversation with God?" I do remember the answer I wanted to all ten questions. Each one was to be the same. "Know the Bible!" "Know the Bible!" "Know the Bible!" "Know the Bible!" I'm convinced that many believers know many of the facts of the basic stories of Scripture but there is a gap in applying them to Jesus and even a bigger discrepancy in how to apply them to their own lives.

The Bible tells the story of God's acts and words as well as human obedience and disobedience. It begins with creation, and the conflict begins with the fall into sin. The overall story shows how God acted to save and restore this people to a right relationship with Him and with the world they inhabit. The story climaxes with Christ's death and resurrection and ends with a preview of the new heaven and the new earth. The people of the Bible were people like us. Our lives now are also part of God's story.

The more we study and know the Bible, the more we know the commands and promises of God, especially in building a relationship with Him through prayer. If we approach the Bible primarily with our own minds, without the Holy Spirit's guidance, it's really not going to mean that much to us or to anyone else whom we might want to approach with it.

This fellow disciple doesn't have all the answers. I have made plenty of mistakes during my journey of life. However, I do want to know and converse with my Lord and Savior better. I hope you can catch my enthusiasm for learning what God has revealed about Himself in Scripture. Also this book is a call to you to experience a life of healthy, significant prayer.

A young Chinese was once asked how his Bible study was and he replied; "I am now reading the Bible and behaving it." This sounds like something I would like to do. Build your life on the authority of the written word of God.

When we go to God by prayer, the devil knows we go to fetch strength against him, and therefore he opposeth us all he can. *Richard Sibbes*

**Personal Reflection Time**

1.  How many passages on the topic of prayer can you say from memory?

2.  Ask God to give you opportunities to share the verses that you memorize in a meaningful way with others. Each time you give the verse to someone else, more of it will truly become yours.

3.  How are you reading the Bible and behaving it?

Prayers not felt by us are seldom heard by God. - *Philip Henry*

# 10

# Helplessness

*Do not be anxious about anything, but in everything by prayer and petition, with thanksgiving, present your requests to God* (Philippians 4:6-7).

As much as the whole visit to Israel provided insights into the life of Jesus, another incident with prayer stands out in my memory. It happened at St. George's Cathedral and hostel where we were staying outside the old city of Jerusalem. Alice and I were visiting with a new acquaintance after tea one afternoon. He was a pastor, who was also spending time in Jerusalem. After sharing details of my plans to become a pastor, I told him of my feelings of fear and apprehension about the future. We did not have the money, a job for Alice, a car, and maybe even the wisdom to succeed. He encouraged us and said the Lord would provide the means. For closure to the conversation he prayed for the Lord's blessing on our family situation. His prayer and our family's prayers were soon to be answered.

On our arrival back to friendly Frankenmuth, arrangements had been made to stay at Marilyn and Roy Bernthal's home. When we entered the door Alice was told to call a former college friend, Chuck Daenzer. He wanted to offer her a teaching job in a Fort Wayne Indiana Lutheran school. A quick trip south to Fort Wayne

God's help is only a prayer away.

was planned. While visiting with Chuck another contact was made, and Alice was finally hired at Unity Lutheran School as a first-grade teacher. We crossed the street to an apartment complex and made a deposit for a place to live. We had driven to Fort Wayne in a car that was given to us by our good friend and financial advisor, Bob Trinklein. Praise God again for meeting our basic needs immediately. Now all that remained was for me to pass Greek and the rest of the courses.

In a previous chapter I mentioned missionary Hudson Taylor. His son Howard noticed that his father, "prayed about things as if everything depended on the praying ... but worked also, as if everything depended on his working." For many years I understood the part about working, much more than the praying part. In many ways I could have been called a workaholic. My interest and ability in sports taught me that I could overcome my lack of natural skill by putting in hours of effort. This was not always good for my family. As I think back, this mental approach to living created worry. I was basically afraid of failure and didn't know how to depend on the work of the Holy Spirit. Therefore I over prepared for whatever I was trying to accomplish.

I knew that God was still in control, I knew that He still kept the world spinning, I knew of His great love displayed through Christ, I knew that He would have the final victory. But I thought Bob Smith could impress God, the world, and avoid failure with working overtime. My effort, not my prayer time, was my priority. I needed better balance between the two. I finally woke up somewhere along this journey of life to realize prayer and helplessness are inseparable.

What do I mean by this? In the end my significance and success depends on God not me. Modern western culture believes effort is enough. A relationship with God is not needed. So many depend on human strength and wisdom, how silly this is. The devil laughs at us in our faces. Our efforts alone are futile.

Someone once wrote this about worry: "Worry is faith in the negative, trust in the unpleasant, assurance of disaster, and belief in defeat...Worry is a magnet that attracts negative circumstances...

We are all weak, finite, simple human beings, standing in the need of prayer.

Worry is like rocking in a rocking chair—it gives you something to do, but you never go anywhere with it."

My recommendation is to go running back to Him in prayer. It's the only way to a more fulfilling life. It is the only way to bearing more fruit. It's the only way that our non-Christian friends are going to see our Christian worldview of peace and composure.

Author O. Hallesby has helped me to understand the role of helplessness. In summary he said: "Prayer and helplessness are inseparable. He is saying a person needs to cry to God for help? Yes. Prayer is for the helpless. A person's helplessness is the very thing which opens wide the door unto Him and gives Him access to all needs. Helplessness can be the secret of powerful prayer. Recall the words of Jesus, *'Without Me you can do nothing'*" (John 15:5).

There is a need for balance between my effort, my work, and my cry for help from God. "*His strength is made perfect in our weakness...*" (2 Corinthians 12:9). God ultimately controls all. It is up to us if we want to be His partner. Open the door when He knocks.

### Personal Reflection Time

1.  Can you think of a specific time in your life when you have felt helpless?

2.  How did God answer your cry for help?

3.  How much balance do you have between your prayer and work life?

I have been driven many times to my knees by the overwhelming conviction that I had nowhere else to go. *Abraham Lincoln*

## 11

# Perseverance

*Then Jesus told his disciples a parable to show them that they should always pray and not give up* (Luke 18:1).

The three years at Concordia Seminary in Ft. Wayne were generally enjoyed by the Smith family. We persevered for these years living a simple life on Alice's low salary. After the first year of adjustment to our new situation, and persevering Greek, we took a short holiday trip to visit our family. Upon return we found that someone had broken into our home through an unlocked window. After investigating we found that only a few things were missing from the boys' rooms. A boom box and a collection of baseball cards were the main items gone. The only person we could think of who knew we were gone was our paper-boy. We decided to go over to his home and ask him if he knew or saw anything suspicious. Before doing this we prayed that the Lord would turn this problem into a blessing.

When we arrived at his family's apartment the father invited us in to talk. His son was not at home. After investigating the situation the father eventually told us that the paper-boy had stolen the items. As a result his son ran away from home for several days. The father asked Kurtis and Eric if they would take over his son's paper route. It became our family project seven mornings a week. The

Kneeling keeps you in good standing with God.

problem turned into an unexpected financial blessing just as God promises in Romans. *And we know that in all things God works for the good of those who love him, who have been called according to his purpose* (Rom.8:28).

The boys were so honest and consistent that one route turned into two routes, and finally we were delivering three neighborhood areas with over 250 papers. However, those were the days when paper boys, still had to go door- to- door to collect the payment for the newspaper. This took a huge amount of time but they weren't quitters. They never joined the Quitters' Club.

You say you have never heard of one of the largest organizations in America? It is quickly becoming known. The reason you've never heard of the Quitters' Club is because they never meet—the members quit coming. There are no dues—the members quit paying them. The Quitters' Club is comprised of people who faced a tough job, a tough marriage, a tough sickness, or a tough failure—and they quit.

God has always honored persistence. Troubles come with God's consent. The Lord is interested in how we respond when the obstacles press and bruise us. It doesn't matter what the causes of our problems. We are to take them to God in prayer. We need to get the greatest spiritual benefits out of them. Troubles can prove a blessing or a curse. It either draws us to prayer and to God or it drives us from God. He can turn all of these obstacles into blessings.

Life can throw nothing at you that God can't use for your benefit. If you totally trust Him, He won't let your life end short of finishing.

Look at the life of Christ and consider what He faced. Jesus had all kinds of difficulties with people who tried their best to make His life miserable. They listen to His every word. They dogged His every step. They opposed Him at every turn. They hated Him. They were constantly looking for a way to do away with Him. One thing that Mel Gibson's movie on the passion of the Christ did for us was to get us in touch with the horrendous suffering Jesus endured at the hand of others.

I've known people who have quit praying because they didn't seem to get an answer. If I walk into a room and flip the light switch,

Don't pray for tasks equal to your powers but powers equal to your tasks.

I expect the light to come on. If it doesn't, I don't curse Thomas Edison and say electricity is a lie. I start looking for the problem. Maybe the light bulb is burned out, or a breaker has been thrown, or the power is out. If it seems your prayers aren't answered, don't quit praying—start looking for the reason. It may be the wrong request, or you may have unconfessed sin in your life, or the timing may not be right. God always answers prayer.

Perseverance is also the mark of true believers. Don't give up, look up! Christ never gave up for you. He endured to the end on the cross. Don't quit—keep on praying persistently! Every time you walk through a door that says PUSH—let God remind you to

### <u>P</u>ray <u>U</u>ntil <u>S</u>omething <u>H</u>appens!

### Personal Reflection Time

1. Have you stopped praying about a need in your life?

2. Are you considering quitting in some area where God has placed you?

3. Can you describe a time when you had perseverance?

It is worth a long term in the school of Christ to learn to pray.

## 12

# Confession I

*Therefore confess your sins to each other and pray for each other so that you may be healed. The prayer of a righteous person is powerful and effective* (James 5:16).

Dr. John Fajen was sent to the Concordia Seminary campus from the St. Louis international office each year. His purpose was to recruit future pastor candidates to serve in the mission field. During a visit I told Dr. Fajen the Smith family would be happy to serve overseas, as long as they didn't send us to the bush. He asked, "What do you mean by the bush?" I quickly responded, "I personally don't want to learn another language. Send me somewhere I can use English."

During May 1985 a special worship service was held for distributing assignments to vicars. As candidates, we were called forward alphabetically by last name. The location vicarage assignment was announced. There were the usual oohs and aahs as the men received their placement at various locations in the United States. Then, toward the end of the alphabet came the announcement; "Robert Smith, Hillcrest School, Jos, Nigeria, West Africa." The entire congregation was in total silence for what seemed to me like a very long time, but in reality it was only a few seconds. Then a sudden simultaneous burst of applause cut through the crowd! I knew again that the Lord was orchestrating another answer to "Send me, send me!" And, oh yes, I was to be the school's chaplain and speak English!

Prayer is the key that opens the morning and closes the night.

As one might surmise, we tried to learn everything we could about Nigeria before leaving the U.S. It never seemed to be enough preparation, even though we spent three additional weeks at Link Care Center in Fresno, California, for missionary orientation. Finally we had to "GO!"

It was fascinating to watch the Nigerians carry heavy loads or burdens on their heads. We were told an individual could carry up to about seventy pounds. The 'tricky' part was getting the load off and on without breaking one's neck or dropping the load. The Nigerians built triangle-like wood structures along the roads. These load bearing structures were designed so people can walk into them. The sides support the load and they can get out from under them easily. This was the place where they could leave their burden.

Hindsight is an eye opener. I had burdens. I could see all the mistakes I made that first year. I often felt the need to be for-given. To be the chaplain of Hillcrest, a missionary kids' school of over five hundred students, was an awesome responsibility. Much preparation was necessary for teaching my classes, as well as for the morning and evening worship services on Sunday. Then, there were also the blunders I made as a teacher, coach, husband and father. I never could reach the excellence I desired. Credit goes to my brother in Christ, Reverend Rich Carter, for taking me aside and teaching me how to lift the burdens of sins from my life. He lived about six hundred miles south of Jos at the Lutheran head-quarters in Obot Idim. He and his wife Miriam came to visit their two children, Nathan and Jeanette, at Hillcrest School. On these occasions Rich and I made an effort to take a long walk together. During these hours we confessed our shortcomings or sins and went through a confessional service. Just as the local Nigerians could lighten their burdens, Rich taught me how to leave my bag-gage of sin at the foot of the cross through prayer. Rich also assured me of forgiveness during our private confessional services.

It has taken me a number of years to fully understand repentance. It is opening me to the fact that I am a sinner. God's law is so perfect and absolute that no one can achieve righteousness. Yet, God's grace

Praying will make one cease from sinning and
sinning will make one cease from praying.

is so great that we do not have to accomplish it. Forgiveness is a gift from God to people like me who don't deserve it. My God is holy, and therefore I stand condemned. This very awareness provides me with God's forgiveness. I am forgiven totally because of the merits of Jesus Christ, who suffered and died for me on the cross. The payment is completely finished and done. His grace is the cure for my sins. Understanding what it means to confess my sins becomes the doorway for approaching my God in prayer.

I first studied about confession when I took confirmation classes in eighth grade. It was also emphasized that before communion or the Lord's Supper a believer should confess his sins. My pastor told me it was important so I did it. However, for many years I did not realize how significant and beneficial it was for my relationship with my God.

Martin Luther in the Small Catechism gives the answer to "What is confession?"

"Confession has two parts.

First that we confess our sins, and second, that we receive absolution, that is, forgiveness, from the pastor as from God Himself, not doubting, but firmly believing that by it our sins are forgiven before God in heaven."

### Personal Reflection Time

1. What do you remember in your life about the role of confessing sins?

2. With what person can you purposely and openly share your sins?

3. Is there anyone you personally need to ask for forgiveness of sins?

I can no longer condemn or hate a brother for whom I pray, no matter how much trouble he causes me. *Dietrich Bonhoeffer*

# 13

# Confession II

*If we confess our sins, He is faithful and just and will forgive us our sins and purify us from all unrighteousness* (1 John 1:9).

I once tried to witness my faith in Jesus and His forgiveness to an older Chinese man who worked as the custodian at Hong Kong International School in Hong Kong. We became great friends. He was convinced that he never sinned. At first I thought it was a translation problem but I did everything I could to explain the word sin. I wasn't successful. He needed to hear the "Law" and not just the "Gospel." He saw no need for being saved by Jesus. From my point of view, I failed. There are others today that believe there is no right and wrong. It is all relative to the situation.

During an internet discussion about confession with our son Kurtis, he shared his views on this topic. They are worth repeating.

> "Confession is about intimacy. The challenge is that today people don't do intimacy well. People aren't sure what to do with themselves. Who am I at my inmost and do I want to share that with anyone—especially, God? It is one of those 'swimming in the deep end' topics. A strong person might be deeply impacted when focused on confessional prayer. Others might flee from God when presented with

Satan is powerless against the power of Christ's prayer.

the topic because it doesn't focus on God but one's own sinful self."

Confession can also highlight generational and theological differences. Confession is associated with older, stoic generations who are acutely aware of the rule of law and role of shame in society. There is a common tendency with today's younger generation to focus on open <u>authenticity</u> rather than confession. Somehow the topic of confession scares people while being authentic doesn't. Confession has taken on negative connotations. While confession is mocked, authenticity—"being real"— is often today regarded as one of the highest virtues. Instead of the privacy of a confessional booth with a priest or a quiet conversation with a pastor of trust, people today lay their lives out in the open for all to see, good or bad and willingly taking the consequences of public opinion. One might find public opinion more open to sin than God.

What I find interesting is that with a focus on authenticity comes a lack of shame. Maybe because authenticity is being balanced by today's highest "virtue," tolerance, young people are being openly brazen without judgment of right or wrong. The "virtue" of authenticity has turned into a public flaunting of the self, whatever the self might be. Of course, confession shares who I am: a sinner. Authenticity mixed with tolerance doesn't insinuate I've done anything wrong, but still allows me to share my inmost being—it's a way to get around that sin thing.

So, how do we bring our society back to confession without alienating people from God's whole message? If people don't consider themselves needing to confess anything— i.e. without sin and just being themselves—then the topic

A man may pray on his knees all day,
but while he preys on his neighbors he will not reach God's ear.

is irrelevant. What does our society need saving from? Meaninglessness?

Maybe we should go out into the desert, wear a camel's hair coat and eat locusts...calling for repentance? Maybe we should start with authentic prayer before jumping straight to the topic of confession. God knows who we are anyway. Let's start from authenticity and then build toward a "proper theological" understanding of our place before God and how to communicate with Him. God knows us. Ultimately, confession is for our own good, not His. "Build toward it."

Kurtis is very correct that God knows all of our sins. Therefore, confession is done for our own personal sake. Let me try one illustration. Suppose a student sees me put down my cell phone on my desk during a class. After class the student walks by my desk and takes my cell phone. He steals it! Another student sees him do it and tells me. The same honest student tells the student who took the cell phone that I now know it. I decide before I see the student robber that he is completely forgiven and he can have it if he wants it. Now the student who took my cell phone comes down the hallway and our eyes come into contact. How do you think the student would feel if his conscience isn't completely dead? If he comes and admits he took the cell phone, confesses his sin and is sorry, who is he helping? You are right, himself. The same is true when we approach God in confession. We help ourselves when we confess our sins and build our relationship with Him.

Self-examination and confession go together because they are one. What is it that keeps me from confessing my sins? It is my own pride. I have to admit that I'm not perfect and I do make too many mistakes. One of the purposes of my confession is to practice seeing myself as God sees me. Sin does not have to separate me from my God, as long as I continue to have self-examination and confession. This is at the heart of a growing relationship with God.

It is very difficult to find a person to share your innermost thoughts. One of the priorities on my prayer list has always been

God is never inconvenienced by our prayers.

to find and have good friends that I can support and uphold. Then I ask them to do the same for me. This means friends that I can trust. The Lord has provided a positive answer to these requests, wherever we have lived in the world.

Confession is not a dark fearful response to an angry God if we don't shape up. Instead, confession becomes an act of anticipation, a response to the unconditional call of God's love. It is the promise that *"...the blood of Jesus Christ His Son cleanses us from all sin* (1 John 1:7)."

Forgiveness leads to life. After confession, the first step is to receive God's forgiveness and let its reality penetrate the deepest part of our existence. Being forgiven and released from everything we've ever done wrong is such a phenomenal peaceful gift. Perhaps one of the hardest lessons for us to understand is the painful point of confession. Our acknowledgement of sins is where life begins and joyful growth continues to becoming His excellent servant.

### Personal Reflection Time

1. Do you agree with Kurtis' statement that the younger generation focuses on <u>authenticity</u> rather than confession?

2. Ask God to bring to light sins you are not aware of so that they can be confessed.

3. Reflect on the sins God has forgiven you through Christ today.

It is good for us to keep some account of our prayers,
that we may not unsay them in our practice. *Matthew Henry*

"No one is a firmer believer in the power of prayer than the devil;
not that he practices it, but he suffers from it. *Guy H. King*

# 14

# Commission

*Go ye, therefore, and baptize all nations in the name of the Father, and of the Son and of the Holy Ghost, teaching them to observe all things whatsoever I have commanded you; and lo, I will be with you always, even unto the end of the world* (Matthew 28:19, 20).

Years ago I heard a church leader made this statement about his life, "I just stood at the corner, and when the trolley car came along I got on and took the ride." To me he was saying to just let God work through you. Be humble enough to admit you need God's help, trust His promises, and then obey His will. I wanted to get on this trolley, take the ride, and live full of obedience. This became apparent to me in Nigeria.

What happened in November of 1986 was no coincidence - God again put all this together. I came to Nigeria to serve my year of vicarage that the Lutheran Church requires. However, my assignment was for two years. At Concordia Seminary I had been allowed to take a delayed vicarage. The ordinary path to a Master of Divinity degree was to complete two years on campus, take a year of vicarage, and then return to the campus for the fourth year. A program for delayed vicarage meant that a student could complete three years on campus and then go on vicarage the fourth year. For family

God's way of answering the Christian's prayer for more patience, experience, hope and love often is to put him into the furnace of affliction. *Richard Cecil*

reasons, I chose the program for a delayed vicarage. After a year of supervision under Reverend Wally Rasch, I was ready to be officially ordained as a Lutheran pastor. My question to my superiors in the Lutheran Church was, "When and where was I to be ordained?" Their answer came back that the Lutheran Church of Nigeria would do it at the 50th anniversary celebration of the first LCMS missionaries coming to Africa in 1936.

My ordination became a historical event beyond anything I could have dreamed. It was the climax of the final worship service for the entire commemoration. The president of the Nigerian Church, Reverend Nelson Uweine, presided at the service attended by over fifty native pastors, over twenty LCMS missionary pastors and families, mission board representatives from the USA, the governor of Cross River State, and about ten thousand of us members. Seven video cameras recorded the event from every angle. The service started early Sunday morning at about 8:00 and lasted until 2:30 that afternoon. Seven choirs sang and danced, including me. I will never forget the representative pastors laying on their hands and giving their blessings. One Nigerian pastor spoke the Great Commission from the King James Version. Fifty years prior to this Jonathon Ekong had come to America and found a conservative Christian church. He eventually was ordained in the USA. Now the Nigerian Lutheran Church was ordaining an American pastor. It was an extraordinary day for them as well as for my family and me.

The timing of these special events was supernatural, as only God's wisdom could bring together. I believe three characteristics are needed to have prayers answered and work like this in lives: humility, trust and obedience. I have learned to pray in humility asking for God's help, then continue praying with trust, and conclude my prayers with obedience. What happened at that ordination, I believe, was totally by God's direction and blessing. Surely God answers our prayers beyond our expectations. Just let God work it out. I don't need to tell God how to solve my problems. I present them to Him and let Him provide the solutions.

Samuel Zwemer said, "The history of missions is the history of answered prayer."

Prayer enlarges the heart until it is capable of containing God's gift of Himself.

Our Lord Jesus Christ has commissioned us to share the good news of the Gospel everywhere. Often we are content to see accomplished in the name of Christ only what we are capable of accomplishing through our own intellect, eloquence, and organizational skills, instead of calling upon the mighty God of the universe and believing in Him for the supernatural.

The disciples knew and prayed to the omnipotent Creator God. In response to their prayers and dedicated lives, He used them as ambassadors of Christ to turn a wicked Roman Empire upside down.

We talk and believe that God can answer prayer. Yet there is a big gap between what we say and do. It is a challenge to revive the spiritual passion and fervor of the Christians to speak boldly as the early Christians. Without a doubt, God wants us to increase, deepen and accelerate now more than ever our witness to the world. We need to be challenged to break the status quo and to break through the barriers of unbelief to a new level of being on fire with prayer. We need to be driven to our knees and into prayer closets, as well as to group prayer. Together we could usher in a widespread awakening for prayer. How many people are praying for the unsaved? Most Christians are praying for the sick which is good. However, have you ever notice that we are more interested in keeping the saints out of heaven than we are the lost out of hell.

We need to grow in the art of praying. We need to pray together like man has never done before in the history of mankind. I believe we need to stir the embers of faith deep in our souls and ignite a fire of vision for what our Lord can do if we simply make ourselves available to be answers to our own prayers. God weeps and grieves over our obsession with busyness, muchness, and manyness. He longs for our presence in prayer. The Lord is searching for people who will yield to Him and will go to Him for help before taking a step into the traffic of the world. Too many of us need to slow the pace of our lives and adjust our priorities and put communication with God as our top priority. Beginning the quest for a wider spiritual awakening in this world begins in the closet of our own hearts. He is waiting for us to say, "Lord, I don't know how we are going to reach the world but I want to go deeper in your presence."

And help us, this and every day, to live more nearly as we pray. *John Keble*

C. H. Spurgeon said, "Whenever God determines to do a great work, He first sets His people to pray."

### Personal Reflection Time

1. It has been said by someone: "More people pray to keep people out of heaven than pray to get them in." Is this true? What is your opinion?

2. What promise is given in the Great Commission?

3. How often and specific do you pray for the unreached non-believers of the world?

To walk with Jesus you must start on the foot of prayer. *John F. DeVries*

# 15

# MK's

*And pray for us, too, that God may open a door for our message...* (Colossians 4:3).

Missionary kids, MK's as they tend to be called, are unique. They often do not seem to fit anywhere. In North America, they are too foreign. Overseas they are considered too American. Actually they are a blend of their parents' North American culture and the foreign culture in which they are reared. Consequently they have sometimes been described as third-culture kids.

One of the greatest concerns of a missionary family is their children's education. Missionary kids were the ones whom we taught and served at Hillcrest School. I had become somewhat an expert, since I had put a great deal of time in writing an independent study on "The Comparison of Alternative Educational Programs for Missionary Children" during my seminary days. This topic was so important to me that I found myself flying to Quito, Ecuador, from Nigeria at the beginning of January 1987. I went there to attend an International Conference on Missionary Kids. The round trip took nine days.

I can remember praying on the lengthy airplane ride from Nigeria to Ecuador requesting God's will again for direction for the

We cannot ask in behalf of Christ what Christ would not ask Himself if He were praying.
*A.B. Simpson*

future of our family. Should we stay and serve in Nigeria for a third year? Where did He want us to serve? I found the answer in South America.

At the conference God guided me to an answer especially through a friend by the name of Dan Peters. He was our sons' pre-field counselor at Link Care Center when we prepared for the Nigerian experience. We sat together for over an hour and talked just before the conference was over. We discussed the advantages and disadvantages of leaving Nigeria after the present school year. At the end of our chat I asked him what he would do if he were the father of Kurtis and Eric. He said he would go back to the USA and let the boys go through an American high school. That was all I needed to make the decision to leave the mission field at that time. On the way back to Nigeria I stopped at a mall in New York City and bought the best football I could find. One of my first comments to our boys when returning to Jos, as I threw them the football, was, "You guys better start practicing because we are going home." Looking back now I am sure God wanted us to return to the USA and have those experiences for the next stages of our lives.

The children of missionaries are vulnerable and open to the attacks of Satan, and they need prayer support. The missionary kids did not choose their lot. They only accompanied their parents who were answering a call from God. As a result, they were forced into situations that most of our children never face and often face problems many of us would never consider. They are children keenly in need of prayer. Satan is also aware that one of his most effective strategies in hindering the Lord's work is to destroy the witness of the family, by taking advantage of the vulnerability of children. Effective, strategic, knowledgeable prayer on their behalf can prevent the significant loss caused by their not adjusting to God's will for them.

Also the educational opportunities for missionary children are severely limited. Usually the only choices are the local international school, which is often very expensive; boarding schools, which means being miles away from parents; and home schooling, which puts additional stress on children and parents. Pray for their education.

If you're too busy to pray for others, you're too busy.

You can also pray for God's work of grace in the MK's life by following the examples of how scripture can be used as a prayer guide. (These examples were found on the internet.)

- Growth in grace: "I pray that (Name of MK) may grow in the grace and knowledge of our Lord and Savior Jesus Christ" (2 Peter 3:18).
- Love for God's Word: "Father, I pray that You will create in _____ a hunger for the Word of God. May he/she find Your Word more precious than much pure gold and sweeter than honey from the comb" (Psalm 19:10).
- Purity: "Create in _____ a pure heart, O God, and cause that purity to be shown in his/her actions" (Psalm 51:10).
- Faith: "I ask that faith will take root and grow in _____ so that by faith he/she may receive what is promised to him/her" (Luke 17:5-6; Hebrews 11:1-40).
- A Servant's Heart: "O God, create a servant's heart in _____ that he/she may serve wholeheartedly as if they were serving the Lord and not men" (Ephesians 6:7).
- Hope: "I pray that You, the God of hope, would cause hope to overflow in _____'s life" (Romans 15:13).
- Humility: "God, please cultivate in _____ the ability to have true humility before You and to show true humility before all" (Titus 3:2; 1 Peter 5:5).
- Responsibility: "Grant that _____ will learn responsibility because each one should carry his/her own load" (Galatians 6:5).
- Prayerfulness: "God, grant that _____'s life would be characterized by prayer. Enable him/her to pray in the spirit on all occasions with all kinds of prayers and requests" (Ephesians 6:18).

Prayer is not a program but a relationship. *John F. DeVries*

## Personal Reflection Time

1.  There is a saying: "Once a MK, always a MK." Do you know any MK's now living near you? Contact them and ask them for prayer requests.

2.  Contact a missionary kid living in a foreign country for prayer requests.

3.  In the list above are wonderful prayer suggestions for any person. Fill in the blanks with the name of someone else.

Prayer is an open line to heaven.

## 16

# Glory

*"Amen! Praise and glory and wisdom and thanks and honor and power and strength be to our God forever and ever. Amen"* (Revelation 7:12).

Two serious needs faced us when we returned to the USA. I was without work and our family of four did not have a home.

The housing problem was amazingly resolved by Ed and Edna Loesel, a musical Christian couple from Frankenmuth. They were our personal prayer partners. I'm sure over the years, they prayed for us as much as anyone we know. Not only was it through prayer that we were blessed but also directly by their gifts. They were kind to let us use their new home for two months before they were scheduled to move into it. Furthermore, as our salary was running out, another Christian friend helped again. Wally Bronner offered employment to Alice - another wonderful answer to our prayers.

It was not easy to wait, but I learned to remember God's promises from His word. My wife has reminded me over the years of Psalm 37:3-7.

*Trust in the Lord and do good; dwell in the land and enjoy safe pasture.*

The great tragedy of life is not unanswered prayer, but unoffered prayer. *KB. Meyer*

*Delight yourself in the Lord and He will give you the desires of your heart.*
*Commit your way to the Lord; trust in Him and He will do this:*
*He will make your righteousness shine like the dawn,*
*the justice of your cause like the noonday sun.*
*Be still before the Lord and wait patiently for Him;*
*do not fret when men succeed in their ways,*
*when they carry out their wicked schemes.*

On the first Thursday in September 1987, before the Labor Day weekend celebration in the US, I received a telephone call from St. John's congregation in Buckley, Illinois. They extended me an invitation to be their assistant pastor. Since the boys were off school that Friday and Monday in Frankenmuth, we drove to Buckley to see if we should accept their challenge.

After driving eight hours to Illinois we were taken directly to the Buckley High School so we might interview with the principal. Unfortunately, the high school did not provide the two extra-curricular activities we thought were so important to Kurtis and Eric, football and track. In addition, the only house available for us to rent in Buckley was not adequate for a family our size. We realized this call was just not suitable for us. At an evening meeting with the call committee it was quite definite we could not accept the position.

As soon as our decision was shared with the group, someone quickly suggested not living in the Buckley school district. A large number of St. John's members lived in the area of Paxton. The following Saturday morning a meeting was arranged with the high school football coaches. With real hospitality the coaches were delighted to meet two outstanding prospective athletes. The main hindrance to the whole situation was that our sons needed to be registered in school by Tuesday in order to play football right away that season. This meant we had to make an immediate decision about the assistant pastor position.

I had experienced a similar situation when my parents moved me from Rock Island to Rockford, Illinois, over a weekend. I had

"God never denied that soul anything
that went as far as heaven to ask for it." *John Trapp*

told myself I wouldn't do that to my family, yet it happened. We announced on Sunday at St. John's that we would accept the challenge and move directly into a motel near the Paxton-Loda High School. Regrettably, our sons never were able to say a formal goodbye to their friends in Frankenmuth. However, they both played that next Friday night for the Paxton-Loda High School junior varsity and varsity football teams.

For the next four years, Paxton was a wonderful place to live and serve - with many answers to our prayers.

During the early 1970's I had become acquainted with an organization called the Fellowship of Christian Athletes (FCA). In those years I started what was called a "FCA Huddle Group." Out of this, both female and male athletes from Frankenmuth attended several FCA summer camps at Central Michigan University and FCA national camp near Marshall, Indiana. I also attended some of the events.

FCA's purpose was and still is to combine people's passion for sports with their passion for Christ. They taught that these two worlds don't have to be separated. This was exactly the kind of influence I wanted for our two boys. Kurtis and Eric were very agreeable to going to the football camps in Indiana. Their attendance was a time of "inspiration and perspiration." As it has worked out over the years FCA has been a powerful inspiration, especially to our son Eric. He has participated and coached football over the last twenty years. He has been equipped, empowered and encouraged by those of FCA touching his life. He in turn has neatly woven his Christian worldview into coaching of young athletes. Eric continues to challenge and develop spiritual values into the lives of players he coaches. Lives have and are being changed. He has learned to play and coach to the glory of God.

We live in a sports-crazed nation. That's where the Fellowship of Christian Athletes comes in. FCA is ministering and making an impact in the hearts of coaches and athletes across the globe.

Prayer is exhaling the spirit of man and inhaling the spirit of God. *Edwin Keith*

## Personal Reflection Time

1. How are your prayers a driving force that shapes the way you do life?

2. How is your life bringing glory to the Father?

3. What athlete can you introduce to the Fellowship of Christian Athletes?

Some go to prayer, not to ascertain the will of God,
but to ask Him to do that on which they have fully set their minds.

# 17

# Blessing

The Lord bless you and keep you;
The Lord make His face shine on you
*and be gracious to you.*
*The Lord look upon you with favor*
*and give you peace* (Numbers 6: 24-25).

In many ways, St. John's Church in Buckley was a miniature of St. Lorenz Church in Frankenmuth. It was in a small rural town with a population of about six hundred. Yet the congregation numbered over one thousand two hundred. At that time Buckley was famous for two main reasons: St. John's Church and baseball. A big billboard sign at the edge of town read: "Home of Giants' Pitcher - Scott Garrelts." These were the years he was at the peak of his career.

Those years were needed to shape me into a "servant shepherd." Again, loving, caring, compassionate Christians surrounded us. These were challenging times filled with more responsibility than I expected or desired. At the beginning I was "assistant" pastor, which was later changed to "associate," but during those years I was asked to be the principal of the school, a physical education teacher, and the only pastor on the staff, after the other pastor accepted a different position. When I look back, it was the prayer support and assistance from my family and other people like

If you want your prayers to reach heaven, make sure you have a good connection.

the Leunings, the Kings, the Abbes, the Dippels, and many others whom the Lord provided, who helped me survive. I needed the experiences and caring confrontations that raised me to a higher level of appreciation for God's constant presence in every situation. It was true what Paul said to Timothy:

> *For this reason I remind you to fan into flame the gift of God, which is in you through the laying on of my hands. For God did not give us a spirit of timidity, but a spirit of power, of love and of self-discipline* (II Timothy 1:6-7).

Kurtis and Eric entered their college years and eventually were both students at Concordia University, River Forest, Illinois. For the first time in twenty years we were empty nesters, without children at home. I especially missed the nightly ritual we had as they grew up. It was my privilege to share a few moments of conversation with each of them and God at bedtime. The content of our prayers changed as they grew, but the "Priestly Blessing" continued through high school years:

> *The Lord bless you and keep you;*
> *The Lord make his face shine on you*
> *and be gracious to you.*
> *The Lord look upon you with favor*
> *and give you peace* (Numbers 6:24-25).

My vision and prayers for our two sons were to help prepare them to be confident, fearless Christian servant leaders for making a difference in the 21st century. I know I was far from a perfect father, but these moments were positive experiences. My daily prayers have never stopped and now include our grandchildren. I believe those few moments of prayer together when they were growing up were so important for them and me. As I analyze those times now, I am able to see insights more clearly, as to what was going on between a father and sons. A few observations are

Prayer - secret, fervent, believing prayer - lies at the root of all personal godliness.
*William Carey*

shared below. At least seven special things and maybe more were happening.

**A deeper relationship and acceptance was being developed.** The bedtime ritual gave us the ability to communicate and demonstrate value, regard, and worth. However, I did not give the boys dignity; I only affirmed God's dignity in them.

**A deeper love and affection was demonstrated.** My father was not one who openly showed his love. Therefore it wasn't easy for me to break out of this mold. With my own sons, one simple way was to draw on each other's back and try to guess what was sketched. The silent sketches conveyed symbols of love.

**A deeper understanding and purpose of a meaningful life was formed.** Most kids believe it is very important that life is meaningful and has a purpose. Yet many young people don't have a purpose and yearn for help in finding the meaning in life for themselves.

**A deeper appreciation and respect for themselves was given through affirmation**. My words and actions provided solid evidence for hope. What words I tried to offer were words of encouragement.

**A deeper ability to be listened to and to be heard was created.** I wanted to model a time of listening so that my sons could develop that skill in their own lives.

**A deeper opportunity was there to help develop a mature faith.** I wanted to pay close attention to my sons to help them grow in their spiritual lives. Help was provided toward closing the gap between belief and practice. It was important to impart firsthand knowledge of the power of God, not just second or third hand information. I wanted our sons to recognize clearly that Christ is alive and active today in their lives.

**A deeper insight needs to be presented in the role of boundaries.** It was serious business to offer guidelines from Scripture for their lives. Practical boundaries provide safety for those swimming in the sea of contemporary temptation.

There is no greater challenge in contemporary society than to pass on to the next generation the mission and vision of following

Unless I had the spirit of prayer, I could do nothing. *Charles G. Finney*

Jesus Christ. It does not happen by accident. The older generation can have a positive impact and blessing on the world today and in the future. We all need to be praying, leading, teaching, and coaching how to follow Christ no matter what our age. Kurtis and Eric are great examples of how this can be done to God's glory.

### Personal Reflection Time

1. Do you include a blessing after your prayers with another individual or group?

2. When are you praying together with someone you want to share your values?

3. What values do you want to share with others?

God comes down to us by His Spirit, and we go up to Him by prayer. *Thomas Watson*

# 18

# Spirit

*Take the helmet of salvation and sword of the Spirit, which is the word of God. And pray in the Spirit on all occasions with all kinds of prayers and requests. With this in mind be alert and always keep on praying for all the saints* (Ephesians 6:17-18).

It was a time when we were willing to accept a call to serve in another situation. Sure enough, God provided this opportunity in July of 1991. It was almost a complete circle. We were going back to the Saginaw Valley in Michigan. To us it was just the perfect location. I had received a call to be the chaplain at Valley Lutheran High School (VLHS) in Saginaw, Michigan. Alice was to teach grades 1, 2, 3 and 4 at Trinity – St. James in Munger, Michigan. Two years later she became the principal. We served the Lord at these locations for the next five years and our lifetime Frankenmuth friends were next door. When we yelled, "Help!" assistance was provided. Little did we know that our previous cross cultural missionary experiences would be so valuable in those next years.

My schedule was full. I was already teaching three courses: New Testament, World Christianity, and Christian Ethics; then came additional challenges. Besides directing the daily chapels, in the springtime I helped coach track, and I also preached at local congregations a few weekends each month. The Lord opened a new

Much keeping company with God will teach us who God is.

door that was beyond anything I had ever dreamed. Chuck Powell, a retired General Motor's executive, came to our school in 1991 to encourage us to begin a pen pal program with Public School #31 of Novgorod, Russia. As a result of this beginning friendship, Galina Zazhorkina, its assistant headmistress, extended the following invitation:

> "In our school there are two thousand pupils. We'd like to change the system of education... we want to teach our students religion... We want some teachers of religion and students to come to us, to speak to the children."

They not only wanted to meet their American friends, but more importantly, they were eager to hear about our Friend and Savior, Jesus. We were delighted to satisfy this wish of Novgorod School #31. This was a miracle of God that opened the door at Novgorod to witness to people in a formerly closed country. These firsthand missionary experiences of students and teachers from both schools were life changing.

VLHS accepted the invitation to visit Russia beginning March 29, 1994. It was a twelve-day trip with the theme: "To Russia With God's Love." A multitude of preparations began a year and a half before leaving. Twenty-two students and ten adults took training in cultural awareness, witnessing and friendship evangelism, learning some Russian, Christian songs, skits, and above all, much prayer.

In Russia on Easter Sunday the group performed a pageant, communicating Christ's passion, death and resurrection. Many of those who saw the pageant said their lives were changed. During the following week over 2,000 English-Russian Bibles were to be distributed at the school in Novgorod to students and teachers. A truck was supposed to bring them from St. Petersburg. The delivery was delayed, and we prayed that the Bibles would get to the school, while we were still there. What an exciting day it was on Thursday, when the Bibles arrived! They were delivered in a green army truck with a bad engine. Most Russian students and teachers held a

Groanings which cannot be uttered are often prayers which cannot be refused.
*C. H. Spurgeon*

Bible in their hands for the first time on that day. Other gifts for the school included sports equipment, a computerized chess set, two large handmade banners for the school, 2000 lapel crosses, 2000 bookmarks, and various other gifts for the students and teachers.

If you recall I mentioned in chapter 6, that in 1978 we read the story called God's Smuggler. It is the life story of Brother Andrew sneaking Bibles into Russia and other countries. His story was so inspirational that it changed our lives. It encouraged us to step out on our own journeys of living on the edge in faith. Now here we were 16 years later distributing Bibles openly in a Russian public school! This was a fantastic event to try to comprehend! Wow, praise God from whom all blessings flow!

In preparation for the trip to Russia, one of my wife's jobs was to coordinate the assembly of 2000 bracelets with seven different colored beads. That added up to 14,000 beads that had to be sorted and strung! The bracelets were used to explain the gospel story. It was an interesting assignment. Her committee shopped to find the best price on colored craft beads and leather strings. The beads and leather strings were counted out and assembled by 1000 children in Lutheran schools throughout the Saginaw Valley. Each bracelet was then packed into a plastic baggie with an explanation of the gospel in English and Russian.

Until this time in my life God had never let me be involved in such a huge opportunity to witness in such a short period of time. Yet it turned out to be what I believe was the fastest and most successful experience I had ever had seeing the Holy Spirit work in peoples' lives. Much had to do with God answering the thousands of prayers from supporters we had across Michigan and other states. Prior to leaving we did two major things: 1) Our group made a combination of over fifty live presentations to churches, schools, organizations, and also to the community through TV programs. 2) We put together a thirteen-day prayer calendar that was distributed throughout Michigan and beyond. Prayer was very much the key to our successful mission trip. Prayer support was phenomenal.

You may as soon find a living man without breath as a living saint without prayer.
*Matthew Henry*

## Personal Reflection Time

1. Who has been an inspiration to you to step out in faith to accomplish something you have never done before?

2. To whom would you like to give a Bible within the next year?

3. How has the Holy Spirit used you specifically to share the Gospel story?

When you pray, rather let your heart be without words
than your words without heart. *John Bunyan*

# 19

# Angels

*For He will command his angels concerning you to guard you in all your ways; they will lift you up in their hands, so that you will not strike your foot against a stone* (Psalm 91:11-12).

Alice had for many years envisioned herself as a courier someday, somewhere, for some unknown reason. She had communicated this desire to God. She was getting eager to travel again, but we could not afford it. I understood what she had in mind but did not think God had any plan for such an adventure.

Our 30th wedding anniversary came on August 7, 1995. How could we celebrate? One day a telephone call came from our son Kurtis. At that time he was attending Concordia Seminary in St. Louis, Missouri. His future wife, Teresa, had met a man named Charles McNutt through her job at the synod's mission department. His request was to find someone to accompany him to give his truck away to a missionary in Guatemala. Kurtis was to have a summer vicarage in New York City and could not go. They decided to ask Eric, his brother. He also had to say no because of plans to go to Loveland, Colorado, for the beginning of his internship as a Director of Christian Education. So this left Mom and Dad Smith to consider the opportunity. We could think of no reason why not to do it. Charles would pay our way there and fly us back to the USA. We prayed, and God answered, "Go!"

The purpose of prayer is not to get what we want, but to become what God wants.

We began our trip south on a Sunday after church from Michigan in June. We drove to Charles' home in Coleman, Alabama, with a one-night stop in southern Indiana. On Wednesday that week the three of us started our trip in the air-conditioned truck with its extended cab. The daily goal was traveling six hours or 300 miles. We would probably have arrived a day earlier, but one day we drove six hours and got lost in Mexico. We finally ended up right back where we had started in the morning. We had driven a big circle in the mountains around Tampico, Mexico. I think Alice and I smiled more than Charles did about that experience.

It took us exactly one week to arrive at our destination in Guatemala, but it included some of the most intense and extended prayer times in our lives. It was like our own week-long prayer vigil. Alice or I, sitting in the back seat was the one who silently prayed for safety. The one who sat next to Charles, our financier, maintained a running conversation. At age 77 he was an interesting character with nonstop stories. He had been an air force pilot during the Berlin airlift following World War II. Unfortunately, his driving was a holdover from his younger risk-taking days. His desire was to pass all vehicles ahead of us. On our very first day of traveling the Louisiana State Patrol decided Charles' foot was too heavy on the metal, thus he got a speeding ticket!

At the passageway through southern Mexico leading into Guatemala we had one of the most dramatic answers to prayer of our lives. We had driven down the beautiful scenic eastern side of Mexico and were told to avoid a certain section due to rebel fighters in the area; so we took the crossing connected with the Pan American highway. We had to go through five checkpoints. While Charles went into a building with our passports, a man named Leo suddenly appeared at my right side; he was licking an ice cream cone. I did not hear him come up next to me. He started a friendly conversation in English; everyone else in the area was speaking Spanish. We found out he did not have a vehicle of any kind there. Eventually Charles invited him to join us in our travel to Guatemala City. He provided the help we needed to get through the government's inspections and

The angel fetched Peter out of prison, but it was prayer that fetched the angel.
*Thomas Watson*

assessments without a hitch. As we drove nearer to our destination, it started pouring rain. Leo directed us in taking the correct turns and ultimately found us a place to stay for the night. It was a beautiful motel. We surely would have missed the place without his guidance. After joining us for an evening meal he excused himself and walked off into the night, never to be seen again. Leo was an answer to prayer that I won't forget. To this day my wife and I have wondered if he could have been an angel, with a sense of humor from God. Of course, our mission was finally accomplished as Charles handed over the keys for the truck to the agricultural missionary, Martin Brodbeck. Our 4,000-mile trip was not easy, but provided a memorable celebration for our thirtieth wedding anniversary.

Leo was not the first angel-like creature experience. In chapter three I mentioned a time when our car stopped running in Nigeria. God provided an individual or someone like an angel to help us fix it. Angels or not, they were answers to prayers.

Yes, I do believe God does send His angels to us to protect and guide us. Scripture is very clear that angels do appear in human form to mortals (see Gen. 19:1-22, 32:1; Matt. 28:2-4; Acts 5:19-20). God loves us so much that He takes care of us in ways we can't even see. Angels are one of these ways. Sometimes God gives an angel a body like a person, so that the angel can do a certain job. To be touched by an angel is good but to be touched by Jesus is the best of all.

### Personal Reflection Time

1.  Have you had an angel-like experience or know of someone who has had one?

2.  It is said that angels are mentioned 273 times in 34 biblical books. Which story about angels is your favorite?

3.  Watching, protecting, guiding, and preparing are among the many functions of angels as they help us experience the grace of God. Have you thanked God for the gift of angels in your prayers?

I beg you to see how absolutely vital prayer is. *C. H. Spurgeon*

# 20

# Praise

*Praise the Lord, O my soul; all my inmost being, praise his holy name. Praise the Lord, O my soul, and forget not all his benefits ...* (Psalm 103:1-2).

On your mark, get set, GO! With bags checked in, and passports in hand, last group prayer, and tearful hugs and good-byes given, we were on our way to Hong Kong and China during Easter break 1996. Twenty-four VLHS students and eight adults were making another mission trip from Valley Lutheran High School. This group included four students from the first mission experience to Russia. Ruth Hessler, Matt Provenzano, Allison Reed and Leigh Anne Rogner were our veteran student advisors. Also traveling with us were our adult veterans from the Russian trip that included teacher Steve (Oh my Gosh!) Zill, Dr. Mark and Connie Davenport, (the medical team), and my faithful wife, Alice. They provided me direct support and input for leading another trip. Dan Sandman and Karen Keup came along too and became right hands on the Michigan end. Karen's parents had worked with us at Hong Kong International School (HKIS) in Hong Kong. Dennis and Donna Oetting, friends in Hong Kong, spent hours making calls and contacts for us with on the Hong Kong side. Their efforts provided a comfortable stay.

The only way to do much for God is to ask much of God.

Musician and composer David Paul Britton also accompanied us on the trip. "First Thessalonians 1:2-3," "God is Everything," "He's Knockin' At Your Door," and "Make a Joyful Noise" were four of the praise songs of a larger selection produced especially for this trip under his direction. He had them recorded on cassette tape by the 1996 VLHS Hong Kong Mission Team. It was a unique, marvelous and successful way to share the gospel message of God's love with Chinese student friends and strangers we met in Hong Kong and Mainland China. To our student ambassadors God was everything and they sang with passion. Amazingly these praise songs were even sung in Communist China on our visit there. More than 1600 tape recordings were given away as our gift to the Chinese people.

It was our hope and prayer that these audio tapes would be used by the Holy Spirit. Music transcends culture, forming a natural bridge to connect people everywhere. Who can know the number of hearts that were touched by these Christian gospel praise tapes!

One area of my prayer life that for the first sixty years I consider to have been very weak was praising God. It was partly because I didn't understand the difference between praise and thanksgiving. Now I want to lift up Jesus, acknowledge Him as King of kings, Lord of lords, and give Him his rightful glory as I come into a period of praying. It has become important to focus on God and praise God for who He is and what He is. I now begin my prayer times focusing on God through recalling words that are names, attributes and characteristics of God and not on myself. Here are just a few.

Prayer is the contemplation of the facts of life from the highest point of view.
*Ralph Waldo Emerson*

Abba, Father

Advocate

All-knowing

All-powerful

Almighty God

Alpha and Omega

Architect and builder

Beloved Son of God

Bread of Life

Bridegroom

Bright morning star

Burden-bearer

Chief cornerstone

Chief Shepherd

Christ Jesus our Lord

Comforter Counselor

Creator

Deliverer

Eternal God

Ever-present

Everlasting Father

Fortress

Friend

Good Shepherd

Great high priest

Guide

Redeemer

Rock

Refuge and strength Ruler

Savior

Servant

Shelter

Spirit of truth

Teacher

True light

Vine

Way

Wisdom

Adoration of God should come before asking of God.

The Book of Psalms was never a book that I appreciated as I grew up. Primarily I think it was due to the reality that I couldn't understand the Old King James version of the Bible when I was young. They contained too many "Thees" and "Thous" for me. I gave up trying to appreciate the poems. It was not until I started to read modern translations did I begin to read the Psalms. I found the book of Psalms is filled with descriptions of God's eternal character and unchanging righteousness as the basis for praise. Praising Him puts your attention on His worthiness.

Someone once said: "Praise is the song of a soul set free." Unfortunately, I think many lifetime Christians don't appreciate the blessings of freedom. Until a person understands what it means to be in bondage, he probably doesn't grasp the full meaning of freedom. Every believer in Christ has been freed from the crushing guilt of sin. Without this insight it isn't possible to sing praise: a song of a soul set free.

### Personal Reflection Time

1. Where do you see yourself in regard to giving God praise?

2. Be still and know that He is God and reflect on His goodness to you. Tell Him you love Him because of who He is.

3. What are several names of God that you use at the beginning of your prayers?

A life of little whispered words of adoration, of praise, of prayer, of worship can be breathed all through the day.

God is never inconvenienced by our prayers.

# 21

# Deeper

*Devote yourselves to prayer, being watchful and thankful*
(Colossians 4:3).

To most Americans it has been forgotten, but to those Korean War veterans it will forever be remembered. It is known as the "Land of the Morning Calm." However, at 4:00 a.m. on June 25, 1950, that calm was shattered by artillery shells exploding on the Korean peninsula. I'm glad I wasn't part of the military that had to serve 50 years before my arrival to Korea. Mountains cover 70% of Korea's land area, making it one of the most mountainous regions in the world. I never expected to help celebrate the 50th anniversary of the Korean War when returning to Frankenmuth, Michigan. Yet approximately 85 war veterans had been gathered by Harry Boesnecker to hear me as the guest speaker on June 28, 2000, for the Korean War Anniversary Celebration. It was a humbling experience to share and provide a link from our Korean American students attending Seoul Foreign School (SFS) to these ex-G.I.'s. SFS students sent postcards with handwritten messages of thanks for the freedom. I saw tears in a few of the men's eyes that night, and there were some in mine, too, as the cards were read.

It was just before our VLHS mission trip to Hong Kong in 1996 that Alice and I were asked to serve at SFS as a teacher and chap-

Prayer is asking for rain and faith is carrying the umbrella.

lain. During the years in Seoul, my prayer life leaped forward to a new level. It was primarily due to a number of experiences. The list begins with the SFS prayer chapel and continues with Jesus Abbey, Moms in Touch, reading many prayer books, a Promise Keepers accountability group, Habitat for Humanity, Missionaries of Charity/ India trips, and a few more that only God knows. I learned to spend time in prayer like never before.

It was the Jesus Abbey Discovery Week trip that challenged me to get my prayer life in order. I was to lead a group of students each year on a five-day prayer retreat to Jesus Abbey, a prayer and meditation center in the Taebeak Mountains of Korea. Father Archer Torrey, an Anglican priest, started this retreat center in 1965. He became a good friend and mentor to me as we visited each year. I knew, if I would be teaching others about prayer, that I had better learn all I could about the topic. Also, "the best way to learn to pray was to pray." Even though the students and I were together from Monday to Friday, the time did not allow me to communicate all I wanted to share. Approximately twenty students joined the group each year. A few months prior to each trip I asked the participating students to write down at least five personal questions regarding the topic of prayer. The questions in Part II of this book are some of those questions. Somehow I underestimated how the power of the Holy Spirit would influence those students during only one week. The testimonies of the students who attended were powerful. Below, I include bits and pieces from the evaluations of their experiences.

- Thomas: "To tell you the truth, Jesus Abbey was my last choice among the Discovery Week choices. I thought it would be a place in which all we would do is work and pray. In a sense... that was all we did, yet there was something that was so different at Jesus Abbey. I could literally feel the presence of God when I was at the Abbey."
- Clayton: "I conclude by saying that Jesus Abbey was one of the greatest experiences of my life and has made a significant impact on the way I see things today."

One can see God in everything, but we can see Him best with our eyes shut.

- Emily: "After maybe a year of neglect in praying, I took a deep breath and started praying. As I prayed, it just struck me that even though I had strayed from my relationship with Jesus; He was still there for me...."
- Phillip: "There was crying. There was joy. There was love and care. We were there with God for sure. There was harmony. We have taken the one less traveled by, Jesus Abbey, and that has made all the difference."
- John: "The most important thing I came to realize from the trip is that I need God's help in my life and in the decisions that I make. I have decided to pray to learn His will. I have also learned the power of praising out loud."
- Alice: (Not my wife) "Faith, Joy, Love. These are three simple words, yet they sum up the emotions that I went through during the five-day trip to Jesus Abbey. It was there that I found myself. The all too prevalent joy that was evident at Jesus Abbey was overwhelming. At times, I found tears of happiness welling up in the deepest depths of not only my eyes but also my soul. My time at Jesus Abbey was truly a special and unforgettable experience that I will savor forever...."
- Ron: "Jesus Abbey was just an overall awesome time where you could have fellowship with other Christians. It was a time... to get right with God... to share my hardships and sins... I could depend on God... I could see how God is with us and see how He works... It was an answer to my prayers."
- Sandy: "One of the things that I learned the most about was the art of prayer. I also came to admit that prayer was one of the hardest aspects of a Christian life to carry out. It is so easy to advertise oneself as a Christian and profess to have complete faith in God to the world. But the essence of that belief lies deeply in prayer, simply speaking, conversations with Jesus..."
- Vicki: "...Thus, Jesus Abbey was a good relaxing experience for me to contemplate about things. Also, I got a chance to pray to God like I've never done before. Since I was able to sit down for a long period of time and actually think about what

God can pick sense out of a confused prayer. Richard Sibbes

I should pray about, I realized that my prayers, so far, have been very shallow and incomplete; I did not allow myself to thank God for all that He's done for me... I still can't believe that I actually cried."

The Holy Spirit worked not only in the SFS students but also in me, the chaplain, during the four discovery week trips which I led. The Korean people are known for being very hard workers, but also many Korean Christians are known for their strong prayer lives. Their enthusiasm for prayer was contagious.

### Personal Reflection Time

1. Which student's witness touched your heart the most? Why?

2. Have you been on any prayer retreats?

3. What activities could help you improve your prayer life?

Any concern too small to be turned into a prayer is too small to be made into a burden.
*Corrie ten Boom*

## 22

# Unity

*"Again, I tell you that if two of you on earth agree about anything you ask for, it will be done for you by my Father in heaven. For where two or three come together in my name, there am I with them"* (Matthew 18:19-20).

B eing with Korean Christian believers on individual prayer mats at Jesus Abbey exposed me to a new fervency in praying that I had not experienced before with Christians in other places. At their prayer services a scripture passage was read and studied. A situation or place was mentioned as how this topic could apply to the world today. Then when it was time to pray, everyone prayed out loud and at the same time. They did not hold back their tears, passion and cries. At first I was surprised, confused, and distracted. The leader gave the signal to begin, and a roar of prayer flooded the chapel until the leader spoke above the noise or a bell signaled that it was time to quit. I could not keep my mind on my own conversation with God. I was listening to the Korean language being spoken by the approximately one hundred people in the prayer service. However, I didn't know the Korean language.

My experience, of course, has been as most Americans. Most often we have conversational prayers led by one person in the

We must move from asking God to take care of the things that are breaking our hearts, to praying about the things that are breaking His heart. *Margaret Gibb*

group. With the Koreans I was experiencing what is called "Concert" prayer. It is very much like playing in a huge orchestra. Everyone plays or prays their notes or prayers at the same time. It becomes a concert like a person has never heard before. I couldn't understand it but I'm sure God could. There was more passion and desire demonstrated than I had ever heard.

Unfortunately, I never did discuss concert prayer with my Korean friends. I just accepted it as being the norm for them. There seemed to be far more power and unity when everyone was praying instead of listening to one person. It certainly removed fear that others would be critical of the words the person was using to speak to God. I do know Korean Christians have popularized this style of prayer. Compared to the Korean Christians, my prayer life seemed to be halfhearted. I left Korea inspired to bolster the fervency of my prayer life.

In Jesus' prayer for all believers in John 17 his heart was set on the unity I observed in those Koreans at Jesus Abbey.

> *"My prayer is not for them alone. I pray also for those who will believe in me through their message, that all of them may be one, Father, just as you are in me and I am in you. May they also be in us so that the world may believe that you have sent me. I have given them the glory that you gave me, that they may be one as we are one: I in them and you in me. May they be brought to complete unity to let the world know that you sent me and have loved them even as you have loved me"* (John 17:20-23).

The oneness of God's people is to be the one way the world is to recognize the influence of Christianity. Unfortunately the devil does everything possible to cause division and strife within the universal church.

Unity has a lot of different meanings or synonyms: oneness, solidarity, harmony, concord singleness and others. Unity knows you don't have to be alone. It gives courage, clarity, and peace of mind to finish every task with no excuse.

Prayers not felt by us are seldom heard by God. - *Philip Henry*

How does a person recognize unity?

- Unity will rise or fall on two main characteristics: humility and love.
- This means that there will be openness & acceptance, leaning & supporting, relating & responding, giving & taking, confessing & forgiving, reaching out & embracing, release & relying, tolerance, understanding and patience.
- Unity is the ultimate expression of interdependence. There is an element of enthusiasm and cooperation that makes others better.
- No role is more important than another.
- The goal is more important than the role.

There is unity because God called us to be Christians for this time in history. Each one tries not to break that unity that we have here. We need unity to plant the seed of the Gospel, then water and harvest it. Maybe the following illustration will help:

"Pull! Pull! Pull!" Twelve grown men were working to coordinate their oars in the South China Sea. Two by two they sat on their six water-logged boards in the rowboat. The team captain urged them on, but inevitably one crew member after another would foul-up the cadence. Six on one side would coordinate themselves and yet the other side wouldn't and the boat would circle in the waves. The captain continually encouraged his crew in spite of their poor skills. "Pull! Pull!" he yelled. Each individual had to focus and work in time for the boat to travel in a straight line and to reach its destination.

In this twelve man rowboat there were eight Englishmen, two Chinese, one Australian, and one American. They had to learn to work together. It was a lesson in international cooperation; each man had to give his best for the effectiveness of the task at hand. Finally, after reaching their destination a huge sense of fulfillment was felt by all of them. It was difficult —

Prayer will become effective when we stop using it as a substitute for obedience.
*A.W. Tozer*

believe me – I was the lone American, and I am proud to say, I did my best to represent the USA and as a member of this team.

Imagine the scene if everyone who shares a common faith in Christ would get into a giant rowboat and coordinate their rowing, so they would all be traveling in the same direction! It isn't just to be done with one oar at a time but in a total cadence together. God, our heavenly captain, has called us together. We are all to be unified TOGETHER in His mission of the Great Commission.

A small boy was given a huge Great Dane dog for his birthday. Overwhelmed at its size, the small boy asked, "Is he for me or am I for him?" His father's answer was, "YES!" So it is in the body of fellow believers. We are for one another. We are to try in every way to pray for and serve the needs of others. God has called us to work together.

- In today's world there are so many who say, "Me... me... I can do it by myself."
- In athletic competition there are those who say "You and Me ... we can do it. We can win."
- The person who is a new Christian says, "Jesus and I... We can do it.
- The person who is mature in faith says, "Jesus and we... We can do it."

### Personal Reflection Time

1. How consistently do you pray with a group of other Christians?

2. Prayer is one way to be united with others around the world. How specific and consistent are you in praying for others?

3. Are you presently doing anything in your life to break unity with other Christians?

I would rather teach one man to pray than ten men to preach. *Charles Spurgeon*

## 23

# Servant

*For even the Son of Man did not come to be served, but to serve, and to give His life as a ransom for many* (Mark 10:45).

We are called by God to be our best, to discover and utilize the magnificent God-given potential within us, and then to give it all away in a lifestyle of servanthood. Our effort to share our Biblical worldview of serving with our family and others has been evident in a variety of ways. I've learned to depend on God to lead me into activities that would teach me how to be a servant. I often prayed the following prayer or similar ones with groups in Korea.

> Dear heavenly Father, forgive me for those times when I failed to serve because I thought I was too good to do a task. Help me to be a humble servant ready and willing to do anything that needs to be done. I want to serve your people. Make me worthy by your mercy. Make me successful by your power. Help me to remember that all my blessings come from you. Fill me with an attitude of love, so that I will willingly share your blessings with others. Open my eyes, my ears, and my heart, Lord, so I may see, hear, and feel the needs of others. Thank you for giving me your love in Jesus our Savior and model of a servant. In Jesus name I pray. Amen.

It takes two feet, prayer and work, to walk with God. *John F. DeVries*

Repeatedly the Bible calls us as followers of Jesus to be servants. Most of us would call ourselves servants. We believe we automatically become a servant when we label ourselves one. Unless we are very cautious of how we apply this issue of servanthood, we may be servants in a very egocentric, self-serving way. Let me illustrate this with a parable, which was told by Dr. Duane Elmer at a conference I attended at our Seoul Foreign School.

"A story is told about a monkey and a fish. It seems a typhoon had stranded a monkey on an island in a secure protected place, while he waited for the raging waters to go down. The monkey spotted a fish in the water swimming against the rapid current. It seemed obvious to the monkey that this fish needed assistance. Being of kind heart the monkey resolved to help the fish. A tree was precariously dangling over the very spot where the fish was struggling. At considerable risk to himself the monkey moved far out on the limb, reached down and snatched the fish from the threatening waters. Immediately the monkey made his way back to dry ground. For a few moments the fish showed excitement. Finally the fish settled into a peaceful rest. Joy and satisfaction swelled inside the monkey. He had helped another creature, and he thought he had done it successfully."

We are struck by the innocence and the tragedy of this parable. We note the monkey's foolishness. The monkey assumed that the fish needed help. He could save the fish in the moment of need and danger. The monkey also assumed the fish was just like him. What was good for the monkey was good for the fish. We are the same, aren't we? Based on assumptions, the monkey did not inquire, seek information, or try to learn about the fish culture. Because the monkey thought he knew, he was free to act, but he did so out of ego centricity. He acted out of his own cultural frame of reference, as we usually do.

What makes this particularly sad is that the monkey had good intentions. He was curious, willing to risk his life for the fish. He

He who fails to pray does not cheat God. He cheats himself. *George Failing*

really wanted to serve the fish. In spite of all these virtues we are happy that we were not the fish.

I have been on a pilgrimage in my own life trying to learn how to be a servant without being a monkey. I'm on the right road, but often I'm doing things from a wrong motive or lack of understanding of what the other person needs. I want to be a loving, humble, obedient, open, accepting servant of Christ with God's love in a culturally acceptable way. Others must feel safe and secure in my presence. When we have this trusting relationship, then I can understand how to meet that person's needs. Unfortunately I often fail.

God wants every person to devote all of life to Him by serving others. Jesus' life was a clear example of service to others in all situations. This is the mission to which we are to devote ourselves. This is God's plan for the world.

How can I learn to be a servant? I look at how Jesus acted as a servant. Our Savior modeled the answer perfectly as the following examples suggest:

- He didn't just preach it.
- He prayed for them.
- He cared.
- He listened.
- He reached out.
- He supported.
- He affirmed.
- He encouraged.
- He walked with people.
- He served.

It takes a lifetime of learning to become a servant. I'm beginning at age 70 to understand the need for openness, acceptance, trust, learning, understanding, and finally serving. Oh, I thought I was a servant years ago, but I didn't truly understand then how much I still needed to be taught. My responsibility is to love others for who they are not for what I want them to become. I am to let the Holy Spirit make the change in their heart. What matters most

The more you pray, the more the Holy Spirit will push you out into service.

is not the strength of my talents and abilities, but the strength of my character, character expressed in service to God and others.

## Personal Reflection Time

1. What do you think are the steps to being a good servant?

2. Who is on your prayer list that you personally need to serve?

3. Have you served someone to the point you have opened the door to witnessing the Gospel in words also?

Prayer is striking the winning blow. . . . Service is gathering up the results. *S.D. Gordon*

# 24

# Servanthood

*You, my brothers (and sisters) were called to be free. But do not use your freedom to indulge in the sinful nature; rather, serve one another in love* (Galatians 5:13).

Imagine you are not watching a parade, but you are the parade and everybody is watching you. That is what many of the citizens of Calcutta, India, do. The poorest people sit and watch. You just happen to be entering a city that is considered the most appallingly polluted city in the world. At least that's my opinion, as your guide. You are coming with a group of twenty students on a service-learning trip from Seoul Foreign School located in Seoul, Korea. (This is a Christ-centered school with a student body of over 1200 and over 45 nationalities represented.) The goal for this week is to learn to adopt the attitude, the thinking, the living, and the loving of a humble Christian servant. You are riding in a hired bus. So far you made it through the maze and congestion at the airport. Right away you are in a traffic jam. It doesn't matter since there is so much to see. So much so, the group is strangely silent - not a word is even being whispered. Then an unforgettable incident happens. A young adolescent boy sits down next to a garbage pile. He very carefully looks it over. He uses his thumb and index finger to pick up a small item from among the rubbish - and he eats it. This street boy continues this with great precision until the bus pulls away. He is never

Prayer is a promoter of activity for it puts one at the disposal of God.

seen again, but he remains indelibly etched in your memory. Yes, this is Calcutta, where Mother Teresa found and served the dying and destitute who otherwise had no one who cared for them.

This is the beginning of a week that left lifetime impressions on my heart and mind. There is so much to smell, hear, see, touch, or to avoid. "Me, Lord, a servant; you got to be kidding! Lord, just help me to survive! I'm supposed to be the leader of this group."

Follow along with our group and enter the city of Calcutta — nicknamed "The City of Joy."

Each student and teacher, every day, observed so much, so fast, that it became like a blur during that one week. A list of observations, images and activities of our team follow:

- Seeing Mother Teresa's burial site
- The beggars living on the street
- Cockroaches and rats on the street and in institutions
- Coming face to face with beggar children
- Being asked to take patients to the bathroom
- First look at the orphanage
- Helping at the orphanage
- Holding the children that I tried to avoid
- Feeding the patients and babies
- Visiting the leprosy colony
- Two little girls who grabbed my leg and would not let go
- Those two pairs of eyes begging for anything I would give them (Oh, I will never forget)
- Handing out food
- Back massages given to the patients
- Smiles from people at different sites when touched and/or greeted
- Washing sick people covered with dirt
- Changing soiled clothes of patients
- Getting hugs from patients at Nabo Jibon
- Seeing the joy of those given something
- The beard of flies on the boy's face

Wherever the Church is aroused and the world's wickedness arrested, somebody has been praying. *A. T. Pierson*

These four trips taken to India were surrounded with prayer before, during and after, by partners in Korea as well as around the world. It was not easy to process the experiences physically, mentally, emotionally, socially, and spiritually. The smiles of the Sisters of Charity and volunteers who continue Mother Teresa's work or the Lord's work shine like bright stars in the darkness of Calcutta. The service we did was only a drop in the ocean, but it was a drop. Finally, it comes down to not how much you do but how much love was put into the action. We walked away with more than we gave.

Fifth grade teacher Evie Slatter describes the children she worked with in an orphanage: "Most couldn't walk or communicate, yet responded to being spoken to, held, and touched. Bodies were small and misshapen, many with oozing sores and scars. Yet, as Mother Teresa would affirm, there was much to be learned from the poorest of the poor."

High school junior James Surh was touched by the irrepressible spirit of Arjun, a young boy he met. "He was a disabled kid who was blind and had TB in his brain. He couldn't walk and he suffered great pain even just trying to sit up straight. Despite his handicap, he was always smiling. He had a smile from heaven... I thank Arjun for teaching me how lucky I am."

Fourth grade teacher Liz Van Duyvendyk summed up the trip in her journal: "Our purpose in being there is not necessarily to help with laundry or do the dishes although that is much needed. Our purpose is to touch someone, to show some love, to give someone a feeling that they are worth something. Our other purpose is to learn from doing simple tasks with a thankful heart. What can I also bring back to my home that I have learned here?"

Over the years I pieced together from others this meaning for defining a servant:

Is prayer your steering wheel or your spare tire? *Corrie Ten Boom*

**Servant** is a person who has the ability to relate to people in such a way that the other person's dignity as a human being is affirmed and that person is able to live his or her life to God's glory.

I asked Brother James, in charge of a home for the dying in Calcutta, "What message should I give others when I speak?" He said, "When you see a person in need, stop and help immediately." It is a simple message. I pray that my eyes and yours don't look the other way. You and I don't need to go to Calcutta to see people in need. Look around today. God stretched me to learn how to serve. My prayers for others and myself have changed since having the Calcutta experiences.

### Personal Reflection Time

1. How can you train your eyes to be more sensitive to the needs of others?

2. Name a person on your prayer list that you personally want to encourage and affirm by serving?

3. Have you participated in a service-learning experience? If not, why not?

I used to ask God to help me. Then I asked if I might help Him. I ended up by asking Him to do his work through me. *James Hudson Taylor*

God's answers are wiser than our prayers.

# 25

# Grace

*And in their prayers for you their hearts will go out to you, because of the surpassing grace God has given you* (2 Corinthians 9:14).

Brief Story: Cedric O' Shea
Found dying on the Streets of Calcutta
Now living and loving at Nabo Jibon

After walking into a large ward for the sick I greeted the men patients who lived at Nabo Jibon, a home for those with TB and for handicapped boys. I heard a response in perfect English come in return. Immediately, I knew there was something different about this man, so I went over and sat beside him on his bed. It wasn't long after, that the Lord opened the doors for me to hear a wonderful Christian witness. His name was Cedric O' Shea. His grandfather had been a well-known doctor who had come to India from Ireland. His father had married an Indian girl, and he was their son. Unfortunately, Cedric had become an alcoholic. His alcoholism eventually led to a life on the streets of Calcutta. He was found almost dead by the Missionary of Charity Sisters of Mother Teresa. They took him to a home called Kali Ghat, where they expected him to die in peace. Instead, the Lord saved his life physically and spiritually, after eight and a half months of love and care.

When we become too glib in prayer we are most surely talking to ourselves. *A.W. Tozer*

Our conversation lasted for over 30 minutes. Soon after our dialogue began several other patients gravitated to nearby beds to listen. Cedric shared a powerful witness of his relationship with Jesus not only to me, but to the group of Hindu that were present. Below are some insights he related to our little group in the drab room of Nabo Jibon.

- "Man always thinks of his own self and how he can benefit first. We have so much to give, but our mind is so much on ourselves. We are very greedy. One should give your gifts to others. I don't mean material gifts. I mean your gifts or talents God has given you."
- "Mother Teresa once said to me, 'Love in your heart was not put there to stay. Love is not love, until you give it away.'"
- "People who volunteer are not changing others, but changing themselves."
- "Keep things simple in life."
- "I don't know if I'll be dead tomorrow, but I am enjoying today. I can get through today with God's strength."

Cedric also told me this story:

"A man kept praying to become rich. Finally a priest told him that he would have a vision of what he should do to become rich. It happened as the priest said. In a dream he saw a hermit, whom he was to go and visit. The hermit would make him rich. So the next day the man saw the hermit. The hermit pulled out a big diamond and gave it to him. The man thought he was now rich. He tried to sell it, but no one could buy it because they couldn't afford it. He became very nervous and afraid someone would steal it - so anxious he couldn't even sleep at night. Eventually he returned it to the hermit and said, 'I don't want the diamond. Please instead, give me the ability you have to give it away. Then I'll be rich.'"

Prayer is not a substitute for work, thinking, watching, suffering, or giving; prayer is a support for all other efforts. *George Buttrick*

What profound meaning is in that story! Cedric had learned to give away his smile and his God given talents. A year later we returned to Nabo Jabon to find him as the gatekeeper with another big smile to welcome us. Cedric is one of the greatest examples of God's grace I have personally ever met.

Christians may often feel compelled to just tell others what type of conduct is not acceptable. They may moralize, evaluate, judge, criticize and preach at nonbelievers. Their messages can convey unacceptance, thinking that by such means those in authority can force Christian growth. Christians cannot push growth. Unbelievers often think that if they act a certain way they are then going to become a believer. A relationship with Jesus Christ is to be introduced, not just information given on how to act or behave.

God is the One who gives and develops the Christian life and faith. He does it as the Holy Spirit works through the Word, baptism and the Lord's Supper. It is through His power a person turns from sin to Him. This is power to *"become mature, attaining the full measure of perfection found in Christ"* (Ephesians 4:13).

It is important to acknowledge the power of God at work in the lives of people like Cedric that can nurture faith through both the Law and Gospel. The Law shows God in His holiness and it is His will that people are to be holy as He is. The Law also shows us that because of sin people cannot achieve holiness. The Gospel, on the other hand, presents God in His love. The Gospel is the good news of our salvation in Jesus Christ. People are made holy in and through Jesus Christ.

Both Law and Gospel are from God. Both are necessary for Christian growth and life. Without the Law the Gospel is not understood. Without the Gospel the Law does not benefit. A balance of both Law and Gospel is necessary.

Cedric recognized he was dead in his transgressions and his sinful ways (Eph. 2:1-3). Therefore, he asked the Holy Spirit to guide him to a relationship with Jesus. He renounced his bad habits and turned the opposite direction, which was to God. By God's grace

To pray is to grow in grace…Christian character grows in the secret-place of prayer.
*Samuel M. Zwemer*

he became a new creation, the old was gone and the new man had come (II Cor. 5:17).

## Personal Reflection Time

1. Describe someone you know personally who has made a 180 degree turn to God.

2. Define the terms Law and Gospel in your own words?

3. How do you apply Law and Gospel to your daily conversations and prayer life?

One secret of effective prayer is prayer in secret.

# 26

# Humility

*He has showed you, O man, what is good. And what does the LORD require of you? To act justly and to love mercy and to walk humbly with your God* (Micah 6:8).

Someone has said, "No one lacks for ways of doing good – only for the inclination." I always thought in life I was modeling the role of the Samaritan in the Good Samaritan story. I came to a shocking reality that too often I have been the priest in the story. I have walked around those in need and avoided touching the untouchable. Calcutta, India has so many beggars and people with needs; a person can't hide and avoid them.

"Washing floors? Yes, no problem, I can do that. Washing clothes? Sure, why not me. Shave an old man? As long as he doesn't mind being nicked a few times. Hair cut? Well, OK. —— Hey, I didn't ask for a man off the street with long hair and full of lice. Lord, you're stretching me." Fortunately, Mother Teresa reminded volunteers of Jesus' five words. "You did it unto Me."

One of our male students said this in our closing circle prayer the morning we left Calcutta our second year: "Lord, I now know why this city is called 'The City of Joy.' When I return home it will be such a joy to be there. I understand your blessings so much

Our prayers should be for blessings in general, for God knows best what is good for us.
*Socrates*

more." Indeed, he returned home with a change in attitude. Personally understanding who this student was, I knew he was going home with gratitude and a humble servant attitude. He wasn't the only one who came home thinking, living, and loving, with a humble Christ-serving attitude. The Holy Spirit was at work in all of our lives, but maybe in mine the most.

Humility is recognizing that God and others are actually responsible for the achievement in my life. We are to remove pride from our hearts and replace it with humility. Humility is one of the keys to a strong prayer life.

Can humility be taught? If so, how is it learned? Yes, I do think humility can be taught. This is what Jesus was doing in the story in Luke 18:9-14 with the Pharisee and the tax collector story; teaching humility. He then went out and lived humility. In fact, St. Paul describes Jesus living out humility in Philippians chapter 2:3-8. Paul tells us to have the same attitude of humility. The way to teach values is to talk about them and show them in action. This is exactly what Jesus did.

It becomes crucial to answer these three questions. My comments are only a beginning.

1. What may humility look like? (A person quietly serves without being noticed or asks to serve regardless of his or her office or position.)

2. What may humility sound like? (A person praises God and others for their help when praise is given.)

3. What may humility feel like? (A person feels an inner brokenness because of imperfections, while also experiencing inner peace and stillness because of God's presence.)

I would like to share four beliefs I have about humility in relationship to prayer.

We must move from asking God to take care of the things that are breaking our hearts, to praying about the things that are breaking His heart. *Margaret Gibb*

1. The humble person has a constant awareness and reverence of who God is.

2. The humble person recognizes his shortcomings; that he falls far short of what he would like to be.

3. The humble person recognizes that his or her accomplishments are carried out with the blessings of God and the help of others. It is okay to yell: "Help!"

4. The humble person does not call himself humble. This leads to false humility. Other people may or may not recognize his humility.

I don't think I can stand up in front of class and say, "today I will teach humility" and expect the students to all walk out of the door and be humble. I am also to be a quiet model of it.

Humility does not have to do with being weak or pessimistic. On one hand John 15:5 says *"apart from me you can do nothing."* On the other hand, *"I can do everything through Him who gives me strength* (Phil. 4:13). Humility is realistically thinking about God and our ability. This is the point where boldness comes into the picture. Do you remember reading the bumper sticker which said, "It's hard to be humble when you are as great as I am." I think some people believe humility is a sign of weakness. *"The fear of the Lord teaches a man wisdom, and humility comes before honor (Pro. 15:33)."* It can be a strength of a person's character.

Also I want to be careful not to advance a theological position that may be interpreted incorrectly. I don't believe that the more "humble" I am the more my prayers will be answered. It is not character that assures one of God's hearing and answering. The Christian remembers and understands that God hears and answers prayer not on the basis of any merit on the part of the one who prays, but solely on the basis of the merit of Jesus.

The prayer that ascends highest comes from the lowest depths of a humbled heart.

When I reread what I have written above I see love, gratitude, humility, to be humble, and to walk (live) humbly. Humility has not been an easy concept to comprehend and write about.

## Personal Reflection Time

1. What experiences have you had to humble you?

2. What steps are you going to take to be a humble believer in Jesus Christ our Savior and Lord?

3. How does humility play a role in your prayer life?

Humility is the way for us to open communication with the merciful God of heaven.

# 27

# Time

*Very early in the morning, while it was still dark, Jesus got up, left the house and went off to a solitary place, where He prayed* (Mark 1:35).

At the close of the fourth school year of serving the Lord at SFS, we again were open to serving anyplace in the world where our talents and skills were needed. It became a daily prayer concern. Where in the world would the Smiths go next? Several contacts came to us during the following year. Venezuela, Jamaica, and Hawaii were all e-mailing us. None seemed to fit perfectly. We both wanted to be involved in serving. Then Darrell Van Luchene, Deputy Headmaster of Sekolah Pelita Harapan (Pelita Harapan means in English "light" and "hope"), contacted us at the beginning of 2001. Alice was asked to serve as a third-grade teacher in the national plus school. I was asked to head the Counseling Department at Universitas Pelita Harapan (UPH). This match seemed to be perfect. After we made a visit to Indonesia, the green light was given by the LCMS to extend both of us calls to serve as educational missionaries.

The habit of praying at the beginning of each day was formed earlier in my life. Consistency in prayer really came for me when we moved to Indonesia. The first item on my agenda still is personal prayer. So, I spend the first 45 minutes to an hour in Bible reading

If you would ever cease to pray, never cease to long for it.  Augustine

and prayer. I have discovered over the years that the most important task I have as a pastor, counselor, teacher, colleague, coach, grandfather, father, husband and world Christian is to pray for the situations and people that I find surrounding me. The second item is that I have found that my prayer list is so long that I need to write down prayer concerns so I do not forget them. I now have made it a habit to write a new prayer list every few months. My desire is to spend time with this list in prayer each day.

God opened doors through UPH for influencing and impacting the lives of faculty, staff, and students. The years brought more responsibility and opportunity to make an impact for Him than I could ever have dreamed. I found myself leading a team of instructors in teaching a course on leadership from a Christian worldview. Then the university gave me the privilege to be the director of the Student and Alumni Department of our 6,000 plus student body. On top of this I built relationships with the students, while coaching the university basketball team. In addition, a university newspaper was started that provided me the space to have weekly editorials on whatever topic I found I wanted to witness. Then we also were coordinating a weekly house church service that was primarily held in our home. During these years I also wrote and published two books. Now why am I listing all these challenges? They were not listed to impress anyone. The excuse of being too busy to pray could have easily been used by me. My intentional conversation with my Lord gave me time to focus on a relationship with almighty God. He provided the strength and guidance I needed. Instead of prayer being a last resort, it was set as my first priority.

As a Godly servant leader I did not pray to inform Him of what was happening. He already knew. I wanted His divine perspective, insight, and direction to accomplish the variety of tasks that faced me in this chaotic world. The focus in prayer was what God could do, not what I could do. It was prayer that was filled with God's presence. Was it perfect? No. Three definite conclusions were made:

1. No leader is greater than his prayer life.
2. Prayer life flows out of an intimate relationship with God.

God never tires of our asking.

131

3.   Make prayer the number one priority in life.

During those five years in Indonesia one book on prayer became very popular around the globe. Its title is <u>The Prayer of Jabez</u> written by Bruce Wilkinson. The book became an instant success. It is based on I Chronicles 4:10: *Jabez was more honorable than his brothers. His mother had named him Jabez, saying, "I gave birth to him in pain." Jabez cried out to the God of Israel, "Oh, that you would bless me and enlarge my territory! Let your hand be with me, and keep me from harm so that I will be free from pain." And God granted his request.*

Jabez's name appears in the genealogy of the line of Judah. In 1 Chronicles 4:9-10, it states that Jabez is more distinguished than his brothers, and that his mother named him Jabez because she had a difficult time during his birth. The name Jabez means "he causes pain," He prayed to God to bless him at his work, to keep him from evil and disaster, and God granted him his request.

Wilkinson's book had a big influence on Christians everywhere. To me, Jabez' prayer is very similar to my small prayer in meaning. You may not see it but compare the two prayers for yourself.

> Bless, Savior dear,
> Be always near.
> Keep me (and keep all)
> From evil, harm, and fear.
> Amen

We need to be careful of making any prayer like these two into sanctified mantras. I have spoken my prayer almost daily for over sixty years. Repeating these words doesn't add strength to the prayer. It is the motive and proper attitude of the heart. I don't want to trust the words more than our all-powerful God. The focus of the prayer is on God and His provision and protection. We receive blessings in accordance to His will.

Do not assume that God will answer prayers for you in the same way as He did for Jabez or does for Bob Smith just because

Strength in prayer is better than length in prayer.

we prayed the same prayer. If this were so, we could take any Bible character and use their prayer and expect the same results. God's will is not the same for everyone. We are all unique. God deals with each of us on an individual basis.

## Personal Reflection Time

1. Where do you place the priority of prayer in your life?

2. How much time at the beginning of the day do you spend in conversation with God?

3. Do you have a special prayer you repeat?

Prayer is our first duty in life and to plead lack of time is an insult to God. *Ronald Knox*

# 28

# Laborers

*Then he said to his disciples, "The harvest is plentiful but the workers are few. Ask the Lord of the harvest, therefore, to send out workers into His harvest field " (Matthew 9:37).*

During Easter of March 2002 Alice and I accompanied Darrell Van Luchene and his wife Sue on a journey. We visited the interior highlands of Papua, Indonesia (formerly known as Irian Jaya) to survey Christian educational possibilities. It is located on the western half of the world's second largest island, New Guinea. The island is known for its wild beauty, and some of the most inhospitable terrain on earth. The population of this most eastern province of Indonesia is listed as about two and half million people. It is composed of a mixture of Christianity, Islam, animists, and a small percentage of Buddhists. About 275 languages are spoken on this half of the island.

We travelled by Garuda Airlines to the island and arrived at the airfield in Sintani where the Mission Aviation Fellowship pilots live with their families. We next flew in a two-engine plane to Wamena and met a teacher and a nurse. They flew with us in a one-engine plane to the mountaintop village of Halowan.

We spotted the village from the air. It was tucked away near the top of the mountain at the edge of a cliff, and consisted of several buildings and huts beside a short dirt airstrip. We circled to land. As

Seven days without prayer makes one weak.

we came in, we noticed that the airstrip was built on an incline. The short hill helped to stop the plane, and to also provide momentum when taking off again. Shortly after we landed, the pilot turned the plane around and took off again. He left us in this village for the next 24 hours, on our own.

A Christian missionary family had lived there for many years and had translated the Bible into the local language. When their work was done, they moved away from the village about ten years earlier. We stayed in the small guest house, which had been their home.

The villagers were very friendly. Some wore no clothes while others wore tattered second-hand clothes to keep warm. We walked around the village with them and they showed us their small church and their school, which were both in poor repair. They also showed us the inside of their huts, which were charred from their warming fires. They gave us gifts of three live chickens, some eggs and some bananas. A villager who took care of the guesthouse butchered two of the chickens and cooked them in a pressure cooker for supper. We ate the eggs and bananas for breakfast. We gave the villagers a box of food, and gifts of money, and bags of supplies for their church and school.

The following day the plane returned to fly us back to Wamena. Each time we flew, we had to weigh everyone and everything to be sure we were within the weight limits for the plane. We boarded the aircraft and sat in the canvas seats. The pilot started the engine and we took off, gathering speed as the plane rolled down the little hill and out over the cliff! Alice thought: "This is how an eagle must feel when it flies!" We just soared out over the valley and followed the riverbed as it wound through the mountains and back to Wamena. It was a beautiful day and we could see several other little villages on other mountaintops. A few of them also had airstrips; otherwise they were only accessible by footpaths. We arrived safely to Wamena, Sintani, and eventually back to Jakarta. We praised God for good health and safety on our trip.

Have you ever seen or read the book entitled <u>From Jerusalem to Irian Jaya</u> by Ruth A. Tucker? I took it along to read. I had read

God may pass by our elaborate programs and outstanding talents, but He will never pass by the prostrate form of an intercessor. *A. A. Wilson*

bits and pieces over the years. It is about missionaries going to the end of the world. Well, I think we have now gone to the end of the world. What a privilege the Lord had given us. Very few people go into the interior of Papua as far we did. I'm having trouble trying to find the right words to express my feelings. What I saw makes me both happy and sad. They do have the Gospel and faith in Jesus Christ as their Savior. Yet their life is so difficult. They were promised by the government to have an education program twenty years ago and it never was provided to any level that would be acceptable in any society today. They live from day to day with little or nothing. My number one memory will be their smiles as I shook their hands and taught them how to whistle with their hands.

The door of opportunity was open. As a result of our trip, we believed the best way to proceed was to help write a curriculum and train teachers. The government of the province was willing to follow our initiatives. A window of opportunity allowed for the educational system to be built on a Christian worldview. The size of this project was huge! It stretched the mind beyond our wildest dreams. Because groups with different worldviews also realize the vulnerability and value of this area, Christians needed to act quickly. This was absolutely the biggest opportunity I had been touched by in my years of serving the Lord.

The harvest is plentiful but the workers are few. Notice what the real issue is here... He says in verse 37: *"Harvest is truly plentiful... But the laborers are few."* In other words, there is much work to be done... But there aren't enough workers to do it...! I regret I have but one life to give to my Lord. As a result of our recommendations Missionary Dennis Denow moved to Papua. His assignment there was to learn the language and coordinate God's work in Christian education.

We have found the people of this world are more ready to receive the Good News of hope than Christians are ready to give it. I challenge you in your prayers and actions to consider the uttermost part of the world – Papua (Irian Jaya) and beyond.

Talking to men for God is a great thing but talking to God for men is the first thing.

## Personal Reflection Time

1. Do you include praying for labors in your daily prayer time?

2. Do you think locally, globally, or both during your prayer time?

3. Do you know of any young person who could use your prayers and encouragement to be a cross-cultural missionary?

Satan trembles when he sees the weakest saint upon his knees.

# 29

# Fear

*I sought the Lord, and He answered me; He delivered me from all my fears* (Psalm 34:4).

Compassion is a hallmark of Christian discipleship and the sign of God's care for us. I see human beings with the same struggles, concerns and worries. Compassion is reaching out to people in trouble and being with people who are in need. This is exactly what God did. He is "with us" in Jesus Christ. God's message is that He sent His Son to be with us and showed us His compassion. Jesus had great compassion! He had enough compassion to sacrifice his life for man's salvation. It provides hope for all human beings. We want to spread this hope.

Do you remember the story of Paul's vision of the man of Macedonia? *During the night Paul had a vision of a man of Macedonia standing and begging him, "Come over to Macedonia and help us" (Acts 16:9).* Paul, with his traveling companions Silas, Luke and Timothy, was on the second missionary journey. They were at Troas. The door was closed by the Holy Spirit in one direction and opened in another direction for missionary work. Paul, in a vision that was more than a dream, was communicated to in a supernatural way. The message was exceedingly simple. A man, a Macedonian, was standing before Paul and asking him to come

The truth is, prayer works.

across into Macedonia. In effect, he kept standing and yelling, "Help us!" The help desired was plainly spiritual help such as Paul was called to bring by means of the Gospel. The Lord was assigning him this Gentile field for his labors.

Amazingly, I believe I personally heard two Macedonian-like calls for help within a period of two months. After traveling to Papua I was asked to go to Afghanistan. Both were to help the Lutheran Church to evaluate possible missionary and humanitarian work for the future. The Papua trip helped to crystallize plans for moving missionary, Dennis Denow, to the province. The Afghanistan trip provided information on what humanitarian work could be done.

I heard the leader of the Christian organizations in Afghanistan say, "Help us!" I heard the local people living in Kabul and refugees living in the Khyber Pass also say, "Help us!"

I was not aware of any other person in the world who experienced a privilege entirely like these two. These calls for help still lay heavy on my heart. How could I personally respond? How could I motivate others to respond to the information that God gave me? After visiting Papua, I thought it alone was enough to think about and digest. Yet, only two months later, in May 2002, I was completely immersed in Afghanistan. In addition to this, I had a clear and challenging opportunity to serve right at Universitas Pelita Harapan.

Let me repeat, the purpose of this team going to Afghanistan in May of 2002 was to identify facts necessary to make wise, informed decisions for establishing humanitarian mission work in Afghanistan and Pakistan. A team of three members, consisting of missionary Rev. John Duitsman "The Team Leader," from Nairobi, Kenya; Afghanistan born Nazifa Atmar "The Undercover Agent," living in Nashville, Tennessee; and me, "The Encourager," from Indonesia were brought together for the task. We were to make specific contacts with those already working there and evaluate other possible projects that could be recommended for the groups we represented. The report was disseminated to various mission organizations. Pakistan was included because it is so vital to the success of anything done in Afghanistan. People of the Book Lutheran Outreach, Lutheran World

Satan is powerless against the power of Christ's prayer.

Relief and Lutheran Church Missouri Synod Missions were the main sponsors. There are so many stories to share that I have decided to record here my top four significant answers to prayer.

1. Living with and learning from Zebi, a Nooristani people group tribal leader, in his private old mansion in Kabul was a blessing. Two months prior to the trip Nazifa had a dream for three nights in a row to contact him. She was led by God to get in touch with him in a refugee camp in Pakistan. He met us at the Kabul airport and provided for our needs while in Afghanistan. John and I ended up staying with him in the Nooristani mansion in Kabul. Zebi was well known in Kabul and even by the Taliban.

2. The visit to Rechmon Mena School and hearing the struggles of the dedicated women teachers was a contact provided by Nazifa. The school had been closed for over seven years. Their response is remembered: "Your visit brings us so much hope."

3. The traveling experience through Khyber Pass and visit to Shalman Ar's Refugee Camp provided a historical perspective. The significance of that area was so very much to try to absorb. Safety was a huge concern, and we were provided an armed guard.

4. Devotional times with John each morning and evening during the trip became a daily highlight. It was experiencing the sense of God's continued peace and presence throughout the entire trip that made available an unexplainable mountaintop experience.

The results were fantastic. Nobody but the Lord could have woven the events together.

As a result of the trip Martin Luther Computer Center (primarily for women) was organized in Kabul. My visits from hearing these two calls for help may not make much difference for the millions of people that live in these two places, but I have been moved and must act. Therefore, my prayers continue for both Papua and Afghanistan.

When the outlook is bad, try the uplook.

I have been asked to speak about Papua, and especially about Afghanistan, many times since my visits. One question I continue to be asked is: "Were you ever scared?" The answer returns to my childhood prayer I started with at the beginning of this book.

> Bless, Savior dear,
> Be always near.
> Keep me (and keep all)
> From evil, harm, and fear.
> Amen

I believe after sixty years of repeating this prayer, almost daily, the Lord answered it again. God kept me "From evil, harm, and fear." My answer is "Yes and no." In several situations I did feel in danger but I was given courage by knowing that Jesus was with me every step of the way. Over the years I have learned this truth. Jesus never will let anything happen to me that He and I can't handle. He knows it all and I know the rest. Ultimately, He is in control. This gives me courage to take risks and do my best in all circumstances. No, I wasn't really afraid. Fear did not keep me from going to Papua and Afghanistan. Faith moved in and fear moved out.

As you develop this attitude of courage you'll be more willing to work hard moment by moment. And you'll be one giant step closer to the use of all your talents for the glory of God.

### Personal Reflection Time

1. Many times God tells us in Scripture not to be afraid. What are you afraid of?

2. (Put your name in the blanks) "Don't be afraid of what other people think of you, _____. I am with you, _____; I will rescue you, _____" (Jeremiah 1:8).

3. Have you ever had any experiences where Jesus gave you peace during fearful situations?

If you can't sleep don't count sheep. Talk to the Shepherd.

# 30

# Death

*No man has power over the wind to contain it; so no one has power over the day of his death* (Ecclesiastes 8:8).

In my office at Univeristas Pelita Harapan (UPH) was a framed batik picture. It is an artist's viewpoint of the story taken from the Biblical parable of the Good Samaritan. It was an excellent reminder for me to meet the needs of others every day. Alice and I were given a real life experience to become Good Samaritans. We accompanied a small group to Banda Aceh. The trip gave us a view of the magnitude of the earthquake and tsunami disaster on December 26, 2004. More than 200,000 people lost their lives in this province in minutes.

The provinces of Aceh and North Sumatra, Indonesia were devastated by an earthquake measuring 8.9 on the Richter Scale and a tsunami (tidal waves) that struck the coastline shortly thereafter. Most of the survivors described three huge walls of water or waves being at least fifty feet high. Experts say they were traveling at least 500 miles per hour.

A disaster aid team was quickly organized by the Lutheran church to go to Banda Aceh. They were Rev. Ted Engelbrecht, Dr. Steve and Julie Lutz, Dr. Keith Harvey and Dennis Denow. They were assisted by their co-workers in Indonesia, the Van Luchenes

There needs be more fear that we will not hear the Lord than that He will not hear us.

and Smiths. Even before everyone arrived in Jakarta, I had set up a number of meetings with special people in order to prepare them for what they would face. Below are a few of their first impressions in Banda Aceh.

"We then went towards the beach and 'ground zero.' The destruction here defies words. Three weeks after the earthquake and tsunamis, some villages in Aceh province still had not been reached by relief aid workers. Food and some basic supplies had been dropped from small airplanes or helicopters, but no organized cleanup or distribution of supplies had yet begun. The enormity of the destruction of the environment, personal property, infrastructure, families, and individual lives will never be fathomed by anyone except those who experienced it personally. Many survivors still walk around in a daze, unable to comprehend what happened to them. Terror lurks in the minds of thousands who can't sleep at night, who desperately try to erase the vivid images of chaos sweeping over them, who endlessly relive the feelings of total helplessness and excruciating panic... How does it feel to lose seven, fifteen, or fifty-three family members in just a few terrifying minutes? How does it feel to survive when they didn't? And what do you do now?"

After the team returned, Alice and I were told we had to go see this if we were going to try to explain it to others. So we went to Banda Aceh in March. Let me give you my reactions.

Whatever you can imagine in your mind as to the scale of the catastrophe, it was worse. Pictures and cameras did not capture the extent of damage or do it justice. Expressions of grief were profound, lonely, and overwhelming. I was told about one man who lost his entire family. He could not find words to express his grief. He said the sadness was so great. His eyes could not shed tears. Also Alice and I sat and listened to a group of teachers give further details about their experiences. One man told us he had over fifty relatives die. The most touching story came from Armin, a school security guard. Our small group listened in amazement as he shared his detailed description of his survival. He lost his wife and two children as the waves caught up with them while they tried to outrun it

Our intercession may be the key to God's intervention.

on his motorcycle. I will remember his final words. "It is healthy for me to tell my story. The pain goes out when I share it. Before this, I never have told anyone."

Missionary Dennis Denow was eventually asked to move from Papua closer to Aceh province and Nias Island, so that he could help plan and oversee several middle and long term development projects in the hardest hit areas. Dennis shared this information.

"It is the most fundamental Muslim area in all of Indonesia. Three years before the tsunami the provincial leaders were given permission by the central government to begin introducing Islamic law in the province. For two years the Indonesian military had been making a concerted effort to neutralize a very strong rebel faction that wanted Aceh to separate from Indonesia and become an independent Islamic state. The fundamental Muslim leaders didn't want any Westerner, because they assume that all Westerners are Christian and will cause problems by trying to evangelize their people. The government leaders didn't want any foreigners in Aceh, because they were afraid that they'll be in danger due to the civil war.

"The earthquake and tsunami burst open the doors to Aceh province, much to the chagrin of the religious and governmental leaders. They had no choice but to allow foreign relief and aid workers in to assist with the overwhelming task of cleaning up, taking care of tens of thousands of refugees, and starting the task of rebuilding. Particularly, the religious leaders abhorred the current situation and were determined to get back to normal as quickly as possible. In the interim they were keeping a very watchful eye on the activities of the foreigners, especially those with connections to Christian or other religious organizations. Concepts such as 'short term' and 'long term' have different definitions in regard to Aceh... and the definitions may be adjusted without notice."

After six years of helping to train Muslim teachers the Lutheran Church was finally refused permission to continue in 2011.

Life is short. Death is certain. Yet we know that God is stronger than every wave of sorrow in this life. He wants to help us through difficult times. There is hope for the future. He can take sorrow and

True prayer will achieve just as much as it costs us. Samuel M. Zwemer tragedy and turn it into a positive future. Alice and I had an overwhelming conviction that God could use this event to unite people around the globe.

Our daily prayers are needed for divine guidance, hope, comfort, and renewal in the lives of those so deeply devastated by any horrific disaster. Many survivors have no knowledge or assurance of eternal salvation through faith in Christ Jesus, our Lord and Savior. Pray that our proclamation of the Good News of Christ will touch lives that have been shattered by devastating events wherever in the world they come.

### Personal Reflection Time

1. "The good were taken. Only the bad are left. I must be one of the bad. I am left here to suffer." How would you respond to the lady that said this in Banda Aceh?

2. Statistics on death are impressive. One out of one people die. Are you prepared for it?

3. Form a prayer in your mind you would say to a person who is dying next to you?

Call on God, but row away from the rocks.

Pray as if your life depended upon it. It does.

## 31

# Defend

*But in your hearts set apart Christ as Lord. Always be prepared to give an answer to everyone who asks you to give the reason for the hope that you have. But do this with gentleness and respect* (1 Peter 3:15).

During the years (1991-1996) at Valley Lutheran High School I taught a senior course called Christian Ethics. I knew I needed guidance of the Holy Spirit to fulfill my responsibilities as an instructor. It was an awesome challenge. I spent time praying for health, strength, safety and five other areas that God would help me. I wanted to learn to:

- Witness Law and Gospel to those who touched my life.
- Lift the dignity of others so they could have hope and glorify God.
- Accept others and build relationships.
- Increase my knowledge, faith, and trust to conform to His will.
- Discern and understand what is right and wrong according to God's will.

"No one is a firmer believer in the power of prayer than the devil; not that he practices it, but he suffers from it. *Guy H. King*

Long hours were spent in class preparation. God molded and blessed my efforts. I slowly began to learn about what it meant to have a Christian worldview in a pluralistic society.

Ten years later God was still answering those prayers when another unexpected opportunity unfolded for Alice and me. God had blessed our son Kurtis with friends, Dr. David and Ingrid Kutsch, in Lincoln, Nebraska. Dr. Kutsch had invited Kurtis to travel to France to attend the Ninth Annual European Summer Study Session of the International Academy of Apologetics, Evangelism & Human Rights. It was held at Trinity Theological Seminary in Strasbourg, France. Each year twenty students from around the world are invited to attend the academy. Actually, it was the second unique chance for Kurtis to learn to defend historic Biblical faith. Two years previously, Dr. Kutsch had attended the academy with Kurtis. As the plans were made for them to attend a second time, Dr. Kutsch decided to back out and told Kurtis to try to find a replacement for him. Can you guess whom Kurtis asked? Right, his parents! The Kutsch family covered the cost for both Alice and me to attend.

The two weeks of classes tested our mental abilities to the fullest. Dr. John Warwick Montgomery served as the director and primary instructor. He is chiefly noted for his major contributions as a writer, lecturer and public debater in the field of Christian apologetics. He holds earned doctorates in philosophy, theology and law. He has authored over 100 scholarly journal articles and more than fifty books. He is often compared to C.S. Lewis and Francis Schaefer. He is considered by many to be the foremost living apologist for biblical Christianity. We thanked God for such an opportunity, the support, and asked for supernatural knowledge for us to learn all that was possible. Let me try to summarize various thoughts that were learned from him on apologetics.

The Greek word at the root of apologetics means defense. In this case it means the rational defense of the Christian faith. It is the attempt to remove barriers to faith by responding to critical attacks. It offers a defense for the doctrinal and ethical content of biblical religion. Christians need to know how to defend Christian truths.

To whip the devil, fall on your knees.

Apologetics deals with the hurdles, difficulties or intellectual side of coming to Christ. Think of the road of salvation as a road that has holes in it. The believer's task is to move non-believers toward the house of salvation. The obstructions along the way are of various kinds. Apologetics deals with the intellectual obstructions. Christians are to keep people moving. We must not let an unbeliever sit down along the side of the road on the basis that there are legitimate objections to continuing or holes in the road. They shouldn't refuse to believe something until they have investigated it. Non-believers owe it to themselves to check out Christianity.

If non-Christians focus attention on Christians' lives they may be disappointed. Christians need to be able to give the reason for the hope and faith within us. We need to give evidence that doesn't depend on us. As Christians we need to shift the attention from ourselves to Christ. Do you remember John the Baptist? *"He must become greater; I must become less"* (John 3:30). We need to be careful that in giving our testimony we don't keep increasing but Christ decreases.

Personal testimony is often the easiest and best beginning point, but it is not the proper stopping place. When witnessing we need to go beyond to the actual facts of the Gospel message.

Let's look at Paul in Athens (Acts 17:16ff). Paul doesn't go on Mars hill and tell the philosophers: "What a great experience I've had." He starts where his listeners are. He quotes the Stoic philosophers' poets. He goes on to share that what is missing in their position is the objective information of Jesus and his resurrection from the dead.

The apologist learns to show that Christ is the answer to the problems of the day. It is a spiritual task to do extra study and reading on what others believe. There should be discipline and perseverance to study and improve our defense of the Gospel. It takes hard work to prepare how to witness to non-believers.

Apologetics is never the starting point. The starting point is evangelism with the Gospel. There is no tension between the work of the Holy Spirit and the apologetics' task. According to Scripture the Holy Spirit is constantly working to convince the world of sin,

If you are strangers to prayer you are strangers to power. Billy Sunday

righteousness and judgment. Wherever the apologetics' task is carried out, the Holy Spirit is working in it. Anytime obstacles are removed from traveling to the foot of the cross it is attributed to the work of the Holy Spirit. It becomes so important for us to include in our prayers the understanding of scripture so we are able to witness with gentleness and respect.

## Personal Reflection Time

1. Believers do not have the choice of witnessing or not. We are called to witness. Believers only choose whether to witness better or less effectively. How effective are you?

2. What steps could you take to expand your knowledge of various belief systems with people with whom you come into contact? (Ex: Muslims or those of a different generation or culture than your own).

3. Are you including in your prayers the ability to understand why you believe what you believe?

Pray often; for prayer is a shield to the soul, a sacrifice to God, and a scourge for Satan. *John Bunyan*

# 32

# Suffering

*And we know that in all things God works for the good of those who love Him, who have been called according to His purpose* (Romans 8:28).

After attending the academy in France, Alice and I flew on to Indonesia and Kurtis returned to Slidell, Louisiana, a suburb of New Orleans. This is where Kurtis, his wife and four children were living. It was not long after that Hurricane Katrina on August 29, 2005 arrived on the scene. It was not until the Christmas holidays when I went there did I fully understand the destruction. (Alice had stayed in Indonesia.)

Winds had flattened the Mississippi coastline and driven a wall of water through the levees of New Orleans. Eighty percent of the city, home to more than 450,000 people, had flooded. By the time the damage had been tallied, Hurricane Katrina ranked as the costliest natural disaster in American history. While visiting Kurtis and family they took me on a tour of Slidell, New Orleans and the Mississippi coastline. Even after several months of recovery time it still took my breath away when I saw Slidell and New Orleans. I thought the devastation in Mississippi was similar to the tsunami in Banda Aceh. For miles and miles along this shore, every standing structure had been crushed.

Many people pray as if God were a big aspirin pill; they come only when they hurt.
*B. Graham Dienert*

Let me give you some excerpts from Kurtis' following Easter letter and other correspondences. They recounted some of the events and reactions to those first few days and the months of recovery that followed:

"Jesus' resurrection means a bit more to us this year as our region takes part in a resurrection of sorts itself. Many thanks to the thousands of people who have given their time, energy and finances to help in the vast clean-up and rebuilding efforts along the Gulf Coast.

"Our family fully returned home to Slidell three months after hurricane Katrina's eye wall hit our community. It had 176 mile/hr sustained winds, 190 mile/hr gusts and a storm surge that came nearly five miles inland. We were able to return home because of the generous prayers, financial aid and help of various family, friends and other 'angels in our midst'. Again, thank you if you were one of those angels.

"To bring you up to speed, Kurtis was hired the same week we returned to Louisiana by Lutheran Disaster Response—an arm of Lutheran Social Services. At that point, the plan was somewhat unclear, but after much prayer and hard work organizing hundreds of volunteers, a tent city was developed that can now facilitate 100-150 volunteers per day in clean-up and rebuilding work along the northern and eastern sides of Lake Pontchartrain... By April 1, over 1500 volunteers had served through the Slidell camp, totaling approximately 70,000 hours of service valued at $1.26 million.

"Because of the positive impact of the volunteers upon our community, LDR received the Slidell Chamber of Commerce organization of the month award this past week...an excellent opportunity for us to witness Jesus' love and the reasons for our service to the community. It has been a tremendous opportunity for our whole family to be involved in some awesome ministries. God has not forsaken us down here. He is alive and flourishing in ways we could never have imagined!

They who pray not, know nothing of God,
and know nothing of the state of their own souls. *Adam Clarke*

"On the home front, we have the house better than ever. We are now enjoying all the little fix ups that have been done to the house after the damage, and we are getting back to somewhat of a 'normal' life.

"The biggest change is that we have converted the small living room area of our home into a 'bunk house'. A handy man from the camp built us two bunk beds from two-by-fours. So, often we have been hosting up to six people at a time. It's like running our own little "bed and breakfast". It is a lot of hard work, but the blessings these people have been in our lives far outweigh the work...

"For all the stress and strain of the last eight months, our family has never been better. We are able to see more clearly how every single thing, and even each breath we take, belongs to God. He gave it to us, and at any moment, He can take it away. We are able to share each Sunday evening with the volunteers from the camp our experiences through Hurricane Katrina. Teresa shares what it is like for a family to go through evacuation and life after the storm. Sophia stands up, as well, and shares. We started out mentioning negative things and then realized that there were actually more positive than negative items. The best thing was that out of the storm people came to share Jesus with other people. Some people are now Christian because of the storm...it's just like the Bible says *'...all things work for the good of those who love God!'* (Rom.8:28)

"Prayerfully addressing disasters brings God's good work into the midst of difficulties. Keeping God as our focus—praying for victims of disasters even if we aren't victims ourselves—allows us to care for people who are in dire need and more often than not, we and they receive blessings from God."

Kurtis concludes...

"Ten years ago I interviewed refugees from a civil war in Liberia, West Africa for a LCMS World Mission video project. I

Trouble and perplexity drive me to prayer and prayer drives away perplexity and trouble.
*Philip Melanchthen*

remember distinctly how, despite the total destruction of their belongings and the loss of life around them, they still found joy. When I asked them where they found joy they simply stated, 'Jesus.'"

The more a believer knows Jesus, the more he will love Jesus. The more the believer loves Jesus, the more he will trust Jesus to turn disasters into good.

### Personal Reflection Time

1. Recall a disaster you have experienced. How did God help you turn it into good?

2. On what can a believer focus when he has the privilege of going through a disaster?

3. What lessons have you learned about praying when suffering a disaster?

The Great Physician is always on call.

# 33

# Desire

*Delight yourself in the Lord and He will give you the desires of your heart* (Psalm 37:4).

After Missionary Ted Engelbrecht came back from visiting the destruction in Banda Aceh, he invited me to attend a meeting in Jakarta with Rev. Nelson Siregar, Human Care Director of the *Huria Kristen Batak Protesten* (HKBP) (Lutheran Church in Indonesia). He was in Jakarta to raise money from the HKBP congregations there to rebuild the Banda Aceh church. He came with the president of one of the three districts. Of all the people we met, he was the most optimistic about the prospect of rebuilding and even growing the church as a result of the tsunami. He called it a 'strategic event.' Upon hearing that I worked at a Christian university in Jakarta, the district president immediately invited me to run seminars on prayer and leadership at the HKBP seminary and college.

For me the desire was there but not the time and means to do it. In the early fall of 2005 Rev. Dr. Richard Carter from Concordia University in St. Paul, Minnesota was taking a sabbatical in India. He contacted us about coming to Indonesia with his wife for two weeks. Through Dennis Denow's assistance and the financial support from LCMS we made plans for Rich and me to lead a one

Don't pray when it rains if you don't pray when the sun shines. *Satchel Paige* day seminar at Abdi Sabda Seminary with approximately 300 seminary students. Additionally, a Church Worker's Retreat with twenty-four church workers from various institutions and congregations in Northern Sumatra was conducted for three more days at a resort on Lake Toba. Topics included Luther's catechism and prayer. The Lutheran Heritage Foundation had already translated Luther's Catechism into Indonesian. Three thousand copies were being stored in our garage. My book on prayer had also been translated into Indonesian. Both books could be distributed to those in attendance. Praise God for wonderful coordination of all these events. We were impressed with their desire for education. The training and books were well received and today there is an open invitation for Lutheran pastors to help with professional growth in Sumatra. Dr. Carter was excellent in presenting Luther's material. We all agreed the money spent for the week was well worth the expense. It was my privilege to present a Christian view of prayer.

I received a special note from Rev. Jaharianson Saragih, head and chairman of Abdi Sabda Seminary:

> "Sincerely, speaking your book on prayer and your experience in praying touched me to pray more and more. You know that your book really inspired our faculty and students to pray more for those who received the books. Actually this is our longing to have a praying seminary.
> "Frankly speaking, due to the lack of your books our faculty and students really would like to ask your favor to send more of your books to Abdi Sabda. We are so glad if you can send us 50 books more so that we can share to representatives of each class and to all faculties."

During those days, Rich's wife, Miriam, and Alice, visited several landmarks where a German Lutheran missionary worked to establish Lutheran churches in the latter part of the 19th century. They came back well informed about the fascinating story of the "Apostle to the Bataks."

In every storm there is a 'Peace! Be still'
Christ will speak where a prayer's call invites Him. *Jack Hayford*

Ludwig Ingwer Nommensen traveled as a German Christian Lutheran missionary to Sumatra in 1862. He worked in the interior among the Bataks, a people previously untouched by either Islam or Christianity. He stood on a mountain, looked out as far as he could see, and prayerfully claimed the magnificent country for Christ. He wrote in his diary with prophetic vision: "In my spirit I can already see Christian churches and schools all over the place... Young and old alike I see walking to the church and hear the church bell ringing everywhere."

After some initial troubles, the mission work began to succeed, with the conversion of several tribal chiefs and their followers. By 1876 there were 2000 Batak Christians. Nommensen translated the New Testament into Batak by 1878. He undertook to preach the Gospel without replacing the native culture by a European one, to develop native Church leaders, and a native order of worship. He died in 1918 at the age of 84. The Christian community he had planted grew and prospered. With the coming of World War II, the missionaries were driven out or imprisoned, and the Batak people took over completely the management of their own church. Today HKBP is the largest Protestant denomination in Indonesia, with a baptized membership of over two and a half million. Nommensen University was established in 1954 and now has over 8,000 students. Also HKBP has over 500 churches in Indonesia.

This combined experience in Medan and Lake Toba was one of the highlights of our stay in Indonesia. The experience of meeting the Batak Christian people was a delight. We would have had a more complete understanding of Indonesia during our five years, had these acquaintances taken place earlier in our ministry.

It is amazing to me that our great God, whose power guides the heavens and the earth, also has time to love and be concerned about ordinary individuals like me. Never is He so busy that He does not have time to listen to me and my desires. Think of what that can mean. This whole trip to Sumatra was begun with a desire to share the Gospel with church workers.

No human heart is outside the reach of God's love. We know God is always with us. How daring are you when it comes to sharing

It is not elegance, but earnestness that counts in prayer.

your desires with God? As we come to Him with our requests, we can be sure that He will hear our petitions and help us. He is never too busy to stop and listen and then answer the prayers of those who delight in Him. When we prioritize God and His values; He will reward and satisfy us in the end.

### Personal Refection Time

1. How do you prioritize God in your life?

2. Recall a desire that God has helped you make into a reality.

3. What are three desires you presently have that would glorify God and model Jesus?

It is mockery to pray for deliverance from temptation, then deliberately walk into it.

## 34

# Crises

*Be joyful in hope, patient in affliction, faithful in prayer*
(Romans 12:12).

O n a Monday night Yuni, a wonderful Christian Indonesian lady who worked with me in the Student Service Department at UPH, talked to her husband on his cell phone around 7:00 p.m. All was going well when they said good night. Dr. Hanafi was leading a US group on a tour of the islands in the Indian Ocean that had suffered from the Tsunami of December 26, 2004. The boat they were on was between Nias and Siberut islands. The good Dr. Hanafi led the LCMS Tsunami Team visit to Nias in January. This man was probably one of the most knowledgeable Christian individuals in all of Indonesia about what needs the people had on those islands. Dennis Denow, the LCMS leader for the redevelopment projects, would work with Hanafi in the future. These islands are inhabited by many Christians.

Tuesday morning Yuni woke up to the announcement that there had been another earthquake right on the spot where her husband was traveling. She desperately tried to contact him. No communication could be made. She did the next best thing a Christian can do. She prayed and started phoning others to pray for Hanafi and the group. With trembling hearts, many joined her in her prayer vigil.

God tells us to burden Him with whatever burdens us.

Well, fortunately, when a person is on a boat during an earthquake it may be a safer place to be than on land. Not long after the earthquake their boat safely arrived at the island of Nias. Our prayers for his safety had been answered.

I talked with him that morning on the phone. He told me the island was paralyzed. The worst conditions were in Gunung Sitoli, one of the big cities on Nias. The deaths were probably over 1000. Many people were caught under buildings. He said damage was all over the island. There were only a few doctors available. The hospitals were almost completely destroyed. Food was lacking and medical supplies were in short supply.

C.S. Lewis once said: "Pain insists upon being attended to. God whispers to us in our pleasures, speaks in our consciences, but shouts in our pains. It is His megaphone to rouse a deaf world." I tried to hear and understand what God was saying to us all through these disasters.

We wanted to find how best to help these suffering people and to share the hope of the Gospel. Before the Tsunami occurred, Concordia University at Seward, Nebraska, U.S.A. (CUNE) and Universitas Pelita Harapan had been in discussion about a joint service project. Bruce Creed, Director of International Education at Concordia and I had been trying to plan an activity with students from both universities. Eventually, after a huge amount of planning, students from both universities executed a joint service-learning project from May 26, 2006 to June 10, 2006.

Several positive reasons directed us to help the people of Nias instead of Banda Aceh:

- The needs of the people were great before and after the tsunami and earthquake.
- Lentura Pelita Harapan Foundation, a part of the same foundation as UPH, was starting a Christian school on the island of Nias.
- More opportunities to witness verbally as Christians were available in Nias than in Banda Aceh. Nias is primarily a

If we do not pray we are only half alive and our faith is only half developed.
*Laurence Freeman*

Christian island, with some estimates at 80%. However, their knowledge and understanding of Scripture was weak.

Three main objectives for the service learning trip were to provide:

- A Christian witness and service to citizens of Nias.
- A cross-cultural relationship building opportunity between universities of different countries.
- A short-term cross-cultural service learning experience for UPH and CUNE students.

Our activities of service included painting churches during the day, teaching classes at an orphanage, and holding prayer meetings with children during the evenings. We also distributed children's Arch Books (Bible stories) that had been translated into Indonesian for children. Finally the group had the privilege to participate in a ground breaking celebration for a Lentura Pelita Harapan Christian school.

Personally, I also held a seminar on prayer with over 60 church leaders attending from across Nias. The Lutheran Church Missouri Synod Project Director, Dennis Denow, was there to provide support and guidance. Vionetta Tong did much of the detailed planning. Family friends who were visiting us from the USA, David Grueber and his sister, Ginny Jesberg, also joined the team. The group of eighteen was "Ablaze" with God's love and hope for those going through a crisis.

In Scripture we are told Moses had crises. God used those crises to act in grace and love. Jacob had troubles. God used those troubles to demonstrate His grace and love. Lazarus, the brother of Mary and Martha, died. God provided a miracle to show His grace and love.

The story of crisis and sorrow is never over, but neither is the grace and mercy of God, as He continues to do miraculous things! He allows hardships, difficulties and crises to come into the arena of His grace and mercy to bring good out of the situation. Every crisis

Prayer means warfare and every time we pray we possess more of the enemy's ground.

is an opportunity to act in grace and love. Words of Jesus Christ bring comfort and hope.

The crucifixion of Jesus Christ was a crisis. Through His suffering and death, He brought us His mercy and grace. He calls you and me to take the crises of humanity to Him and return to them the grace and mercy of Jesus Christ!

## Personal Reflection Time

1.  What crises situation have you experienced in your life?

2.  Sometimes life's upsets can make people more open to the Gospel. Do you know anyone in a crisis situation? How do you plan to serve them?

3.  How often do you pray for self-control and patience in your prayers?

Soldiers of the lord are doing real fighting when they are on their knees.

## 35

# Celebration

*This is the day the Lord has made; let us rejoice and be glad in it* (Psalm 118:24).

Two celebrations highlighted the school year of 2005-2006 for Alice and me. The first occurred on Sunday, August 7, 2005. It was our fortieth wedding anniversary. I had the opportunity during the spring to bid at a silent charity auction on a classy planned party. It was to be put on by the local country club for 100 people. The starting price was half of what it was worth. I decided it would be my gift to my bride of forty years of magnificent married life. At the end of the night I had been the only one who bid for it. This opened the door for a wonderful evening on our anniversary date to give thanks and praise God for blessings. It was a great joy to have over 100 friends in Indonesia to witness to and share our special day.

Prayer has always been a part of our marriage, from the first night on our honeymoon until today. We have prayed consistently and specially for each other every day. I can't imagine a better partner or closer friend. Without prayer the success of our relationship would have been on our own wisdom and effort and would have come up short. Without prayer a marriage is left up to chance. That is not good enough. We have seen miraculous answers to our prayers too numerous to mention. The truth is; our prayers for each

The less I pray, the harder it gets; the more I pray, the better it goes. *Martin Luther* other were not always long and detailed. They were often short and to-the-point. Yet, we had a third partner who listened to them and provided guidance. Praying is so crucial for a marriage. God wants marriage partners to join in prayer together. Prayer makes a difference.

"**Wow!** I HAVE BEEN NAMED THE DISTINGUISHED LUTHERAN INTERNATIONAL TEACHER OF THE YEAR 2006!" Alice was humbled, shocked and blessed to receive this award. It was the first of its kind from the Lutheran Education Association (LEA). I was also extremely proud of my wife. She had taught school in the USA, Hong Kong, Nigeria, South Korea and Indonesia. Dr. Jonathan Laabs, the Executive Director of the LEA, traveled from River Forest, Illinois along with Mr. Kurt Bucholz from the international office of the LCMS in St. Louis, Missouri to Indonesia to present the award at a ceremony on May 17, 2006. Every teacher should be blessed at their retirement with such a wonderful experience! As a lifelong learner, her enthusiasm was caught by colleagues and students alike.

In a letter of support, one of Alice's colleagues wrote, "The children in Alice's classroom are bilingual and come from many religious backgrounds. As a Christian school teacher, this makes for a very challenging classroom environment. Mrs. Smith is well adapted to such a classroom, modeling her teaching skill to other teachers in the school and providing solid instruction for the children." Confirming this assessment, a parent said, "Mrs. Smith incorporated many songs in her daily devotions and Biblical Studies classes, which have helped [my son] tune in to all the lessons since he loves singing. This has undoubtedly helped [my son's] spiritual growth as he learns more about God's love and the Christian community through singing."

Regarding her ministry, Alice said, "It has totally been the Holy Spirit who inspired and directed me to minister in a Christian school. In this age of uncertainty and terrorism, it has totally been the Holy Spirit who inspired and directed me to minister in an International school. I never dreamed of it or at any time aspired to it, when I was a young person. As a child, I always wanted to be a teacher,

Prayer is the key that unlocks the resources of heaven and the resistance of hell.
*John F. DeVries*

but I never had a vision of my classroom being on foreign soil. I must say, it has been quite an adventure! I pray 24/7 about every aspect of my work. I know the Lord inspires and directs all of my work. I always pray that my actions and words will reflect the love of Jesus. When I fail, I admit it and ask to be forgiven. Every day is filled with new opportunities to forgive and to be forgiven. As a lifelong learner, I continue to engage in daily Bible study, devotions and prayer. To God be the glory!"

God is pleased when His people gather to celebrate in His name. People are really celebrating His victories, His faithfulness and His grace. God is exuberant and we are not always quick to join in celebrating or inviting others to celebrate with us. Celebrating is the response of those who are passionate about the mission Christ has given us. God is looking for people who will join Him in rejoicing over His blessings. He is looking for believers who know how to throw a great party!

Take time in your life to celebrate even the small victories in living out your Christian worldview. What we are celebrating is His life, the life He offers us. Let there be a celebration today. Why wait?

### Personal Reflection Time

1.  If you are married do you pray with your partner?

2.  Make a list of the top ten things you can celebrate today.

3.  Rejoice, relax and throw a party for someone else or yourself and share how God has blessed.

It is not so true that "prayer changes things"
as that prayer changes me and I change things.

# 36

# Silence

*Be still, and know that I am God* (Psalm 46:10).

A man was observed driving a large truck through a crowded city. At each stoplight he got out and began to beat on the truck with a big stick. He had done this several times when someone became interested and followed him. The observer noticed him beat on the truck several more times before he finally stopped in a parking lot. The now very curious observer got out of his car and asked about the strange behavior. He wondered what could be in the truck he was beating upon so often. The answer surprised him!

"I've got a whole load of canaries," was his quick reply. "In fact, I have four tons of canaries, but the truck is only a two-ton capacity. So I have to make sure that half of them stay in the air at all times otherwise I'd be over my weight limit!"

Isn't life sometimes like that for many of us? At times we've got many more activities, commitments, and/or problems than we can possibly handle. So, like the truck driver or a juggler, we try to keep some of them up in the air at all times. Actually we aren't handling the problems. We are just putting them off. Eventually we will have to do something about them. They are in the back of our minds causing us stress and can result in burnout.

When we become too glib in prayer we are most surely talking to ourselves. - *A.W. Tozer*

We enjoyed every moment of being in Indonesia, but the last six months were hectic for us. We needed a break and a time to reflect, refocus, and relax, before heading into the challenges that faced us, as we were about to relocate in the USA.

Therefore, during July, 2006, we spent one week at a health and wellness center and the following week at a Catholic Retreat Center in Chaing Mai, Thailand. After that, we traveled to Bangkok to attend the wedding of our longtime friend, Dennis Denow and his new bride, Monta. Finally on July 17, we flew to the USA to begin a new chapter in our lives called retirement.

The two weeks in Chaing Mai were certainly new experiences. The first week was for the physical body and the second week was for the spiritual. The pace of life the previous six months was one of running at 90 mph. We needed some down time to recuperate and set the proper perspective for our future. The physical exercise and organically-grown vegetarian food of the first week was good but the second week of silence was a new and rewarding experience. It gave us time to meditate and center our thoughts on God. We knew the transition in our lives was positive but change still caused stress.

For many people, the pace of life has picked up speed so radically, that it demands we take a solid look at our life-style. We need to learn how to give ourselves permission to relax, to play, to enjoy life, and enjoy God for who He is. A time for silence can be included.

The most frequently overlooked dimension in the professional literature on stress is the spiritual. It is not surprising that many stress management programs fail. They do not address the spiritual component of stress. When we deny our spirituality we deaden ourselves to the reality that there is a God who created us and calls us to live in personal relationship with Him.

People often have difficulty trusting that God will supply for their needs. They become victims of countless fears, insecurities, and guilt. We may have difficulty "letting go" and "letting God." We want to be in control, rather than letting God be the supreme ruler of our lives. When we "let go," we admit our powerlessness – we admit that the outcome is not in our hands. All we need to do is admit that we need God's help and trust that God will equip us.

Prayers not felt by us are seldom heard by God. - *Philip Henry*

When we surrender our stressors to Christ, He uses them for our growth and His glory. Christ has reconciled us by setting us free from sin, fear, and the need to justify ourselves. He has done enough. Jesus said that He came to give us both abundant and eternal lives. Christ came to set us free from the stress syndrome.

The scriptures are full of promises to reassure a believer of help from God. Below are several passages from Scripture to use when facing stress.

- *Come to me, all you that are weary and burdened, and I will give you rest* (Matt.11:28).

- *Call on me in time of trouble. I will rescue you, and you will honor me* (Ps. 50:15).

- *Cast all your anxiety on Him, because He cares for you* (1 Peter 5:7).

Meditating on His attributes is one way I found to face the future. Focusing on the strengths of His character can give one comfort and strength. Reviewing who God is provides reassurance to get through stressful circumstances. God is: all powerful... all knowing... everywhere... Maybe we have a lot of stress in our lives, because we do not really believe in the sovereignty of God. Perhaps we are placing too much importance on ourselves and what we are doing.

We have the resource of prayer. Prayer has power. Does this mean that our prayer words, by themselves, can make things happen? No, there is power in prayer because God, for Jesus' sake, promises to hear and answer the fervent prayers of a righteous person, a person made righteous by Jesus Christ. The power of prayer is available to overcome stress.

The key question is: "In what do I place my confidence?" Place God at the center of your stressful life. He is your best Guide in finding ways to reduce stress.

Our short prayers in public owe their point and
efficiency to the long ones in private that have preceded them.

Our aim for the silent week was to enjoy God more than ever before. Our silent prayer retreat offered just that. We had plenty of time to meditate, read, contemplate, walk and relax in a peaceful atmosphere. The silence of the retreat was a gift we gave ourselves. We had come to slow down, to be still, and to get serious about our conversations with God. It was exactly what we needed to refocus, be refreshed, and to recharge before our next leg of life's journey.

### Personal Reflection Time

1.  What is causing you stress?

2.  How do you refocus, be refreshed, and recharge?

3.  Where could you go for a silent retreat with God? When do you plan to do it?

Prayer is when you talk to God; meditation is when you listen to God.

We cannot ask in behalf of Christ what Christ would not ask Himself if He were praying.
*A.B. Simpson*

# 37

# Coaching

*However, I consider my life worth nothing to me, if only I may finish the race and complete the task the Lord Jesus has given me—the task of testifying to the gospel of God's grace* (Acts 20:24).

A man on his ninetieth birthday was quoted as saying that he didn't think he became valuable until he was sixty. Could that be true? At the time of this writing I am about to celebrate my 70th birthday. Maybe I'll never celebrate my ninetieth birthday. Maybe the other saying is also true: "Old too soon, smart too late." At this point in my life I realize that my opinions can provide spiritual guidance to my family, especially to our grandchildren, and other brothers and sisters in Christ. This is why I'm spending time writing this book. By the way, I've discovered it is easy to write a book. All you have to do is sit in front of a blank computer screen until you sweat blood.

My responsibility to mentor or coach others increases with age while Christians and non-Christians look to me for answers as I pastor, counsel, teach, coach and just chat about life. One discovery I've made is, others can not argue with me about my personal experiences. Therefore, I share how God has answered prayers in my life. Perhaps my passion and strong desire for spending time in prayer will be understood and caught by those who listen or read my spiritual autobiography.

God gives peace to those who are quiet before Him.

The purpose for sharing my stories is to glorify God. In my opinion, one of the most important ingredients to my significance or success is not just natural talent and hard work. It is due to the men and women God put into my life to help me in my journey. God provided mentors for our family wherever we lived.

Now it is my turn to be in the right place at the right time for others. My experience as a pastor and head of Universitas Pelita Harapan Coaching and Counseling department opened up opportunities for me to do one-on-one counseling, coaching, mentoring and discipling. These terms, to me, are often used interchangeably and overlap. I prefer to use the term coaching since I was called Coach everywhere we lived in the world. From somewhere I have adopted this definition of "coach:"

> "Coaching for life is the art and practice of guiding a person from where they are toward greater competence and fulfillment that they desire."

Coaching helps people expand their vision, build their confidence, unlock their potential, increase their skills, and take practical steps toward their goals. Coaching is about the future, about asking questions, about clarifying values, about encouraging, and discovering the new. Coaching for life is what I want to do with our sons, their wives, our grandchildren and anyone who touches my life. It is an impossible mission made possible only with the Holy Spirit's guidance and direction.

It is discouraging to hear and read research that some Christian youth are giving up their faith. Some of it has to do with the older generation. Do they see us demonstrate the kind of mature, passionate faith we would like for them to have? How shall we witness successfully? Become a life coach or mentor. Build a relationship with a younger person. They need to know they are personally, absolutely and unconditionally loved by and reconciled to God in Jesus Christ.

It is our task to show others that Jesus is the Messiah in the way we confidently live and speak. We want them to look at our lives to

It is easy to discuss prayer and to read books about it.
But the actual practice of prayer is difficult.

see what Christ does for people by hearing our conversation and by seeing our conduct. The way we live and speak should conform to our beliefs. God can and will work powerfully through us.

The Apostle Paul prayed for those he coached:

- He prayed that the Holy Spirit will help them in their weakness (Romans 8:26, Ephesians 3:16).
- He prayed that they would not do what was wrong, but will do what was right (2 Corinthians 13:7).
- He prayed that the eyes of their heart would be enlightened (Ephesians 1:18).
- He prayed a prayer of thanksgiving for them (2 Timothy 1:3).
- He prayed that they would increase in knowledge and depth of insight (Philippians 1:9, Colossians 1:9).
- He prayed that they would be able to avoid anxiety and turn their concerns over to God in prayer (Philippians 4:6).
- He prayed that God would fulfill their every good purpose and that the name of the Lord Jesus would be glorified in them (2 Thessalonians 1:11-12).
- He prayed that they would be active in sharing their faith (Philemon 1:6).

Think of some person in your life that you could coach. Use the prayers of the Apostle Paul as your prayers for the young person or friend you have chosen to coach.

I believe young people are searching for adult relationships they can trust. We can help them to get a grip on the changeless truths of the Bible, God's word. Otherwise they are at risk to be blown away by other worldly beliefs. They need to understand what they believe and why they believe what they believe. My commitment is to be an "enabler, encourager, a can do" Christian coach. In all cases, I want to convey clearly the saving message of Jesus Christ as the Lord and Savior. The key to coaching wisdom is to identify someone and reach out to him or her. In each of our lives, another person is waiting for our approach no matter how young or old you are.

Prayer is not an exercise. It is the life of the saint. *Oswald Chambers*

## Personal Reflection Time

1. The secret to effectively sharing God's word and living His will is privately feeding on it. You are to be the best model and reflection of Christ that you can possibly be. Are you willing to meet the challenge?

2. God has reached down with the "walking stick" of His Gospel and has snatched us old antiques (my generation) out of the trash heap while we were still dead in our trespasses and sins. In His grace and mercy we all need to TELL OUR STORY!

3. What impossible mission do you have right now that is only possible with the Holy Spirit?

Prayer does not equip us for the greater work, Prayer is the greater work.

# 38

# Success

*...The Lord doesn't see things the way you see them. People judge by outward appearance, but the Lord looks at the heart* (1 Samuel 16:7).

During my junior year at Concordia College I started coaching basketball for a local recreational league. Since then, I have had the opportunity to build relationships through coaching a variety of sports right up through today. In the mid seventies Ruth (List) Elbers one of St. Lorenz girls' basketball players asked me this question: "What is success?" I don't remember having a very clear answer for her. At that same time Coach John Wooden of UCLA became famous during the 1960's and early 1970's. He designed what was called the Pyramid of Success. Basically, it was a moral guideline by which he thought everyone was to live. Along with it he had a definition of success that he penned way back in 1934:

> "Success is peace of mind that is the direct result of self-satisfaction in knowing you did your best to become the best that you are capable of becoming."

Beloved, it is not our long prayers but our believing God that gets the answer.
*John G. Lake*

From this beginning Bob Smith's definition evolved over the next thirty years:

In Hong Kong I included "in the time and the place God has called me." In Nigeria, I tacked on "to God's glory." At the Calcutta airport after my fourth service learning trip, I added the word "servant" to the definition. Later in Indonesia, while teaching a leadership course at the university, I added the word "leader." This resulted:

"Success is the peace of mind knowing I did my best to be the best servant leader I could possibly be, in the time and the place God called me, to His glory."

This definition was used extensively during the years with the Valley Lutheran High School football team. Our son, Eric – the head coach at that time – gave me the privilege to be the chaplain for the team. It was special to be his assistant and to minister to the spiritual needs of coaches and players. The challenge was not easy since society looks at the win column as to success. Here is the definition I gave the team:

"Success is the peace of mind that you did your best to be the best VLHS football player you could possibly be in the time and place where God called you, to His glory."

In the 2007 season VLHS football team suffered a heartbreaking loss of a football game in a double overtime 40-34. It was a tremendous effort by every player and coach. Could we have done things differently? Yes. Hindsight is always more clear for us. Emotionally it was not easy to accept that final score. We all wanted desperately to win but it wasn't to be. As their spiritual leader I shared these few thoughts:

"It is important for us at these times to remind ourselves of our Christian perspective of winning and losing. It helps to answer this question again: 'What do we consider is the total athlete or coach?'"

"Prayer as a relationship is probably your best indicator about the health of your love relationship with God. If your prayer life has been slack, your love relationship has grown cold." - *John Piper*

Forty years ago, I learned this definition from Athletes in Action organization: "A total athlete is one who uses all of his God-given abilities of body, mind and spirit to the ultimate, for the glory and honor of God."

Throughout our preparation for every football season we worked for excellence. Coaches and players of VLHS football team knew they were going to honor God whether we won or lost. We were going to give God the glory. We left our ultimate effort on the field and honored Him in doing so. The "winning-is-the–only-thing" phrase wasn't true on this team. What was most important was going into a contest and giving maximum effort. Could our play selection, execution, and actions have been better? Sure, we never wanted to stop learning and improving.

God already knew our desire to win. We wanted our players to be "winners" in God's sight and secondly in the world's view. The fans couldn't see our attitude. Only God can view our hearts. We encouraged players to play to win, but first and foremost we wanted our team to honor God by doing our best and controlling our emotions in positive ways. We prayed for the fullness of God's blessing, presence, influence, and protection. Those were good requests for football players and for our lives in general.

Some of VLHS players or parents might have been asking, "Does it really help to pray?" Without any doubt it helps to talk to our Father who loves us. *"The prayer of a righteous man is powerful and effective"* (James 5:16). A righteous man is one who has a relationship with Jesus and has been made righteous by Him. We have found that a tenacious endurance is often the key to a successful prayer.

Another major point of concern might be valid. We didn't want prayer to become viewed as a good work that merits God's favor. Just because we prayed, didn't mean we were going to win. We knew for sure some other teams' players, coaches and parents would also be praying before and after games. This is very positive for all.

We did encourage everyone involved with this team to begin their prayers with *humility*. Continue their prayers with *trust*. Conclude

Money millionaires have a poor rating alongside prayer millionaires.

their prayers with *obedience*. Jesus has invited everyone to ask Him for wisdom, and He says He will give it to you. In one way or another God will answer. There are times when He answers in different ways than what we are expecting. No one person really knows why sometimes God doesn't answer prayers the way we think they should be answered. We have to trust that what He does is best for us.

Mother Teresa was motivated by God's love and sacrifice for her through Jesus Christ. That relationship helped her pick up the first poor person in need. It is interesting what Mother Teresa once said when asked, "How do you measure the success of your work?" She looked puzzled for a moment and then replied, "I don't remember that the Lord ever spoke of success. He spoke only of faithfulness in love. This is the only success that really counts."

### Personal Reflection Time

1.  How do you define success in your personal life?

2.  How could you be more successful in your prayer life?

3.  What role does humility, trust, and obedience play in your prayer life?

Prayer is not overcoming God's reluctance, but laying hold of His willingness.
*Martin Luther*

## 39

# Witnessing

*"Come, follow me," Jesus said, "and I will make you fishers of men"* (Mark 1:17).

What do you wish to accomplish through your prayer life? How do you see God working in your life through prayer? I believe setting goals, objectives, or having a vision serves to inform and inspire. Vision clarifies purpose and gives direction. It helps to reflect the uniqueness of a person, to serve as a guide to strategy and action for improving your prayer life. I would hope that your vision for prayer is so powerful that it would shape your prayer life each day. For example, what are your most critical prayer concerns? Does it include prayer for opportunities to witness? Does it include particular people whom you would like to share the Gospel? Once a person has an understanding that witnessing is a priority for the future then a plan can be made, possible obstacles predicted, and prayer supporters recruited. I believe the most important time I can spend for all people and situations in my life is to spend time in prayer. A strong approach to praying for open doors to witnessing can be achieved. Envision yourself praying in the future and God accomplishing a difference through you. Picture the impact! Be in tune with the power of God through prayer.

Prayer will promote our personal holiness as nothing else, except the study of the Word of God.

In 2009 Rev. Roland Wells personally introduced a small group of which I was part to the "Mission Shift" Video series produced by the School of Urban Ministry in Minneapolis, Minnesota. The series focuses on the emphasis the new international immigrants pose to the Twin Cities and Minnesota churches. It presents the challenge of reaching new international neighbors in the midst of the greatest human migration in the world. Six sessions are included in the total program. Permit me to share just a little bit from the first video class entitled: "The Whole World Has Changed and the Church is Asleep."

Rev. Wells explained that the coming change in society will be greater than the fall of the Roman Empire, the Black Death, World War II and the Nuclear Age. He continues to point out a "Perfect Storm of Change" is coming to the world. The first condition of that change is urbanization. What did he mean? He says that over 70% of the world will be living in huge mega cities by the year 2025. This in itself will cause huge relationship problems. The second condition is migration. We are witnessing a complete mixture of cultures in every part of the world. This will create many needs. The third condition is fluidity of capital, labor, and information. What can and will the church be doing to heal the hurt and anger this storm of perfect change is creating?

Here are some other observations to add to Rev. Wells opinions. Other subtle shifts have taken place that face Christians today. One involves secularization or specifically the belief system that denies the reality of God. Another shift in Western culture comes in the form of community to individualism. It is a shift from the "We" mentality to the "Me" mentality. Another change has been a severing in the connection from our beliefs to how we behave. Christians do not behave according to Christian beliefs.

The task at hand is to take the changeless Gospel and communicate it in a relevant and meaningful way to an ever-changing world – to take the first-century message and communicate it to the 21st-century citizen.

As I continue my journey up the King's highway, I have witnessed some eye-opening situations in the church today. The Lord

It is not well for a man to pray cream and live skim milk. - *Henry Ward Beecher*

has allowed me to observe some troubling and positive signs of the times. The church cannot be lukewarm or fall asleep. We need to be in a revival mode not a survival mode. The responsibility begins with me.

J. Hudson Taylor is credited with saying the following: "I used to ask God if He would come and help me. Then I asked if I could come and help Him. Finally I ended by asking God to do His own work through me." This sounds like a pretty good idea to me.

Below is one of my favorite poems that is based upon the biblical story of the feeding of the five thousand. I rewrote the poem into a prayer and now connect it to my witnessing. Could this be helpful to you and others?

How long will it take us to learn that our shortest route to the man next door is by way of God's throne? *A. T. Pierson*

**Five Loaves and Two Fish**
By: Philip Clarke Brewer

God uses
What you have
To fill needs which
You never could have filled.

God uses
Where you are
To take you where
You never could have gone.

God uses
What you can do
To accomplish what
You never could have done.

God uses
Who you are
To let you become who
You never could have been.

**Five Loaves and Two Fish Prayer**
By: Philip Clarke Brewer
Rewritten for Praying
By: Robert W. Smith

God use
What I am
To fill needs which
I never could fill.

God use
Where I am
To take me where
I never could go.

God use
What I can do
To accomplish what
I never could do.

God use
Who I am
To let me become who
I never could be.

## Personal Reflection Time

1. Are you praying for open doors to witness?

2. A new word being used is G L O C A L-Think globally act locally. How do you and your local church work glocally?

3. Go back and use **Five Loaves and Two Fish Prayer** as a prayer right now.

All great soul-winners have been men of much and mighty prayer...
*Samuel Logan Brengle*

# 40

# Love

*"But I tell you: Love your enemies and pray for those who persecute you"* (Matthew 5:44).

While living in Indonesia, a family from Jakarta attended our house church. The father was from Afghanistan. He shared his life story with us. As a young boy, he lived with his Muslim family. Eventually, he was accepted to study at a university in England. A Christian group at the university asked him to join their Bible study group. His father found out and immediately called him back to Afghanistan. Upon return he was given an ultimatum to make a choice: Muslim? Christian? Which was it going to be? Later that night he walked out of his home in Kabul and for three days walked through the Khyber Pass into Pakistan. There he found a Christian church and pastor, who offered him a room to rest and recuperate. After a few days he walked into the community and saw a newspaper in a news stand. On the front page was his picture. Under it was the inscription: Wanted Dead or Alive! His father had asked the newspaper to print the announcement. Our friend never returned to his home town nor did he ever see his father again. In God's timing, he became a Christian pastor.

Unfortunately, his story is more common than we would like to believe. Worldwide, Islam uses fear and threats to discourage

The men who have done the most for God in this world have been early on their knees.
*E. M. Bounds*

those, who might have an interest in Christianity or any other religion, from openly pursuing it.

Because my wife and I lived in Muslim majority nations, it provided us opportunities to know and become friends with many Muslims and former Muslims. Therefore, upon our return to Michigan, we were invited to share our experiences, knowledge, and understanding of Islam.

Islam is a very hot topic for the speaking circuit. Just what is the Muslim faith all about, and what can the average Christian do to reach out and share the Gospel with a Muslim?

This is a time of great suspicion between Muslims and Christians. We need to increase our understanding of Islam and extend genuine love and servanthood, so we can reach out to our Muslim neighbors. We need to bridge the gap between Muslims and the Gospel.

The twenty-first century wholelistic approach to witnessing includes the Gospel, fulfilling a need, and building a relationship with those being served. The principles of deep friendship, God's word, and mercy are all needed. The task the Lord Jesus has given to us is to testify to ALL people. Muslims are included in the Gospel of God's grace.

First, in my Muslim encounters, I try not to see a Muslim. I try to see another human being. Second, I see a potential friend. Then I see one whom I can serve and share God's love. Muslims hope that Christians can respect them. Karl Menninger, a famous psychiatrist, says, "Love is the medicine of the world." As a Christian I try to resist the temptation to be caught up in generalization, anger, hate or fear toward anyone.

My experience has found that most Muslims are kind, peaceable people. A few Muslims are not. Our attitude should be built on the former, but we also have to deal with the latter. Not all Muslims are terrorists. Most Muslims are moderate and conservative and are not extremists.

In the Muslim mind, Christianity is directly associated with something called the West. We must insist on the distinction between westerner and Christian. The government is to protect the

We must move from asking God to take care of the things that are breaking our hearts, to praying about the things that are breaking His heart. *Margaret Gibb*

country. The Church or Christians are to witness God's grace, love and compassion.

Our outreach to Muslims will take far more patience, time, and focus than outreach to other religious blocs and ethnic groups. While some principles do overlap with Christianity, a Muslim will need to hear the Gospel many times before he or she will even begin to consider it. We must reach out and go to Muslims. This requires a relational approach. Once a relationship is built, Muslims need to have many discussions with a Christian. Both sides need to spend plenty of time listening. We, as Christians, have to take the first step in our relationship with Muslims. We must cultivate genuine friendships. To love Muslims is not just a strong feeling – it is a decision.

Here is the challenge: Muslims, who are no longer simply "over there", but are now "right here." The growth of numbers of Muslims in the West means that Christians who live where Muslims live now have witnessing opportunities they never had before. Muslims are coming to faith in Christ because they rub elbows with Christians. More Muslims are converting now than ever before, because God has given Christians a new opportunity. The October issue of Christianity Today 2007 reported a study of 750 Muslims surveyed, who became Christians between 1991 -2007. Its title was "Why Muslims Follow Jesus."

First, the lifestyle of Christians is the most important influence in their decision to follow Christ. 1. Love of Christians 2. Treatment of women 3. Adaptation of simple lifestyle – local customs.

Second, the power of God in answered prayers and healing. Closely related was the finding, that some noted deliverance from demonic power.

Today Christians in the West have an opportunity to learn about Islam and pray for Muslims in ways that we never did in the past.

Let us not fall asleep or be naive on this issue. This is going to be more important for our children and grandchildren than it ever was for my generation. The last full day we were in Nigeria in 1987 we had lunch with the head of the "Great Commission Movement of Nigeria." I asked him what he wanted me to tell Christians in

Faith and love are vital to effective prayer.

America. Tell them this: "I just saw the list of six steps on how Islam is going to take over every nation in the world. They have already started in Nigeria. Get prepared." Be ready to listen, listen, listen; pray, pray, pray; and love, love, love!

### Personal Reflection Time

1.  It has been said that for every million Muslims in the world there are about two Christian evangelists. True? False? What do you think? Are you one of them?

2.  Are you praying for strength and protection of missionaries who work in Muslim nations?

3.  Are you praying for a better understanding how to witness to Muslim neighbors?

Pray hardest when it is hardest to pray.

# 41

# Heart

*Be joyful always; pray continually; give thanks in all circumstances, for this is God's will for you in Christ Jesus* (1 Thessalonians 5:16-18).

In a Bible class I once attended, a Liberian who recently moved to the United States was asked to share his personal story. With many others, he lived through war and bloodshed in his homeland. He suffered greatly as a young person. He found great hope and comfort when the Gospel of Jesus Christ was shared with him by Christian missionaries. As a new Christian, he studied the scriptures and memorized Bible verses to carry in his mind and heart, giving him strength for each day and courage to face the future. He spoke about his faith with conviction and confidence.

He was asked if he noticed any differences between Christians from Liberia and Christians in America. "Yes, he said, African Christians pray and know that God will supply their daily needs. The American Christians believe that God and their credit cards will supply their daily needs."

Recently I received an announcement for "World Prayer Assembly 2012." It will be held in Jakarta, Indonesia and co-hosted by the Indonesian and Korean prayer movements during May 2012. My wife and I lived in Korea for five years and in Indonesia for five years. I have personally observed the enthusiasm for prayer by Christians in these places. It is contagious! I've never experienced

Real prayer comes not from gritting our teeth, but from falling in love. *Richard Foster*

anywhere such intentional and deliberate prayer as in these places. The main thing I learned from Korean and Indonesian people is that I am <u>not</u> too busy to pray. Many in the western church will give busyness as an excuse.

Membership in Christian churches is growing on several continents. It is interesting to me that two continents on the planet where church growth does not seem to be taking place are North America and Europe. Could this have any connection to prayer? I think there is a link to the priority placed on prayer. We are experiencing a prayer crisis today in the western church. In general, prayer is not a priority. How many prayer mountains or prayer retreats or prayer vigils have you heard about lately in the USA? How often have you been getting up at 4:30 or 5:00 a.m. to spend an hour or two in prayer?

All over the world men, women and children have proven the power of prayer. God calls us to partner with Him through prayer. He wants to transform our own circumstances and our world through prayer. God does shape the world through prayer.

It is time to connect more intentionally to God with prayer. We do not want to wait till there is a crisis in our lives or the world, but to pray with passion now. I will say this again, there is nothing greater we can do for our family, our church, our land, our world, and ourselves than to pray.

Often we have a gap between what we know is right and good, and what we do. Our challenge is to close the gap. We want the presence of God to move beyond theory to living reality.

Paul doesn't just encourage us to act in certain ways, to rejoice, to pray, to give thanks – no, he wants more, he wants these believers and us to do these things "always," "without ceasing," "in all circumstances."

Maybe this sounds impossible, even undesirable, to some believers. Nobody can think of God all the time. Who would even want to? Life is complicated enough.

Look at the world and see the need for prayer. Martin Luther is given credit for the following quote: "He who does not see the need for prayer evidently goes through life with closed eyes."

*Sometimes we think we are too busy to pray. That is a great mistake,*
for praying is a saving of time. *Charles Haddon Spurgeon*

What is such a life of prayer that never ceases? The attitude of the person praying is what counts. It is your whole relationship with God – It is never losing contact with God. It is an open conversation that never really stops with a period.

Prayer is the conversational part of a loving relationship with God. Faith gives birth to prayer. Faith and prayer are the two sides of a coin. One is not without the other.

Finally it comes down to a heart attitude. The relationship is in the heart and is put there by the Holy Spirit. The key to all successful prayer is the presence of the Holy Spirit. It is undoubtedly an entire sacrifice of one's life to God's Kingdom and glory. If a believer tries to pray without ceasing, because he wants to be very pious and good, he will never succeed. Yielding ourselves to live for God and His honor, enlarges the heart and teaches us to regard everything in the light of God and His will. We instinctively recognize the need for God's help and blessing in everything around us, and an opportunity to glorify Him.

What is meant by requiring us to make every aspect of our lives a prayer? Often for us, prayer is defined as an occasional activity, like eating and sleeping. These are things we must do sometimes, but that by definition we cannot do all the time. This is not wrong, it is just inadequate. Pray always? Again, it is never losing contact with God. Therefore it becomes a heart attitude. It is an attitude that informs all we do. Everything becomes a response to what God has done and is doing. Unceasing prayer is an attitude in which a believer views the world and all that is going on in life, all that occurs, and all of it translates into prayer. Something good is seen, and, immediately, praise rises from the heart. Something negative is seen and, immediately, goes forth a prayer for help with the situation. Everything is weighed and tested by the one thing that fills the heart: the glory of God. To forget about self and to live for God and His Kingdom among men is the way to learn to pray without ceasing.

Jesus is the key to prayer because He removed the sin barrier between God and humanity. By His blood, Jesus leads us into the immediate presence of God. By the Holy Spirit's power we live

In all thy prayers, let thy heart be without words, rather than thy words without thy heart.

there. Living so close to God and knowing we have been taken there to bless those who are far away, we cannot help but pray.

Christ said, "I have set you an example." Christ teaches us to pray by showing us how He does it, by example, by doing it in us, and by leading us to do it in Him and like Him. Christ is everything. He is the life and the strength for a never-ceasing prayer life. Because His life is our life, praying without ceasing can become the joy of heaven here on earth.

We need to be reminded that unceasing prayer is hidden prayer, the prayer of the closet. Others may not know we are engaged in it. We know the only source of help is God. It becomes a way of life. We start our day with prayer. We pray through the day. We end the day by praying as we fall asleep. Very often these petitions rise silently from our hearts to the throne of God.

Prayer, an ongoing conversation with God, is not a work or a burden, but a joy and a triumph. It becomes a necessity and a second nature. It can become a way of life.

### Personal Reflection Time

1. Do you believe this statement is true? "The American Christians believe that God and their credit cards will supply their daily needs."

2. Why do you believe church membership and attendance is dropping in the United States?

3. Can you explain to someone else how to pray without ceasing?

Prayer must not come from the roof of the mouth but the root of the heart.

## 42

# Thankfulness

*Enter His gates with thanksgiving and His courts with praise; give thanks to Him and praise His name* (Psalm 100:4).

Traveling outside of my comfort zone has given me a thankful perspective on blessings I have received. My family has had protection and safety in so many situations around the world. I am humbled and amazed as I look back through my life's calendar. As the opportunities unfolded for us to travel the world, we realized what amazing things God has done. He has showered us with His spiritual and material riches. The older I grow the more thankful I become.

Thanksgiving differs from praise. Remember praise recognizes God for who He is, while thanksgiving recognizes God for specific things He has done. Giving thanks turns our hearts and heads upward. Every experience one encounters is a reason to give thanks. So start counting your blessings. You will run out of time before you exhaust the list of blessings. Someone once said "Giving thanks is like swimming in the ocean. There is no end."

"I have reason to thank God," a man once said to a friend. "As I was crossing a narrow open bridge on horseback, my horse stumbled. I fell from the horse and almost drowned." The friend answered, "I have a greater reason to thank God. As I traveled on horseback, my horse did not stumble at all."

Prayer requires more of the heart than the tongue. *Adam Clarke*

This story reminded me of Cecil Blanck and his wife, Lily. They were members of St. John's congregation which I shepherded in Buckley, Illinois years ago. They were in a serious car accident. After the event I talked to them and they were praising and thanking God for His protection and few injuries. This was certainly appropriate. If I remember correctly, however, Cecil especially was thanking God for the fact that his new glasses weren't broken on the first day he received them. For four years I traveled the same road every day and I didn't thank the Lord enough for His safety and protection.

The presence of danger causes us to appreciate God's providence and protection, but we fail to notice the daily absence of danger. We can easily start thinking: "A gift regularly and freely given soon becomes a demanded right."

Giving thanks is a style of living. Saying thank you is easy. We teach our children and grandchildren from the beginning to say "Thank you." When a person says thank you it says two things. It first says: "I know you are there." And the second thing thank you says is: "I know goodness comes from you."

Now think what your heart is saying when you turn to God and say, "Thank you." Your heart is saying: "I know you are there. I know goodness comes from you."

God has always been there. He is here now and He will be there in the future for me. "Thank you, Lord."

Thanksliving is a whole style of living with an attitude of giving thanks. My attitudes, values, hopes, dreams, and commitments - all of these focus back to my relationship with Jesus. I can stand tall in my thankfulness to God for I am His child and He is my Father. Yielding my life to the baby born in Bethlehem is positive. He grew up and won the victory I needed. Thanksliving is truly understanding that we are significant to Jesus Christ. I am humbly thankful for His blessings and our relationship.

The ancient Greeks used to say "Whatever good you do, record it on sand. But the good others do to you, carve it on marble." Our sinful nature, however, urges us to reverse the procedure. We remember our kindnesses to others, but we forget their kindnesses

I have lived to thank God that all my prayers have not been answered. *Jean Ingelow*

to us. We forget the harm we do to others, but we remember the harm others do to us.

This attitude shows up not only in our interpersonal relationships with others, but also in our relationship with God. His kindnesses toward us are countless. They are so numerous, varying, and constant, that we fail to identify them. They escape our attention. But we never seem to fail to notice any lack we may experience, no matter how small.

I have so much to be thankful for, yet find myself being irritated and dissatisfied. I don't like the direction things are moving politically, socially, culturally or economically. Left unchecked, though, my attitude dissolves into anger and even fear. A thankful person is a joyful person.

When you awoke this morning, what was the first thing you did? Did you pause to thank God for the sleep you enjoyed, your health, and the privilege of life for another day? Or have these become so common place that you are not impressed by them? Beware of ingratitude in the midst of plenty which is taken for granted.

### Personal Reflection Time

1. What have you been taking for granted lately?

2. Do you remember the ancient Greek saying I quoted? Permit me to change it. Whatever good you do, record it on sand. But whatever good God does for you, carve it on marble, and then say: "Thank you, Lord."

3. What in your prayers can you thank God for today?

Are you living for the things you are praying for? *Austin Phelps*

# 43

# Troubles

*Praise be to the God and Father of our Lord Jesus Christ, the Father of compassion and the God of all comfort, who comforts us in all our troubles, so that we can comfort those in any trouble with the comfort we ourselves have received from God* (2 Corinthians 1:3-4).

- Moses *"failed"* at the beginning to help his people. He went off for 40 years. He eventually came back to lead an entire nation out of slavery.
- Joseph *"failed"* on several occasions, ended up in prison, and then rose to a position of power.

The list of Bible characters who seemingly failed at first could continue. Each of these godly people learned lessons that gave them wisdom for greater works, which God planned to accomplish through them. When I review the road journeyed these many years there are more shortcomings than I would like to admit. My troubles seemed like needless suffering. The obstacles that invaded my life caused me too often to ask myself, "Who needs all this grief?"

What does "trouble" or *"failure"* teach us? Should we avoid it at all costs? Does failure chip away at our fragile ego, causing feel-

To give thanks in solitude is enough. Thanksgiving has wings and goes where it must go.
*Victor Hugo*

ings of insecurity, isolation or humiliation? Most people try to avoid failure as though it were a bad disease. They cringe at the prospect of failure and may choose to stay in a safe but unchallenging position. Is there a better way?

I remember while teaching physical education in St. Lorenz gym picturing an audience of one sitting on top of the bleachers watching me. It was God. He was always watching my every instruction and move. In my whole life He walked with me around the world. God is always with each of us. He is the one who understands a person's motivation. God tests us to see if we look to Him for daily and future help. We are to commit our works to the Lord. God permits affliction so God's works may be displayed! He has a plan that is far different from anything you or I could dream. He has a way to accomplish His purpose in this world. He frequently permits uncomfortable situations and events to occur in our lives. He is constantly training us to understand and cope with life. He offers comfort in our troubles so that we can lead others to understand His mercy and encouragement.

Could God use a failure in your life as a transformative experience and an opportunity for His majestic light to clearly shine through you? Only the Lord sees in advance the whole picture of your life. The illustration of the pearl fits well with the study of adversity in our lives.

> *Again the kingdom of Heaven is like a merchant looking for fine pearls. When he found one of great value, he went away and sold everything he had and bought it* (Matt. 13: 45-46).

Do you know how a pearl is formed? It is truly fascinating. A foreign object, often a grain of sand, somehow makes its way into the tightly sealed oyster. Instead of spitting out this irritating object, the oyster absorbs it and covers it with layer upon layer of a substance secreted from its own body. After months or even years, a beautiful pearl is formed. The longer the pearl remains in

What we usually pray to God is not that His will be done, but that He approves ours.
*Helga Bergold Gross*

the oyster, the more valuable it becomes, due to the continuing layers of secretion.

How do we as Christians handle irritating obstacles in our lives? Remember, the greater the irritant, the thicker and more beautiful the pearl becomes as a result of continual washing. Like the oyster, we want to surround the irritating troubles in our lives with layers of prayer and recall of Scripture. It is our faithful response of poise, patience, and grace that develops over time with the help of the Holy Spirit. Cultured with these attributes, we can witness the love of Christ to those who may not know the story of His love.

Cultured pearls are known for their virtue of luster. Luster is the beauty of light reflected from the surface of the pearl. The ability to reflect light determines its value. You can become a pearl of great value! How will you reflect His light today, tonight, tomorrow, next week and for a lifetime?

What has been the most difficult experience of your life? How will you face troubles in the future? Your determination to carry through and accomplish a task regardless of opposition is a lifelong challenge.

The world will poke fun at us. The world never sees tribulations and afflictions as helpful. Even some Christians may say, "God is love. Why is He doing this?"

We are being used by God to influence the lives of many, some of whom do not understand how to live with trials and tribulations. Life is tough. When we feel discouraged, take it to the Lord in prayer. We can be assured that God is with us, even as He was with faithful men and women of the Bible. God is exercising our faith. We cannot understand this through the power of reason. This is a matter of faith. The joy of the Lord becomes and is our strength.

He who does not pray when the sun shines, knows not how to pray when the clouds come.

## Personal Reflection Time

1. Remember a time in your life when you failed. What lessons did you learn?

2. What would you share with a person who is going through a time of trouble and tribulation?

3. What troubles, trails, and tribulations are you taking to the Lord in prayer today?

When you're in trouble and your knees knock, kneel on them.

"Some people think God does not like to be troubled with our constant coming and asking. The way to trouble God is not to come at all. *D. L. Moody*

# 44

# Safety

*For I am the LORD, your God, who takes hold of your right hand and says to you, do not fear; I will help you* (Isaiah 41:13).

We gathered around the car, held hands, and prayed for safety for those who were traveling on the Nigerian highways. This was a common practice for Nigerian Christian missionaries before extended trips in cars. We all knew the dangers on Nigerian roads.

Players, coaches, parents, and fans prayed for safety of both teams before football games. We all knew the possibilities of injuries that could take place.

Safety has been one of my most common prayer petitions for myself and others during my entire life. Maybe it has been the same for other Christians. Here are a few prayer requests that Kurtis, our son and his wife, Teresa, posted on their blogs from Huanuco, Peru during 2010 – 2011:

- For health, safety, and peace for our family.
- For safety, healing and justice of the thousands of young victims of violence and abuse.
- For evil to be bound and cast out, especially where practices of witchcraft and other demonic activities are occurring.

God's ear lies close to the believer's lip.

- For our family and local staff to be safe and protected from crime. (The Paz y Esperanza office was robbed twice this past year.)

Permit me to expand on this topic of safety and protection with Peace and Hope or Paz y Esperanza (its name in Spanish) in Huanuco, Peru.

*If anyone causes one of these little ones...to stumble, it would be better for them to have a large millstone hung around their neck and to be drowned in the depths of the sea* (Matthew 18:6 NIV).

Colleen Beebe Purisaca, Co-International Director, of Peace and Hope shared this sad commentary on the verse above through their website:

(http://www.peaceandhopeinternational.org/)

"Most Christians are familiar with Jesus' warning to people who mistreat children – it would be better for them to drown in the depths of the sea. Based on the prevalence of child abuse around the world, one can only conclude that we don't really take this warning very seriously. Perhaps, if Christians knew more about the problem of child abuse, the profound damage it causes, and that we are commanded by God to stop injustice, we would be compelled to do more to stop it...

"While exact statistics are difficult to obtain, studies suggest that Latin America and the Caribbean have some of the highest rates of violence against women and children in the world—manifesting itself in physical punishment, sexual abuse, neglect and economic exploitation (a form of human trafficking). Further, much child abuse is unreported and more widespread than it appears in the region. Child abuse in Latin America and elsewhere cuts across social classes, race, ethnicities and gender."

If a matter is big enough to worry about, it is big enough to pray about!

Safety was the most frequent prayer request we heard from those we talked with while on our trip to Huanuco, Peru. Pastor Adjon, chaplain for "The House of Good Treatment," a shelter for abused women and children administered by Paz y Esperanza was asked, "What is your biggest prayer concern?" His answer, "Safety is the biggest concern for the abused women and children staying in the shelter. Also the workers of Paz y Esperanza have been threatened by those who are being prosecuted. We need prayer for their safety as well."

The Paz y Esperanza lawyers are attempting to handle 250 to 300 cases of abuse presently on the books in Huanuco. This is a city of more than 500,000 residents. It is reported that 50 cases of abuse are happening per week in this area. Over 70% of the families communicate violence towards women and children.

A handful of Christian lawyers, psychologists and pastors decided to respond to the growing numbers of people affected by the extreme violence in Peru. They established Paz y Esperanza a biblically based independent non-profit organization in 1996. Since then, Paz y Esperanza, has grown from five people in one Lima office to over 125 people in 10 offices in five countries. *Paz y Esperanza* in Peru is one of the largest and one of the most important human rights organizations in Peru. Their work is base on this scripture mandate:

*And what do I require of you? To do justice, love mercy and walk humbly with me* (Micah 6:8).

From all the evidence I saw this very professional organization of Paz y Esperanza is reaching their vision. It is going beyond what they had hoped would happen. They are seeking to transform society by eradicating injustice wherever it is found. Psychological, social, economic, and spiritual rehabilitation, legal representation, education and training are occurring like never before in the history of Peru.

As we place our feet on the floor each morning we pray that God would provide the physical protection for others we love and

You can do more than pray, after you have prayed,
but you can never do more than pray until you have prayed. *A.J. Gordon*

ourselves. In everyday formal and casual conversations with God we ask for protection and safety. Missionaries who are on the front line of fighting the devil especially request and need the protection of angels to accomplish their tasks. We don't have to live in fear as God does answer prayers to provide the safety we pray for everyday. I do believe safety is not the absence of danger but the presence of the Lord. Every missionary I had the opportunity of personally knowing can provide a story or two how they have had God's arms protecting them at some time in their lives.

### Personal Reflection Time

1. Recall a time in your life when you are sure God provided help and safety for you.

2. Take time to investigate the growing problems around the world of abuse and slavery of women and children.

3. Who needs your prayer for protection and safety right now?

Prayer is not merely an occasional impulse to which we respond when we are in trouble; prayer is a life attitude. *Walter A. Mueller*

## 45

# Authority

*I urge, then, first of all, that petitions, prayers, intercession and thanksgiving be made for all people— for kings and all those in authority, that we may live peaceful and quiet lives in all godliness and holiness* (1 Timothy 2:1-4).

Living, working, volunteering, and visiting a variety of countries has been a unique privilege. This has provided some opportunity for me to compare the way countries are governed. Think about the differences in freedom and the ability to witness between United States, China, Russia, Afghanistan, Israel, France, Nigeria, Guatemala, South Korea, India, Indonesia, and Peru. I can draw on these examples from personal encounters. Here are some of my snapshot opinions of the present world:

- **There are a lot of people in this world.** People are moving to the big cities causing urbanization – People from everywhere are living everywhere else. There is a huge migration of people.
- **Communication has changed.** Communication takes place from everywhere to anywhere instantly. Yet, there are all kinds of communication problems between spouses, different generations, languages, and world governments.

You need not cry very loud; he is nearer to us than we think. *Brother Lawrence*

- **The world is evil.** Injustice, corruption, and bribery in governments are rampant. Yet governments have the responsibility to protect their citizens.
- **An overwhelming number of people are suffering in this world.** An estimated 27 million people are currently enslaved around the world as a result of human trafficking. That is only one example of suffering.
- **Everyday people are dying.** Individually and in groups people are dying from natural catastrophes such as earthquakes and tsunamis. Also other innocent people are losing their lives in such situations as murders, wars and persecution.
- **This world is "Hungry for Hope!"** This world needs HOPE! Jesus Christ is the answer to that Hope! God is a loving and compassionate God. There is an urgency to spread this message of hope.

We are living in an age of religious pluralism, especially here in the USA. What do I mean by that? People all over are having ethical disputes. This is an age with a variety of views. What comes along with pluralism? It is individualism or widespread self-interest. Now we need to ask ourselves what implications this has for us as Christians. Is this positive or negative and is it a challenge or an opportunity?

Christians have the opportunity to be "the salt of the earth." Therefore, our position on earth is to be God's ambassadors representing heaven's government. It is through prayer and intercession we begin administering the authority that is ours in the name of Jesus. In the face of all the waves of sorrow mentioned above it is our responsibility to witness and demonstrate that Christ is Lord of lords. We need leaders who say what they mean and stay with it. For one, I try to vote for the person who has the greatest "character." I mean honesty and integrity. Consistency is important. Issues will change over time. Therefore the character of the person is imperative.

Prayer is the spiritual gymnasium in which we exercise and practice godliness.
*V.L. Crawford*

Paul gives us directions for a ministry of prayer:

> *I urge, then, first of all, that petitions, prayers, interces-*
> *sion and thanksgiving be made for all people— for kings and*
> *all those in authority, that we may live peaceful and quiet*
> *lives in all godliness and holiness.*(1 Timothy 2:1-4).

God is concerned that we pray for "all people." Also He expects us to pray for "all those in authority." This may be summed up in the single word, the government. Unfortunately, I am convinced that many who claim to be committed Christians never pray seriously for the government of their nation.

Why do we want to pray for our government? Paul says: *"that we may live peaceful and quiet lives in all godliness and holiness."* Let me share an example of the contrast between the two govern-ments of North and South Korea. The growth and vibrancy of the government and church in South Korea is well recognized around the world. The largest churches in membership in the world are found in Seoul. Their members are famous for the amount of time spent praying. But there is also a church in North Korea under cruel dictatorship and no freedom of worship. The group Open Doors says there could be 400,000 Christians in the North, with possibly 40,000-60,000 in prison labor camps. For the 9th year running, the "Hermit Kingdom" of North Korea has once again topped the Open Door World Watch List. This is an annual ranking of the world's worst persecuting of Christians countries. It is reported in 2010 one small house church in Pyungsung province was raided by the police. Three members were immediately sentenced to death. The other twenty were sent to prison. Let us pray that the Lord would encourage and shine through all of those disciples, those who are free and those who are in camps. Christians in the United States and other free countries should forever be thankful *"that we may still live peaceful and quiet lives in all godliness and holiness."*

The will of God is good government. Why does He want good government? It is easier to preach the Gospel effectively. Bad gov-ernment hinders it. God has made it possible for Christians by their

To influence leaders for God, intercede with God for leaders.

prayers to insure good government. Today many citizens criticize their government. Pointing fingers and blaming individuals are not the answers. The answers lie in God's people praying for His will to be accomplished. So long as believers fail to pray, they have no right to criticize.

There is a nondenominational Christian ministry called The Presidential Prayer Team. They believe that the prayers of its members can transform the nation. The materials that they produce are up to date and very beneficial.

This group believes that one of the most important missions to be accomplished today is the prayer for those in leadership. They have faith that God influences leaders and that prayer to God impacts what happens. Therefore, the mission for The Presidential Prayer Team is to encourage and motivate people to pray for the President and other leaders of the United States.

Even though there are a lot of negative things about the USA I still believe that America is the greatest country in the world. We are blessed to have been born and raised in a country with the freedoms the constitution provides.

### Personal Reflection Time

1.  What are some specific views you have about today's world?

2.  Pray that North Korea would somehow open their doors to the world and stop persecuting followers of Christ.

3.  Are you a person who includes government leaders in your personal prayers? If not, why not?

As long as there are tests, there will be prayer in schools.

# 46

# Vision

*Where there is no vision, the people perish* (Pro. 29:18a).

Praise God for Pak (Mr.) Bul Penyami. He was one of the most visionary men I have ever met. On my arrival in 2001 at UPH, a university with over 6,000 students, Pak Bul asked me to help with teaching a new course, which was eventually called "Becoming a Leader." It amazed me that the course was started after the semester was in progress. We just put up a couple of signs and 24 students started coming to class. We kept preparing creative lessons one week ahead of the students' arrival. It turned out to be magnificent. Each semester thereafter it improved and became one of the most popular courses on campus. Pak Bul was the leader of teaching the art of successful leadership. I was assigned to provide consistency and direction as to what and how it was to be taught. We had the vision that this course would be the most valuable course of each student's life. It would be the foundation for the attendees to become "Great Godly Servant Leaders" with a Christian worldview. This class was to become a prime national resource for empowering students to develop good character and attitude and to glorify God.

When we talk to God, we're praying. When God talks to us, we're schizophrenic.
*Jane Wagner*

About a year before Pak Bul died he was asked to do a leadership seminar at Petra University, another Christian university in Indonesia. He was too ill to do it and asked Pak Roy and me to take his place. I asked him to share ten thoughts on becoming a great leader that he wanted me to present to those students. Believe me they came from the heart of a great Christian visionary leader. Pak Bul sincerely wanted students to become not only leaders of Indonesia but also of the world. His enthusiasm for creativity and leadership was contagious. Pak Bul said that if he were young again and became a leader today, he would do these 10 things:

I would:

1. Think deeply about my personal leadership vision and mission, so that there would be more clarity between my existence and my relation with God.
2. Try to understand the meaning of humility and apply it in my life.
3. Try to learn more about my own temperament profile and other people's around me, so that I could know more about myself and other people, and understand and respect their strengths and weaknesses.
4. Try to understand my group's needs, especially their need to be listened to and to be understood.
5. Try to understand my talents and other people's, and do my best to delegate tasks according to each person's talents.
6. Prepare my successor strategically.
7. Establish the group's vision and mission and routinely discuss them with my group members.
8. Try to understand and apply Jesus' teachings about leadership.
9. Try to learn about theories and the art of leadership.
10. Leave everything in God's hands, and submit myself to Him – because I am weak and know nothing...

Prayer is the "pump" that makes everything go. *Jeff Dahl*

Oh, one more saying, from Pak Bul that he placed on the walls of UPH: **"Responsibility begins with me."**

As I reflect on my life I humbly realize I have been a dreamer or visionary person. By the time I reached the point of teaching leadership at the university level I realize I had been putting my dreams into words and actions. Let me give you two examples from St. Lorenz days.

Many years ago I was given the responsibility of directing St. Lorenz Spartan Day Camp in Frankenmuth. Terry Laubsch was the camp's assistant director. Beginning in the early part of January, Terry and I would unveil an elaborate vision for the coming summer day camp. Each year there was a new special theme: "Treasures of the Sea," "Rendezvous in Space," "Paul Bunyan," or another. Together we set a mental/spiritual image of what we thought God wanted the camp to be the next season. It was way above what many others thought to be too ambitious. Yet, it was our understanding of what God wanted to do through us. We understood that in order to be successful God would have to be trusted to guide and direct the results.

At the same time the St. Lorenz Physical Education program was becoming well known for its superior quality of instruction. God opened the door for me to become St. Lorenz's first full time physical education instructor. During the 1970's we were able to have over 700 students in the school from grades one through eight be instructed in physical education every school day. The President's Council on Physical Fitness and Sports recognized the program as the first parochial demonstration center school in the country. This opened up a flood of visitors. There were as many as sixty college students and teachers per day who came to observe how we were applying the Christian worldview to the teaching of physical education.

Those visions were bigger than our abilities and pulled us out of our comfort zones. Hours of prayer and work went into the preparations. Our visions had amazing results. Hundreds of volunteers bought into the visions and contributed to making the day camp weeks and physical education program successful. It was well worth the effort. God blew us away with His blessings!

Prayer is the acid test of devotion. *Samuel Chadwick*

My personal vision is to be the best servant leader I can possibly be in the time and place where God has called me to His glory. I want to be a person who views the world from God's perspective, who exercises His gifts and talents with excellence and perseverance, and who strategically plans to serve others. My mission then, is to confirm the dignity of every human being that my life touches by providing openness, acceptance, trust, understanding, encouragement, service, hope and prayer.

To be this significant person stretches me beyond what I believe are my limits. Because I need God's help and guidance, my desire to be significant has become a daily prayer petition.

### Personal Reflection Time

1. Have you formed your own vision for your life? If not, try doing it now.

2. Is your present personal vision consistent with God's plans as recorded in God's word?

3. Have you prayed that your vision will be clear, concise, easy to understand, remember, and communicate?

I pray on the principle that wine knocks the cork out of a bottle. *Henry Ward Beecher*

# 47

# Fasting

*Moreover, when you fast, do not be like the hypocrites, with a sad countenance. For they disfigure their faces that they may appear to men to be fasting. Assuredly, I say to you, they have their reward. But you, when you fast, anoint your head and wash your face, so that you do not appear to men to be fasting, but to your Father who is in the secret place; and your Father who sees in secret will reward you openly* (Matthew 6:16-18).

We don't hear too much about fasting in Christian churches here in North America. For the first half of my life fasting was foreign to me. Those strong Christians I knew never talked about any fasting they did or suggested the practice. It was not until I moved to another continent that I became acquainted with Christians who fasted. They understood the focus the Scripture placed on fasting. Also, while living in predominately Islamic countries, I observed and read much about fasting. Of course, their motivation was different than what Christians would hold. Let me share a story that our son returned to tell after going to Africa for a filming project:

"When we were working on the video for the 100th Anniversary of LCMS World Mission, we were interviewing

Prayer fastens the soul to God. *Monica Furlong*

Liberian refugees about the growing church in West Africa. After several other interviews, we met with Kenety Gee. He told an incredible story of hardship in his personal story of fleeing from rebel forces when members of his extended family were massacred. He then proceeded to witness his faith in his answers with Scripture as if he were the Apostle Paul himself. It was our best interview by far and became the central story of our production.

"Later I asked missionary John Duitsman how come this particular interview went so well and he told this story: Kenety heard that our video crew was coming and had decided to fast and pray about his answers for the ten days before our arrival. He wanted to speak wisely in his answers and glorify God as he shared his story with the American audience. He gave up food in order to focus on Jesus and his message to be told across the world."

Christians around the globe are practicing fasting, and not only in the season of Lent. When I preached in Huǎnuco, Peru, the church members, particularly among leaders, had been fasting for several days before a planning ministry meeting for the coming year.

Fasting isn't normally done with intent to change God. Instead, it is largely done in order to bring oneself into closer communion with God and His will in one's life. As a replacement for focusing upon the bodily needs of nourishment, fasters are able to spend extra time upon their spiritual lives and listening to God. Physical hunger reminds fasters of their focus during their time with God. It prioritizes the relationship with God, and strengthens the bond of commitment.

Fasting is a spiritual discipline that is very closely related to prayer. Fasting is not commanded but seems assumed in Scripture. Jesus, in His sermon on the mount, taught with the assumption that God's people are people who fast. *"When you fast..."* (Matthew 6:16-18). He did not say "If you fast," but "when." There's an expectation implied in His Words... perhaps even an invitation.

Put the power of prayer in your hands. Read the Bible.

I might have been more inclined to practice this spiritual discipline early in my own life if I had understood Scripture. Perhaps you have heard about the church bulletin that ran the following announcement: "The cost for the National Conference on Prayer and Fasting includes meals."

This space won't be taken to exhaust the subject, but I do hope to spur us on to a lifestyle of fasting. So let me start by giving the definition of fasting.

Fasting can be defined as going without food, drink or certain other pleasures voluntarily in order to give oneself more attentively to God and to prayer. A person can fast by skipping one meal and spending that time in prayer, or he can fast for an entire day, or, in some serious cases of need, several days.

Fasting is not simply a state of the stomach, but a state of mind and a state of heart that quietly pursues God in a way that enlarges one's capacity to hear from Him and to receive from Him all that He desires for us. God delights to respond to His people when His people humble themselves and seek His face, His person, His kingdom, His righteousness. So whenever God's people encounter a gap between what is and what ought to be, that encounter is God's special invitation to fast and pray... to lay aside something natural in order to lay hold of something supernatural.

I guess my bottom line is to challenge each person to embrace a lifestyle of fasting. How a person fasts, when he fasts, from what he fasts, the regularity with which he fasts, is really between that individual and the Lord. So as believers talk about living out God's kingdom priorities - loving God, loving one another, and reaching out to the world with the Gospel fasting can be part of Christian discipline. Consider seriously taking the next step by embracing a lifestyle of fasting in some manner. Just be sure the motivation is correct. A follower of Christ can't buy blessings from God.

Prayer is more discussed and less practiced than any other doctrine.

**Personal Reflection Time**

1. Do you know of anyone who fasts and prays?

2. Have you experienced a personal time of fasting? It not, why not?

3. Make a plan for a time to fast.

Our prayers must mean something to us if they are to mean anything to God.
*Maltbie D. Babcock*

## 48

# Caring

*Cast all your anxiety on Him because He cares for you*
(1 Peter 5:7).

While I was chaplain at Seoul Foreign School (SFS) in Korea, I was given the privilege to teach a course called: "Peer Counseling." This instruction was to provide beginning counseling skills that would enable students to be the initial caregivers to classmates who had a variety of problems. We studied listening, caring and confrontation skills, and a body of knowledge designed to inform us about some of the key issues commonly faced by students. In particular, I was committed to providing a caring Christian environment consistent with the highest Christian values of compassion, tolerance, forgiveness, and reconciliation at SFS.

We tried to identify the causes, effects, the Biblical perspective, and responses to many issues such as suicide, self-esteem, stress, depression, rape, drugs, alcohol, racism, abuse and others.

Each class member was asked to do a research paper on one of the topics and present it to class. The abortion topic seemed to make a lasting impression on me. This topic carried over from teaching Christian Ethics in the United States. It had become a prayer concern from years previous. Now I was hearing Korean statistics on abortion from more than one of my students. The

Pray not for lighter burdens, but for stronger backs. *Theodore Roosevelt*

Korean Times reported on November 23, 2000 the following information:

- "As many as 1.5 million abortions were carried out throughout the nation in 1994, 4,500 a day, according to data from Gallup."
- "The figure is more than twice that of total annual births which number about 700,000. This means that one is aborted every 20 seconds."
- "Unofficial figures show that over 2 million fetuses are aborted in Korea annually."
- "The enormous number of pregnancy terminations is attributed to a variety of factors such as the failure of contraceptives, governmental policies to control population size and the deep-rooted preference for boys."

When I moved to Indonesia and became the head of the counseling department at Universitas Pelita Harapan (UPH) I became even more aware of the world statistics on the number of abortions. My colleague, Miss Suriani Arifin, shared information from the Indonesian National Family Planning Bureau. It indicated that over two million babies were aborted in Indonesia each year. Teenagers were behind the rate climb with about one third of the abortions, 750,000, involving teenage mothers.

Not long after my arrival at Universitas Pelita Harapan I met one of the most enthusiastic young Christian male students on campus. We became great friends and he felt comfortable visiting my office. One day he asked if he could bring a female friend with him. They were not dating and were just friends. She had confided in him that she was pregnant and was planning to abort the baby. He had tried to convince her otherwise but had no success. Now it was my turn to try.

She said she was a Christian so I began with prayer that the Holy Spirit would be present and guide our discussion. I continued with the counseling techniques I taught in Korea, such as listening, understanding, questioning, and summarizing what she was really saying,

Our thanks to God should always precede our requests.

feeling, and meaning. I attempted to inform her of the Biblical perspectives of abortion. They were interspersed over the hour and a half session. The statements below summarize my thoughts of six biblical arguments against abortion:

1. A child in the womb is referred to as a child.
2. The unborn child in the womb is always a human person.
3. God values the life of the unborn as highly as the adult.
4. God is involved in the creation and the development of the unborn child.
5. Jesus was both God and man from the point of conception, not birth.
6. Anyone who willfully destroys human life commits murder.

My heart breaks and tears come to my eyes to tell you that not many days after I had this counseling session, the young lady had an abortion. After all was said and done I realized I could have been much bolder and followed up better. If I had to do it all over again, I would have tried harder.

Fortunately there is spiritual healing for all women who have had abortions. Also for the men who have promoted the evil of abortion. As with any other sin we can come back to the reality of what God says about our lost and hopeless condition. God tells us there is salvation and that redemption is found in His Son. It was Jesus who took all the wrath of God meant for you and for me. All of that was taken on Himself. He cared and will always care for each one of us.

*For as high as the heavens are above the earth, so great is His love for those who fear Him; as far as the east is from the west, so far has He removed our transgressions from us* (Psalm 103:11-12).

I don't know of anything else that can bring relief and freedom to a woman who is torn and burdened, heavy laden with the reality, and guilt of what she has done in having had an abortion. Nothing can solve that problem except what Jesus offers.

Prayer is weakness leaning on omnipotence. *W. S. Bowden*

"Thank you, God, for the healing care of Jesus and God the Spirit, who ministers comfort, restoration, hope, trust, and rest."

### Personal Reflection Time

1.  Worldwide abortion is the main cause of death. So what can you do to effectively fight this battle? The first thing is to pray for God's mercy on America and the rest of the world. How often do you include this pro-life issue in your prayers?

2.  Do you know anyone who is considering an abortion? Be ready to share your Christian worldview.

3.  We all can do many other practical things locally to express our love and to advance a pro-life ethic in our city, state and nation. What will you do?

We have to pray with our eyes on God, not on the difficulties. *Oswald Chambers*

**49**

# Commitment

*Though one may be overpowered, two can defend themselves. A cord of three strands is not quickly broken* (Ecclesiastes 4:12).

Figure this out: my wife, Alice, and I were married on 8 - 7 - 65. How many years have we kept our marriage vow of commitment to each other?

One of UPH's students asked me in a coaching - counseling session; "Can old people who are married still have romance?" I was quick to reply with a positive answer because I have personally experienced it. My wife and I have creatively spent time and effort at trying to keep our marriage romantic and loving. Have we been perfect in showing our love to each other? No, of course not, there have been times of failure for both of us. Yet, we have been quick to ask for forgiveness and to give it. Also, we have had a lifetime commitment to pray for, serve and love each other.

Most couples walk into this unity with very little understanding, guidance and help. One thing I found out for certain: a successful marriage takes work with good communication. Permit me to share a few views and thoughts of what I think my wife and I believe it takes to have a romantic and happy marriage union.

Let us count the ways using the Bible passages from Philippians 2:2-3, our wedding text: *Then make my joy complete by being like-*

Daily prayers lessen daily cares.

*minded, having the same love, being one in spirit and purpose. Do nothing out of selfish ambition or vain conceit, but in humility consider others better than yourselves.*

1. **"like minded":** The more a couple begins their marriage and continues to have shared values from the same cultural background, same faith, same ethics and same attitudes less problems will arise. Problems are surmountable but they can cause huge family and marital conflicts.
2. **"same love":** Love, to us, is finding the needs of your spouse and serving them. It is great to be trying to out serve the other person. Try to do everything possible to make the other person successful.
3. **"being one in spirit and purpose":** Couples thrive when spouses focus on what is good and true in each other. Positive trust and expectations exert a tremendous force or spirit to the marriage. From this comes a joint purpose and vision for the future.
4. **"do nothing out of selfish ambition or vain conceit":** Change your middle names to "Flexible" and learn to change actions or goals. Most successful couples experience crisis in their marriage and adjustment becomes necessary. This often involves times to repent, saying "I'm sorry," which means asking for forgiveness.
5. **"but in humility consider others better than yourselves":** It is important to define roles and responsibilities within the marriage. There need not be a struggle for power or status. Considering your partner better is not that your spouse is superior or more talented, but that your love sees the other person as worthy of special treatment.

During the last forty-five plus years Alice and I have worked at improving our marriage. We have been proactive in the attempt to prevent marriage problems. We have spent large amounts of time effectively working on better communication. We have resolved arguments and conflicts peacefully. There are tools to learn through

Abba, Father (Mark14:36).

"Marriage Encounter," "Marriage Enrichment" courses, and marriage counseling books. One of the methods is to ask each other the right crucial question at the correct time. Over the years we have improved.

Finally a word is given on the importance of sex. It is positive but over rated in today's society. A good marriage does not rest upon sex but upon friendship, respect, love, communication and a commitment to sexual purity. These are what make a happy lifelong marriage possible. Yes, there can be romance after years together. I can't imagine a better friend or closer partner. Divorce is not in our vocabulary. We have made a commitment for a lifetime to surrender to God and each other.

Without prayer the success of marriage becomes our own effort. Praying invites God to do great things in our lives. God wants marriage partners to join together in prayer and experience the joy, the satisfaction, and the dynamic power that comes from such a union. Praying together as a couple can improve and strengthen every marriage, and at the same time deepen the couple's relationship to God. *"A cord of three strands is not quickly broken."*

As the years have passed we were blessed with two sons for whom Alice and I asked God to intercede into their lives. Eventually God brought brides into their lives who have common commitments to Christ. From these two families have come eight wonderful grandchildren, four girls and four boys. We have made a commitment to praying for their world. We are daily inviting God to come into their situations and give them the gifts of the Holy Spirit; love, joy, peace, patience, kindness, goodness, faithfulness, gentleness, and self-control. I am confident God hears and answers these prayers.

If God is not first in our thoughts in the morning, He will be last in our thoughts all day.

## Personal Reflection Times

1. When was the last meaningful prayer time you have had with your family?

2. What are the common obstacles that keep your family from praying together?

3. What specific prayers have the Lord answered for your family over the last several months?

Pray and let God worry. *Martin Luther*

# 50

# Wisdom

*If any of you lacks wisdom, he should ask God, who gives generously to all without finding fault, and it will be given to him* (James 1:5).

Living in other countries so far away from loved ones has prevented us from closer daily contact with our family in the United States. This circumstance has presented opportunities for me to offer some advice from a father to his sons in several letters. In the process of writing to them I was reminded of a continuous prayer I have asked God to answer: "Lord, I need wisdom."

God has answered this repeated request. I have to give credit to several Christian authors whose books God guided me to read and study in addition to the Bible. They include E.M. Bounds, Oz Guinness, Charles Swindoll, John Maxwell, Jeff Meyer, John Wooden, Walter Wangerin, Jr., and especially missionaries whose writings have personally touched me and have helped to shape my thoughts. They have put into words what I have experienced trying to live intentionally and with a purpose. It has taken time to consolidate my thoughts. Additionally, some ideas have faded with time.

In 1966 I enrolled full time at Central Michigan University to get my masters degree in physical education. At that time I decided to begin a study of the book of Proverbs. This began a search for what

Prayer may not change things for you, but it for sure changes you for things.
*Samuel M. Shoemaker*

is wisdom, how I could obtain it, and apply it to my life. At that time I had very little confidence in my talents and abilities. I concluded if I were to become successful or significant in this life I was going to need all of God's help I could get.

In many ways I was similar to Moses or Jeremiah or Gideon who each gave excuses why they couldn't achieve the vision that God placed before them. I, too, put a lid on my abilities. Moses and others, I think, were acting like humanists, trying to define themselves. Their self-assessment caused them to say "no" to the God of the universe. I think God was extremely displeased with them and me, not because they had a wrong view of the world, but because they had a wrong view of themselves. I, too, have given a lot of excuses why I couldn't do some things in my life. My self-imposed barriers prevented me from achieving God's highest purposes for my life.

It was the encouragement of God, primarily given through my wife, Alice, that I eventually changed my focus to Christ IN me and not on my talents, abilities and effort. Or saying it another way, God intervened, showing me that my identity was in HIM, not in what I perceived that I could or could not do. I eventually learned that I need God to help me in every way every day!

My opinion is that it takes time to become wise. It is a combination of knowledge, faith (trust) and righteousness (obedience). But how does the word WISDOM lead to purpose, confidence, honor and all the other good things we desire? Proverbs taught me that it begins with the fear of the Lord. Wisdom expresses God's delight as I thoughtfully and skillfully live out His design.

It is possible for a person to gain clarity about direction in life. With Godly wisdom a Christian can live the life God intended. Wisdom for me is the supernatural knowledge and understanding of life given through Scripture to guide me to know what is right and wrong. This discernment gives me a definite line for separating good and evil. It acts as an umpire in my life and blows the whistle on that which is false.

Wisdom comes not from trying to do great things for God but more from being faithful in the small, obscure tasks few people

Private place and plenty of time are the life of prayer. *E. M. bounds*

ever see. Wisdom comes with right decisions, Godly reactions, and the application of scriptural principles to daily circumstances. The concept of learning to be wise is a lifelong task. It is not like a one-time conversion experience that has become so popular.

Some assume that anything a person needs to know can be put into the content of a university course or two, or even a self-help book. The progression toward wisdom is a function of on–going maturity. How long does it take a person to learn all the things the Lord has taught? I, as a Christian, assume that there is always more to learn. It is going to take me a lifetime, no less.

*Teach us to number our days aright, that we may gain a heart of wisdom* (Ps. 90:12). As I enter the autumn years of my life, I am beginning to understand WHO I AM IN CHRIST. I am His child. I am His light to a dark world. I am an heir with Christ. I am united with Christ in one spirit with Him. I have been bought with a price and He lives in me. I am a new man. I am firmly rooted in Him. I am special to God. He has designed me, thought about me, and planned a mission for my life. I have been made complete in Him. I have been given a spirit of power, love and good judgment. Now THAT'S a God-given identity! I didn't realize this soon enough in my life. The wise person knows where to find wisdom. It is in a relationship with God. This is the wisdom I searched for since the springtime in my life. The more I understand this, the more I want to carry on a conversation with Him.

God has blessed me with wonderful ability and will use it until the day I die. I think the most important thing in my life was and is my baptism, and because of it my attitude can be positive. Therefore, I try to remember my baptism every day. It seals me to Jesus. With this wisdom I can do the next thing I have to do with my whole heart, and find delight in doing it.

It is so important that each Christian takes his or her passion for fulfilling God's will to the Lord. Then, walk forward without fear. Try to meet the obstacles with courage, enthusiasm and His strength. Move into each day of abundant living, growing, and maturing in conversations with God. Expect to find weak areas where you can improve. The goal is not prayer itself. The goal is to reach a better

A man is what he prays. *Alan Ecclestone*

relationship with God. Prayer is where one begins to achieve the understanding on how to be a Godly servant leader. Incidentally, the next time we meet, share with me what new insights you have learned about prayer. I look forward to hearing your wisdom.

### Personal Reflection Time

1.  What excuses have you given for not using your talents?

2.  How do you define wisdom?

3.  What passions are you taking to the Lord in prayer?

The prayer life consists of life that is always upward and onward and Godward.
*G. Campbell Morgan*

# 51

# Significance

*Therefore, since we have been justified through faith, we have peace with God through our Lord Jesus Christ* (Romans 5:1).

M y father looked forward to retiring from his job at the age of 65. However, he had a stroke and died less than a month before his sixty-fifth birthday. My mother passed away before my father at the age of sixty, before Alice and I were married. Neither of my parents had the opportunity to experience retirement. It has been different for their sons and daughters.

After tearful goodbyes, closure came to serving in Indonesia in 2006. It was time to mark the new season of life's journey into our retirement or as some call it repositioning. Alice and I were repositioning ourselves back into the Saginaw Valley of Michigan. We eventually purchased a home only a short distance from where we bought our first one in Frankenmuth in 1968.

We were aware of possible reverse culture shock with this move. Making a major move can be one of the most insecure times we face in life. Pulling up roots in one place and trying to put them down in another can be depressing. After living in two foreign countries for the previous ten years our anticipation of returning to the USA created mixed feelings. On one hand, we were looking forward to being with family and friends. On the other hand, we

Be thankful that God's answers are wiser than your answers. *William Culbertson*

would miss our friends we had grown so close to in Indonesia. We had two major challenges: To re-establish our personal identity and to re-enter the culture. For many, this is the most difficult hurdle in the cycle of international life.

Purchasing and furnishing a home, baby sitting for grandchildren, coaching football, preaching, speaking, and attending Bible classes kept us busy. Not every day flowed smoothly but the love, care, compassion and friendly welcome of family, old, and new friends helped for an easier transition. Yet, when coming back from overseas I saw America as a foreigner might see it. I had to be careful not to say too much which could be taken inaccurately.

As I walk this path of retirement I think it could be simple for me to experience the fear of not being a significant person. It is easy for a Christian missionary to develop feelings of self-importance. Often missionaries are put on pedestals by other Christians. Yet, they are no better in God's eyes, just different. No longer am I in a location where I am one of a few American Christian pastors. Now, being back in the United States, I am just one of many pastors. I have needed to re-examine the foundational truths that motivate me to live out my life for Christ rather than for the approval of other people. This takes much prayer, meditation, self-examination, and Bible reading. I believe the emphasis shifts for many believers who are retired from **doing** to **being**.

While living in Korea, our son, Kurtis suggested I use the word significance in place of success. I began to use significance in my daily prayers at that time. "Help me, Lord, to become a significant witness to someone today." Retirement has become a time to again search for how to be significant. Below is my short summary on how I, as a Christian, can remember to have a lifetime of significance:

I need to remember:

1. My baptism. (Romans 6:4**)**
2. All of my sins are forgiven through Christ. (Romans 5:1**)**
3. I want to obey God's will in my daily living. (2 Corinthians 9:13)

Cold prayers shall never have any warm answers.

4. I will bear fruit by the Holy Spirit's power. (John 15:5)
5. To pray without ceasing. (1 Thessalonians 5:17)

My true value is not based on my behavior or the approval of others but on what God's Word says is true about me. Separated from God and His Word, I have only my abilities and the opinions of others on which to base my worth. My worth has been given to me by God. I'm still loved and accepted by Him even if I am not approved by others. Christ is the source of my significance. As I grasp this unconditional love of God, then serving Him becomes more and more my passion. Gradually in my life I have learned to take attention off of myself and place it on Him.

Since retiring, my attitude or outlook has become even more important to me than before retirement. It defines who I am and who I will be. It shapes my actions and reactions to the events that are happening in my life. There are always two ways for me to look at everything that happens to me – the positive way or the negative way. A problem can be looked at as a privilege God has permitted me to go through. I can treat the situation as a process of learning and as a challenge. The end of the condition hasn't arrived until God is glorified.

Don't let yourself be dragged down by negative thoughts, words, and actions of other people. Negative attitudes are contagious. So, too, are positive attitudes. Have a positive attitude! Look for the best in other people and the best in every situation. Let others catch your attitude of enthusiasm for life. Then you will know you have had a significant day.

### Personal Reflection Time

1. How are you becoming a significant person?

2. What is your attitude toward life? Positive? Negative?

3. Have you caught the peace that can come with conversations with God?

Where prayer focuses, power falls.

# 52

# Future

*For I know the plans I have for you, declares the LORD, plans to prosper you and not to harm you, plans to give you hope and a future* (Jeremiah 29:11).

The Swiss theologian, Karl Barth (1868-1968) once said, "You can never have a new beginning, but you can start today to make a new ending."

Hillcrest School was located in Jos, Nigeria, West Africa. When Alice and I were teachers there, over 40 countries were represented in the student body. This gave us the opportunity to teach a variety of students from all over the world. One of the topics at the end of the year for my senior class in religion was centered on forgiving others. It was important for the seniors not to leave the high school while carrying the extra baggage of unforgiveness the rest of their lives. Most of them were leaving Nigeria to return to their parent's home country and to attend a university somewhere to further their education. The majority of them would never see their classmates again. Part of making closure to this episode of their life was to be sure that any hurt or abuse previously suffered was properly forgiven. Departing students were encouraged to mend relationship problems with classmates, teachers, or others before leaving for new adventures.

He never rises high who does not know how to kneel.

*Be kind and compassionate to one another, forgiving each other, just as in Christ God forgave you* (Ephesians 4:32).

Below are some of the highlights on forgiving others from those lessons:

- Never in the Word of God do you find a sin too great to forgive.
- Forgiving is something you do for yourself. An unforgiving spirit can poison your soul. You need to forgive so you can move forward in life.
- Forgiving can be a long road indeed, but at its end lies freedom and an abundant life in Christ.
- The beginning point is to emotionally accept the fact that you have been hurt. Christians often try to deny or cover up their pain.
- Realize that God has forgiven your sins, plus those who have offended you. Ask Him to help you make the decision to forgive those who sinned against you.
- Decide that this person's offenses cannot change your view of yourself and your God-given mission.
- Ask God to reaffirm His purposes for your life. The stronger your sense of mission, the easier it will be to quickly recover from hard blows and press on.
- "I forgive, but I can't forget." Forgetting past offenses is difficult to transfer into your real-world experience. Only God can forget sin. However, memory does not have to bring pain. Take the past offenses and marvel at the wonder of the shed blood of Jesus Christ for forgiveness. Thank your heavenly Father for giving you the grace and strength to forgive.
- Forgiveness is not a feeling. It is a decision. You choose to cancel the debt.
- Forgiveness revolves around canceling debts. You must proclaim that the person doesn't owe you anymore.
- Forgiveness paves the way for you to love your enemies and pray for those who have persecuted you.

The neglect of prayer is a grand hindrance to holiness. *John Wesley*

The late Dave Pollock, founder of Interaction International, became a personal friend and introduced the concept of RAFT to me. It is an acrostic denoting a pre-departure process that I have added to the lesson on forgiveness:

**R- RECONCILIATION** - Begin building your raft by asking yourself if you have any relationships that need mending. This is the time to give and receive forgiveness. Mend your fences!

**A- AFFIRMATION** - This is the time to thank the people who have been involved in your life. Affirm the relationships you have made and what they have meant to you.

**F- FAREWELLS** - Say good-byes to people, places, pets and possessions that have mattered to you. Take lots of pictures.

**T- THINK DESTINATION** - Think and dream about where you are going and what it will be like. Be honest with yourself about how you feel about this transition. Put concrete plans in place.

When a trapeze artist jumps to catch the next trapeze bar he doesn't hold on to one bar while grabbing the next one. This would result with one hand on each bar. It would cause him to hang and be stranded in the middle. Instead, he lets go with both hands and flies through the air to catch the other swinging bar with both hands. In the same manner we can't jump into the future by holding too much to the past. One thing we learned from moving so many times is to let go of the past. We tried to live to the fullest wherever we found ourselves in this world to God's glory.

The fear factor often comes up when thinking about the future. Jesus talked about fear more than any other topic. Fear is the perception that life is out of control. However, Jesus is the one who controls life. God does not give me a spirit of fear to face the future. I face the future by keeping my eyes on Jesus.

Just pray for a tough hide and a tender heart. *Ruth Graham*

As I walk the last steps of my life's journey with prayer, I am asking God to help me to do it with courage, excellence, poise, and perseverance. What do I mean?

**Courage:** Living with courage is resistance to fear. Overcoming fear has been one of the most difficult hurdles to overcome in my lifetime. Courage recognizes fear but I proceed in the face of it with calmness and firmness. My security is in God. The result can be a total performance that reaches ones' potential with excellence.

**Excellence:** I want to have the self-discipline to reach my full God-given potential by using all of my abilities of body, mind and spirit to the ultimate, for His glory and honor. I want the quality of my character to be one of excellence no matter what the situation.

**Poise:** I want my life to demonstrate confidence, self-esteem, composure, and self-control under any situation. Poise keeps me true to God and to myself. I won't try to be someone I am not. I choose to be authentic as I project coolness, calmness and stability. Poise is a choice. I want to choose to be poised in every situation.

**Perseverance:** My baptism gives me hope and my Christian hope fuels the strength to bear the pressures of daily living, resulting in a life of significance.

Courage + Excellence + Poise + Perseverance = Significant
Godly Life

God has demonstrated in my life's journey that He truly answers prayer. It would be foolish for me not to pray. There have been many principles He has taught me over the years about prayer. The key now is to act on them. I envision a radical way of living and a radical way of praying. My job as God's child is to be a mirror of Jesus. Each time I fail or sin the mirror gets cloudier and God's reflection grows dimmer. My heart's desire is for my life to reflect Jesus and His love to all I meet. My life is a gift from God to you who come after me, especially my family. I have had and you also still do have His promise:

God will do nothing but in answer to prayer. *John Wesley*

233

*For I know the plans I have for you, declares the LORD, plans to prosper you and not to harm you, plans to give you hope and a future* (Jeremiah 29:11).

### Personal Reflection Time

1. Is there anyone you need to forgive before walking into the future?

2. What characteristics do you want to reflect to others day after day for the rest of your life?

3. After reading the entire Section One containing fifty-two chapters what questions do you still have about prayer? Now see if they are answered in Section Two.

Nothing lies beyond the reach of prayer except that which lies outside the will of God.

The main lesson about prayer is just this: Do it!  *John Laidlaw*

## Section II

# PRAYER QUESTIONS

## "QUESTIONS I WOULD LIKE TO HAVE ANSWERED ABOUT PRAYER."

Seoul Foreign School sponsored Discovery Week during 1997-2001. Students from grades nine through twelve were given a variety of options to participate in local and international courses planned by SFS teachers. It was my privilege to organize and lead five days of prayer and meditation for four years. These annual challenges enabled me to clarify my own understanding and beliefs about prayer. Here are my answers to students' questions during those years. I have purposely tried to keep answers short. Supporting biblical passages are provided. In addition are quotes from authors of many books I have read on the topic of prayer. Their ideas relate to the questions, as well as providing additional insights into prayer. May these questions and answers stimulate your own answers and insights into prayer, help you to converse with God, and discover what can be expected when you do.

Nothing lies beyond the reach of prayer except that which lies outside the will of God.

### 1. How do you define prayer?

*My Answer*

It is the heart-to-heart conversation part of a loving relationship with God in words and thoughts. It is the way to talk to God. Jesus primarily communicates with us through the Bible. Prayer allows us to personally communicate with Him.

*Bible's Answer*

*Let us then approach the throne of grace with confidence, so that we may receive mercy and find grace to help us in our time of need* (Hebrews 4:16).

*Additional Answers*

1. Prayer is communion with God. Communion means communication that includes direct, close relationship. *Leith Anderson*
2. Prayer is our response to what God has done. *A. L. Barry*
3. First and foremost, prayer is talking to your Father in heaven and getting to know Him.... How do you develop and grow in your relationship with God? The same way you do with anyone else. You spend time together. *John Maxwell*
4. Praying is simply a two-way conversation between you and God... prayer is not our using of God; it more often puts us in a position where God can use us. *Billy Graham*
5. True prayer is God the Holy Spirit talking to God the Father in the name of God the Son, and the believer's heart is the prayer-room. *Samuel Zwemer*

6. Prayer is the chief way we express our love to God and the chief way we receive God's love for us. *C. Peter Wagner*
7. Complexly, the complete prayer is made up of four acts, four discrete parts, two of which are ours, two of which are God's... yet often all four acts occur in such swift succession that complete prayer is revealed as a single, unbroken event and so it is. It is communication.

> First, we speak,
> While second, God listens.
> Third, God speaks,
> While fourth, we listen. *Walter Wangerin, Jr.*

8. Prayer is submitting ourselves to and seeking God's will, trusting that His will for us is very good. *Rick Osborne*
9. Prayer is not a substitute for work, or merely preparation for work. It is work. *Ronald Dunn*
10. Prayer is the center of the Christian life. It is the only necessary thing (Luke 10:42). It is living with God here and now. *Henri J.M. Nouwen*
11. Prayer is work (Col. 4:12; Heb. 11:6)! *Edith Schaeffer*
12. Prayer is the key that unlocks all the storehouses of God's infinite grace and power. All that God is, and all that God has, is at the disposal of prayer. *R. A. Torrey*
13. Prayer is primarily learning to be still and listen to the voice of Jesus through His word, people and circumstances. *Tom Parrish*
14. Prayer is the Holy Spirit finding a desire in the heart of the Father and putting that desire into our hearts and then sending it back to heaven in the power of the cross. *Adrian Rogers*

*Your Answer*


## 2. Why do we pray?

*My Answer*

We are the dearly loved children of God. Our Creator and Savior deeply desires to hear what we have to say. He also commands us to pray, and He promises to hear and answer us. We invite God to be in our lives. We do not pray to impress God or inform Him.

*Bible's Answer*
*Devote yourselves to prayer, being watchful and thankful* (Colossians 4:2).

*Additional Answers*
1. Prayer's first goal isn't to change God's mind to do things my way. It is to change me to do things God's way. *Leith Anderson*
2. Prayer is not the cause of our relationship with God, but a result. Prayer does not produce faith, it flows from faith (Prov. 28:9). *A. L. Barry*
3. This invitation to pray is the cause of our prayers (Rom. 8:14-15). A. L. Barry
4. The chief object of prayer is to glorify the Lord Jesus. *Cynthia Heald*
5. It is Jesus who moves us to pray. *O. Hallesby*
6. Know that God wants our communion and encourages us to pray. *Cynthia Heald*
7. When we learn His purposes and make them our prayers, we are giving Him the opportunity to act. *S. D. Gordon*
8. We have been taught that we should pray, and we believe that the quality of our spiritual life is dependent in large part on our life of prayer. *Ronald Klug*
9. Prayer guides us in a middle way between two extremes-complete irresponsibility on the one hand ("Oh well, God's will be done."), and taking matters into our own hands on the other ("Modern man has come of age, so don't expect God to do anything for you. God helps those who help themselves.") Prayer is the middle way of doing things together with God. *Brad Long & Doug McMurry*
10. You must learn to call. Do not sit by yourself or lie on a couch, hanging and shaking your head. Do not destroy yourself with your own thoughts by worrying. Do not strive and struggle to free yourself, and do not brood over your wretchedness, suffering, and misery. Say to yourself: "Come on, you lazy bum;

down on your knees and lift your eyes and hands toward heaven!" Read a Psalm or the Our Father, call on God, and tearfully lay your troubles before Him... Here you learn that praying, reciting your troubles, and lifting up your hands are the sacrifice most pleasing to God. It is His desire and will that you lay your troubles before Him. He does not want you to multiply your troubles by burdening and torturing yourself. He wants you to be too weak to bear and overcome such troubles; He wants you to grow strong in Him. By His strength He is glorified in you. *Martin Luther* (LW 14, 60-61)

11. The Word generates prayer because when it speaks of God, we long to commune with Him. When it speaks of blessing, we long to praise Him. When it speaks of promise, we long to receive it. When it speaks of sin, it leads us to confess it. And when it speaks of hell, it leads us to pray for the lost. The Word of God causes prayer. *John MacArthur*

12. "Whenever God determines to do a great work, He first sets His people to pray." (C. H. Spurgeon) *John Maxwell*

13. Prayer begins with God's promise of mercy toward us... Because we know that He is merciful, we pray. *Andrew Steinmann*

14. Prayer is designed to help us transcend our problems and troubles by focusing on God Himself. *Andrew Steinmann*

15. Seventeen Reasons for Prayer

    1. God's repeated command to do so 1 Sam. 12:23; Rom.12:12; Col. 4:2;     1 Thess. 5:17; 1 Tim. 2:8
    2. The example of Christ     Heb. 5:7
    3. The example of the early church     Acts 1:14; 2:42; 6:4; 12:5
    4. The example of Paul     Acts 9:10-11; 16:25; 20:36; 21:5; Rom. 10:1
    5. Prayer defeats the Devil     Luke 22:32; 1 Pet. 4:7
    6. Prayer saves the sinner     Luke 18:13
    7. Prayer restores the backslider     James 5:16
    8. Prayer strengthens the saint     Jude 20

9. Prayer sends forth laborers      Matt. 9:38; Acts 13:2-3

10. Prayer heals the sick      James 5:13-15

11. Prayer glorifies God's name      Rev. 5:8; 8:2-4

12. Prayer accomplishes the impossible Matt. 21:22; Mark 9:14-29;      Acts 12:5-7; James 5:17-18.

13. Prayer gives good things      Ps. 102:7; Matt. 7:7-11

14. Prayer imparts wisdom      James 1:5

15. Prayer bestows peace      Phil 4:5-7

16. Prayer keeps one from sin      Matt. 26:41

17. Prayer reveals the will of God      Luke 11:9-10

*H.L. Willmington*

*Your Answer*

## 3. What's the purpose of prayer?

*My Answer*

People have felt the need to be more intimate with God. God gave us prayer as one of the ways to fill this special need. We are able to receive His blessings through prayer. Ultimately we are here to glorify God by doing His will. Prayer helps us obtain direction to do this.

*Bible's Answer*

*I keep asking that the God of our Lord Jesus Christ, the glorious Father, may give you the Spirit of wisdom and revelation, so that you may know Him better. I pray also that the eyes of your heart may be enlightened In order that you may know the hope to which He has called you, the riches of his glorious inheritance in the saints* (Ephesians 1:17-18).

*Additional Answers*

1. The underlying principle of prayer, which overwhelmed me, is that God desires to be intimate with me, and He wants this

relationship so much that He invites, encourages, and helps me to pray. *Cynthia Heald*

2. … the Bible's idea of prayer is that we may get to know God Himself. *Oswald Chambers*

3. When we learn His purposes and make them our prayers, we are giving Him the opportunity to act. *S. D. Gordon*

4. By our prayers we sensitize our own spirit and open the way for the power of God to be released wherever His children are in need. *Ronald Klug*

5. Jesus is the bridge to the Father. This is important for prayer, because Christian prayer is different from all other prayer. It grows from a personal love relationship with God. If prayer does not grow out of such a relationship with God, it is not Christian prayer. *Brad Long and Doug McMurry*

6. Let this be said as an exhortation to pray, that we may form that habit of praying with all diligence and earnestness. For next to the preaching of the Gospel (whereby God speaks with us and offers to give us all His grace and blessings) the highest and foremost work is indeed that we, in turn, speak with Him through prayer and receive from Him. Moreover, prayer is in truth highly necessary for us for we must, after all, achieve everything through prayer; to be able to keep what we have and to defend it against our enemies, the devil and the world. And whatever we are to obtain, we must work here in prayer. *Martin Luther* (LW 24, 389)

7. We pray to conform our hearts to His will, which is always to bless those who are obedient. *John MacArthur*

8. Prayer brings us into agreement with His will. *John MacArthur*

9. The focus of Biblical praying is the glory of God and the extension of His kingdom. *John MacArthur*

10. The glory of the Father must be the aim, the very soul and life of our prayer. *Andrew Murray*

11. God the Father wants to release the work of Jesus through your prayers. *Dutch Sheets*

12. Dad taught me to praise Him when something good happened, ask Him questions when I was confused, cry to Him when I was hurt, and thank Him when I was blessed. And any time we had

to make a decision, Dad's first words were always, "Let's just stop right now and pray about it." Dad and Mom taught me that the most effective and contented Christians made prayer a part of their lifestyles. *John Maxwell*
13. ...and we know that prayer is a chief instrument for releasing God's purposes into reality. *C. Peter Wagner*

*Your Answer*


## 4. Why is prayer important?

*My Answer*
Prayer helps a person reach his/her potential in serving God in the short time that one lives here on earth. We do not pray to God to impress Him. We do not pray to inform God but to invite God into our lives. He also commands us to pray.

*Bible's Answer*
*He will call upon me, and I will answer Him; I will be with Him in trouble, I will deliver Him and honor Him* (Psalm 91:15).
*Then Jesus told his disciples a parable to show them that they should always pray and not give up* (Luke 18:1).

*Additional Answers*
1. (I'm going to use an answer given to me by teacher Jack Moon of Seoul Foreign School and a few of his students he mentored: "We have been looking at sections of a book entitled *The Complete Works of E.M. Bounds on Prayer.* It has been motivating to say the least.")
   A. Prayer gives us perspective on life: it establishes our God's sovereignty and our need for Him; it places us in a position of humility.
   B. Prayer helps us set our priorities: in the tyranny of the urgent it allows us to weigh the importance of relationships and activities in terms of eternal significance.

C.  Prayer establishes our faith: by interceding specifically we allow God to act on our behalf confirming His reality in our lives.

D.  Prayer spurs us to action: it allows us to be aware of needs and sensitive to issues that demand our attention as well as God's.

E.  Prayer sustains us when little else can: God knows we are by nature ones who vacillate in our commitment; prayer confirms His faithfulness and spurs us on.

2.  (E.M.) Bounds considers prayer for pastors so important that he says, "Air is not more necessary to the lungs than prayer to the preacher." *C. Peter Wagner*

3.  There is a twofold use of prayer. One is to obtain strength and blessing for our own lives. The other is the higher and true glory of prayer ...intercession... *Andrew Murray*

4.  John Calvin was not exaggerating when he said that it is almost impossible to explain how necessary prayer really is. *C. Peter Wagner*

5.  Therefore let the man who fails to pray not imagine that he is a Christian. *Martin Luther* (SL 9, 1254)

6.  For indeed, the Christian Church on earth has no greater power or work... What matters is not the places or buildings where we assemble but unconquerable prayer alone, and our really praying together and offering it to God. *Martin Luther* (LW 44, 66)

7.  (Speaking of prayerful meditation on the Word) - Make room for such thoughts, listen in silence and under no circumstances obstruct them. The Holy Spirit Himself preaches here, and one word from His sermon is far better than a thousand of ours. Many times I have learned more from one prayer than I might have learned from much reading and speculation. *Martin Luther* (LW 43, 198)

8.  Everything starts from prayer. Without asking God for love, we cannot possess love, and still less are we able to give it to others. Just as people today are speaking so much about the poor, but they do not know or talk to the poor, we too cannot

talk so much about prayer and yet not know how to pray. Mother Teresa *(Jaya Chaliha and Edward LeJoly)*

9. Prayer is a joy. Prayer is the sunshine of God's love, prayer is hope of eternal happiness, prayer is the burning flame of God's love for you and for me. Let us pray for each other, for this is the best way to love one another. Mother Teresa *(Jaya Chaliha and Edward LeJoly)*

10. "Give me 100 preachers who fear nothing but sin and desire nothing but God, and I care not a straw whether they be clergy or laymen, such alone will shake the gates of hell and set up the kingdom of Heaven on earth. God does nothing but in answer to prayer." John Wesley *(John Maxwell)*

11. ...there is nothing we need to study and practice more than the art of praying. *Andrew Murray*

*Your Answer*


### 5. How powerful is prayer?

*My Answer*

Jesus answered the disciples' question as to why they couldn't do miracles: their faith was too small. Yes, prayer is powerful. There is no measuring stick for its limits. Prayer can do anything that God wants to do.

*Bible's Answer*

*He replied, "Because you have so little faith. I tell you the truth, if you have faith as small as a mustard seed, you can say to this mountain, 'Move from here to there,' and it will move. Nothing will be impossible for you"* (Matthew 17:20).

*Additional Answers*

1. "When you give your life to prayer, your name goes on a bulletin board in hell." (Dick Simmons) *Brad Long & Doug McMurry*

2. He wants them to understand that prayer is not to be selfish; it is the power through which blessing can come to others. *Andrew Murray*

3. The most under-utilized source of spiritual power in our churches today is intercession for Christian leaders. *C. Peter Wagner*

4. He usually answers <u>big</u>. His answers are much larger than our asking! God is not small! He is never stingy! Along with every answer He gives us more than the answer. Saul of Tarsus was both filled with the Holy Spirit and healed of blindness at his conversion, when he had simply prayed, "Lord, what wilt thou have me to do?" (Acts 9:6) *Armin Gesswein*

5. Christ never said the mountain would be removed. But He did promise that the mountain would move. Every mountain I've ever faced – and there have been a few – has moved when I prayed on the positive-thinking level. *Robert H. Schuller*

6. The power of prayer is like turning on a light as it illuminates God's purpose for our lives. There is no greater connection to knowing His will other than the word. *Thomas Kinkade*

*Your Answer*

## 6. If I have not prayed before, what could you recommend me to do?

*My Answer*

Commit your life to Christ by admitting you are sinful and cannot succeed without Him. God will welcome you. We pray to God, through Jesus, and in the Spirit. You don't have to think up something to say to your heavenly Father. Just be honest and talk about what's going on in your heart and life. Faith and prayer are two sides of a coin. One is not without the other. Faith opens the way for approaching God in prayer.

*Bible's Answer*
*And without faith it is impossible to please God, because anyone*
*who comes to Him must believe that He exists and that He rewards*
*those who earnestly seek Him* (Hebrews 11:6).

*Additional Answers*
1. How do we learn to pray? When Jesus was asked by His disciples how to pray, He did not teach them any methods or techniques. He said that we should speak to God as to our Father,
   a loving Father. Let us say this prayer and live it. Our Father...
   *Mother Teresa (Jaya Chaliha and Edward LeJoly)*
2. How do we learn to pray? By praying. It is very hard to pray if
   one does not know how. We must help ourselves to learn. Pray
   with absolute trust in God's loving care for you, and let Him fill
   you with joy that you may preach without preaching. *Mother
   Teresa (Jaya Chaliha and Edward LeJoly)*
3. To pray the prayer of faith we must, first of all, study the Word
   of God, especially the promises of God, and find out what the
   will of God is and build our prayers on the written promises of
   God. *R. A. Torrey*
4. And to learn of prayer is at the same time to learn faith. *Walter
   Wangerin, Jr.*
5. ... our preparation (for prayer) must be a genuine humility!
   *Walter Wangerin, Jr.*
6. Faith and prayer are so inter-linked that faith is prayer and
   prayer is faith. You cannot separate them. You could not have
   the one without the other. *A. Lindsay Glegg*

*Your Answer*


**7. To whom should we pray?**

*My Answer*
   Direct your prayers to the Triune God: Father, Son and Holy
Spirit. We should not pray to idols, saints or anything God has
created.

*Bible's Answer*

*We know also that the Son of God has come and has given us understanding, so that we may know Him who is true. And we are in Him who is true—even in his Son Jesus Christ. He is the true God and eternal life. Dear children, keep yourselves from idols* (1 John 5:20-21).

*Additional Answers*

1. The Scriptures also clearly indicate that only prayer offered to God through our Lord Jesus Christ is acceptable to God (John 14:6, 13-14). *A. L. Barry*

2. You are to look closely at this command and stress it, that you do not consider prayer an optional work and act as if it were no sin for you not to pray and as if it were enough that others pray. You should know that praying is earnestly enjoined, with the threat of God's supreme displeasure and punishment if it is neglected. It is enjoined just as well as the command that you should have no other gods and should not blaspheme and abuse God's name but should confess and preach, laud and praise it. He who does not do this should know that he is no Christian and does not belong in the Kingdom of God. *Martin Luther* (*What Luther Says* 2:1075, entry #3432)

3. Who is it to whom people pray? It did matter then, and it does matter now (I Kings 18:18-24). *Edith Schaeffer*

4. It is the prayer that is to God the Father, through Jesus Christ the Son, under the guidance and in the power of the Holy Spirit that God the Father answers. *R. A. Torrey*

*Your Answer*


## 8. Does God really listen?

*My Answer*

He has called you His beloved child. In Jesus He has demonstrated that He loves you. A loving Father listens to His child. Having heard you pray, He will answer. The Lord never referred to unanswered prayer. He taught that prayers were always answered and therefore He must listen.

*Bible's Answer*
*Before they call I will answer; while they are still speaking I will hear* (Isaiah 65:24).

*Additional Answers*
1. Not only does Jesus give us the invitation, but He himself makes a way for such praying…. *Walter Wangerin, Jr.*
2. … it is the listening of the Lord God which makes our mumble a prayer…. *Walter Wangerin, Jr.*
3. What you utter God hears. What God hears becomes through grace and compassion a prayer. *Walter Wangerin, Jr.*
4. We can commune through prayer with a God who is powerful, majestic, faithful, loving, holy, and gracious. *John MacArthur*
5. The first reason for not praying to a false god is that there is not another god who can hear and answer…There is one God… *Edith Schaeffer*

*Your Answer*


### 9. How can God hear everyone at the same time?

*My Answer*
When you walk into a dark room, flip a light switch, presto the room Is bathed in light. You flipped the switch, but are you the source of that light? Do you understand how it all works? I can't explain electricity. If I could understand everything about God, He would be too small. We are not told in the Bible how God can do all He is able to do. I'm glad I have a God who is beyond my comprehension.

*Bible's Answer*
*This is the confidence we have in approaching God: that if we ask anything according to His will, He hears us. And if we know that He*

*hears us—whatever we ask—we know that we have what we asked of Him* (1 John 5:14-15).

*"Can anyone hide in secret places so that I cannot see Him?" declares the LORD. "Do not I fill heaven and earth?" declares the LORD* (Jeremiah 23:24).

*Your Answer*

## 10. Can God understand all languages?

*My Answer*

God knows whatever language a person can speak. He even knows our heart's desire before it is expressed.

*Bible's Answer*
*Do not be like them, for your Father knows what you need before you ask Him* (Matthew 6:8).

*Your Answer*

## 11. When people are praying out loud, how should others listen?

*My Answer*

We should listen with concentration. We want to make it our own. I love Walter Wangerin, Jr.'s illustration for using other people's prayers: "It is no less a prayer if we take their words and make them our own, for one may build a beautiful house, then gives it away so that another one might live in it."

*Bible's Answer*
*May the words of my mouth and the meditation of my heart be pleasing in your sight, O Lord, my Rock and my Redeemer* (Psalm 19:14).

*Additional Answers*
1. Praying aloud increases that communion and fellowship and makes the prayer time profitable. *David Yonggi Cho*
2. I've discovered it helps to pray aloud. When prayer is totally thought, the mind is inclined to wander. It drifts from a dialogue with God to plans and programs, an argument, a discussion, something read... But if I address myself to God aloud, if I say the words aloud or in a whisper, my own ears keep order. *Majorie Holmes*

*Your Answer*

## 12. With the help of prayer, can a group of people become more harmonious?

*My Answer*
Yes, when people pray for one another they are bonded together with the love of Christ.

*Bible's Answer*
*They devoted themselves to the apostles' teaching and to the fellowship, to the breaking of bread and to prayer* (Acts 2:42).

*Additional Answers*
1. Nothing tends more to cement the hearts of Christians than praying together. *Brad Long & Doug McMurry*

*Your Answer*

## 13. What do you do if your heart isn't in prayer?

*My Answer*
Don't wait until a special feeling comes to spend time in prayer. It may never come. Let the feelings follow the Bible study with prayer time. Make the commitment to continue in prayer every day. That

commitment or habit controls the emotions that hinder prayer. Many people have the habit of brushing their teeth and combing their hair on a daily basis. The same type of commitment can be made to praying every day. A person misses God's blessings when s/he does not pray.

*Bible's Answer*
*You want something but don't get it. You kill and covet, but you cannot have what you want. You quarrel and fight. You do not have, because you do not ask God* (James 4:2).

*Additional Answers*
1. Though all Christians believe in Jesus Christ, most of them do not know how to pray effectively. *David Yonggi Cho*
2. I learned by heart the point that Archer Torrey once made in an interview: "I think the Lord wants me to make the point that intercession is hard work, not always exciting, but desperately important, and needs doing by faithful, regular intercessors." *Brad Long & Doug McMurry*
3. The size of our calling is not the important thing. More important by far is whether we take up the tools God has given us - prayer being chief among them - and go to work. *Brad Long & Doug McMurry*
4. I've learned that no one is born a prayer hero. They are shaped and refined on the practice field of life. *Dutch Sheets*
5. Trust in God leads to prayers that are able to bring all our concerns, pains, frustrations, and worries openly to God. *Andrew Steinmann*
6. Prayer will never rust for want of use. People will pray. *Walter Wangerin, Jr.*
7. ... the deepest desire behind our praying must be that the Lord be glorified by a manifestation for his sovereignty! *Walter Wangerin, Jr.*
8. Fall on your knees and grow there. There is no burden of the spirit but is lighter by kneeling under it. Prayer means not always talking to Him, but waiting before Him till the dust settles and the stream runs clear. *F.B. Meyer*

*Your Answer*

## 14. What does it mean to pray in the Spirit?

*My Answer*

When you become a believer in Christ you are filled with Holy Spirit. He will give you the power and energy you need to pray. The Holy Spirit and you are praying together. We pray to God – through Jesus – in the Spirit. When you pray does the Holy Spirit have you?

*Bible's Answer*

And pray in the Spirit on all occasions with all kinds of prayers and requests. With this in mind, be alert and always keep on praying for all the saints (Ephesians 6:18).

*Additional Answers*

1. When we receive Christ as Savior, He enters every life by virtue of the Holy Spirit... It is the Holy Spirit whom Christ has sent to live inside us... Rather than praying under our own influence, we are to pray under the influence of the Holy Spirit. *Fred A. Hartly*
2. We receive salvation as a gift that we can't earn and don't deserve, and the filling of the Holy Spirit is also a free gift... I tried desperately to pray and read the Word, yet it was dry and lifeless. Then a light went on, and I realized that being filled with the Spirit was not something I did to myself but some-thing God did to me. *Fred A. Hartly*
3. The evidence that should characterize and dominate everyone who has genuinely been filled with the Holy Spirit and is con-tinually being filled is a radical, all-consuming love for Jesus. *Fred A. Hartly*
4. No one has ever been filled with the Holy Spirit who didn't first believe he could be filled with the Holy Spirit. *A. W. Tozer*
5. The Holy Spirit is not only our teacher, our inspirer and our revealer, in prayer, but the power of our praying in measure and force is measured by the Spirit's power working in us, as the will and work of God, according to God's good pleasure... The secret of feeble praying everywhere is the lack of God's Spirit in His mightiness... Ask for the Holy Spirit – seek for the

Hoy Spirit – knock for the Holy Spirit. He is the Father's greatest gift for the child's greatest need. *E.M. Bounds*

6. All true prayer is exercised in the sphere of the Holy Spirit, motivated and empowered by Him and depends totally on Him. *Archie Parrish*

7. The greatest need of the church today is more of the presence and power of the Spirit of God. O that Christians were roused to greater earnestness and importunity in prayer! I believe that the greatest revival the church has ever seen would result. God help us, each one, to be faithful in doing our share. *D.L. Moody*

*Your Answer*

## 15. What if you just don't enjoy praying?

*My Answer*

Pray anyway. Spend time praising God for who He is. Dwell on the positive things of life and not on the negatives. When you come to Him, He will come to you. Lack of desire can be a sign of God's absence from the heart!

*Bible's Answer*

*Rejoice in the Lord always. I will say it again, Rejoice! Let your gentleness be evident to all. The Lord is near. Do not be anxious about anything, but in everything, by prayer and petition, with thanksgiving, present your requests to God. And the peace of God, which transcends all understanding, will guard your hearts and your minds in Christ Jesus. Finally, brothers, whatever is true, whatever is noble, whatever is right, whatever is pure, whatever is lovely, whatever is admirable—if anything is excellent or praiseworthy—think about such things (Philippians 4:4-8).*

*Additional Answers*

1. For Christians, the number one priority is prayer! Number two is prayer! And number three is PRAYER! *David Yonggi Cho*

2. We have the wonderful invitation that must be responded to; we may choose to pray. *Edith Schaeffer*
3. God's Word, the Scriptures, is the foundation upon which prayers are built. *Andrew Steinmann*

*Your Answer*

## 16. What does God do when you don't pray?

*My Answer*

He waits patiently. When God seems far away, we know who should move closer.

*Bible's Answer*

*But for that very reason I was shown mercy so that in me, the worst of sinners, Christ Jesus might display His unlimited patience as an example for those who would believe on Him and receive eternal life* (1 Timothy 1:16).

*The Lord is not slow in keeping His promise, as some understand slowness. He is patient with you, not wanting anyone to perish, but everyone to come to repentance* (2 Peter 3:9).

*Your Answer*

## 17. How can prayer help with my relationship with God?

*My Answer*

Many people keep a record of answers to their prayers. By doing so, they learn how personally God is involved in their lives, thus deepening their relationship with their Lord. Finally, it comes down to trusting God's promises to answer prayers. Trust perfected is prayer perfected.

*Bible's Answer*
*But you, dear friends, build yourselves up in your most holy faith and pray in the Holy Spirit (Jude 1:20).*

*Additional Answers*
1. First and foremost, prayer is talking to your Father in heaven and getting to know Him…. How do you develop and grow in your relationship with God? The same way you do with anyone else. You spend time together. *John Maxwell.*
2. When God is deaf to our prayers, it is we who are unable to hear or understand. *Andrew Steinmann*
3. The primary purpose of prayer is to bring us into such a life of communion with the Father that, by the power of the Spirit, we are increasingly conformed to the image of the Son. *Richard J. Foster*
4. I can take my telescope and look millions of miles into space, but I can lay my telescope aside, get down on my knees in earnest prayer and I can see more of Heaven and be closer to God than when I am assisted by all the telescopes and human powers on the face of the earth. *Isaac Newton*

*Your Answer*

## 18. Does it really help to pray?

*My Answer*
Without any doubt, it helps to talk to a Father who loves you.

*Bible's Answer*
*Therefore confess your sins to each other and pray for each other so that you may be healed. The prayer of a righteous man is powerful and effective (James 5:16).*

*Additional Answers*
1. How do we begin that love, that peace and hope? The family that prays together stays together; and if we stay together,

naturally we will love one another and want each other. I feel today we need to bring prayer back. Teach your children to pray, and pray with them. *Jaya Chaliha and Edward LeJoly.*

2. Yes, there are many secrets to our growth, but the most important secret is prayer. *David Yonggi Cho*

3. You can do more than prayer, after you have prayed. But you cannot do more than pray until you have prayed. (S. D. Gordon) *Cynthia Heald*

4. Prayer is striking the winning blow...service is gathering up the results. *Dutch Sheets*

5. Bounds said: God shapes the world by prayer. The more praying there is in the world the better the world will be, the mightier the forces against evil... The prayers of God's saints are the capital stock of heaven by which God carries on His great work upon earth. God conditions the very life and prosperity of His cause on prayer. *Dutch Sheets*

6. I have found that a tenacious endurance is often the key to victory in prayer. *Dutch Sheets*

7. "...intercessory prayer is one of the most important elements of successful ministry today." *C. Peter Wagner*

8. Let us abound in prayer. Nothing under heaven pays like prevailing prayer. He who has power in prayer has all things at his call. *Lance Wubbles*

*Your Answer*


## 19. Where is God when you pray?

*My Answer*

Wherever you are, God is listening to your prayers. God is everywhere. God is a spirit. Also, God is in heaven. Where is heaven? Heaven is to be in the presence of God.

*Bible's Answer*
*Praise the LORD, all His works everywhere in His dominion. Praise the LORD, O my soul* (Psalm 103:22).

*Your Answer*

## 20. What is the point of praying in tongues?

*My Answer*

   The gift of tongues was the special ability that God gave to certain members of the body of Christ (a) to speak to God in a language they have never learned and/or (b) to receive and communicate a message of God to his people through a divinely-anointed utterance in a language they have never learned. I know people who say they speak in tongues. They are my friends. However, I do not have this gift. Nothing in Scripture says a person has to have this gift to be saved.

*Bible's Answer*

*...to another miraculous powers, to another prophecy, to another distinguishing between spirits, to another speaking in different kinds of tongues, and to still another the interpretation of tongues* (1 Corinthians 12:10).

*For this reason anyone who speaks in a tongue should pray that he may interpret what he says. For if I pray in a tongue, my spirit prays, but my mind is unfruitful. So what shall I do? I will pray with my spirit, but I will also pray with my mind; I will sing with my spirit, but I will also sing with my mind. If you are praising God with your spirit, how can one who finds himself among those who do not understand say "Amen" to your thanksgiving, since he does not know what you are saying? You may be giving thanks well enough, but the other man is not edified. I thank God that I speak in tongues more than all of you. But in the church I would rather speak five intelligible words to instruct others than ten thousand words in a tongue* (1 Corinthians 14:13-19).

*Additional Answers*
   1. Well, after spending seven years studying this question and reading all sides of the issue that are in print, and after

spending many hours discussing it with Charismatics and trying to evaluate it from their perspective, I am convinced, beyond all reasonable doubt, that tongues ceased in the Apostolic Age nineteen hundred years ago. *John MacArthur*

2. Summing it up, Paul says, *"Let all things be done decently and in order"* (1Cor. 14:40). The word "decently" refers to harmony and beauty, and the word "order" refers to things being done in sequence. Well, since God is a god of harmony, beauty, and order, Paul says, "Let your assembling together manifest those characteristics of God." And as the church manifests God and is edified, it will also be multiplied. That's God's promise. *John MacArthur, Jr.*

*Your Answer*

## 21. What can prayer do for me spiritually and mentally?

*My Answer*
An active prayer life leads to a stronger and deeper faith. Additional blessings are mental calmness and peace.

*Bible's Answer*
*...because those who are led by the Spirit of God are sons of God. For you did not receive a spirit that makes you a slave again to fear, but you received the Spirit of sonship. And by Him we cry, "Abba, Father"* (Romans 8:14-15).

*Additional Answers*
1. Another major point of concern, valid today, is that prayer may become viewed as a good work that merits God's favor ... the only means by which we receive God's grace and forgiveness are obscured. If prayer becomes a way to earn God's grace, then the work of Christ on the cross is no longer the only way of salvation. *A. L. Barry*
2. God has created us to love and to be loved, and this is the beginning of prayer - to know that He loves me, that I have

been created for greater things. Mother Teresa *(Jaya Chaliha and Edward LeJoly)*

3.  What room may be furnished more beautifully than the heart where prayer is. For in that room God is. *Walter Wangerin, Jr.*
4.  Better an ounce of divine grace in prayer than a ton of worldly goods. *Lance Wubbles*

*Your Answer*

### 22. Is prayer really needed?

*My Answer*

God did not create puppets. Humans were made a little lower than God and above animals. We may choose to have God's blessing or not. Yes, God is sovereign. However, God does work through man. I believe man is to be God's link to authority and activity on earth. From creation on we were to be given dominion over the earth. He waits for man to ask for His help. Elijah's prayers really did produce rain and stopped it. This was not coincidental. Yes, prayer can change history. Yet, I don't completely understand God's sovereignty and the freedom to pray for His blessings. My mind is too small and God is too great. Finally, I think it comes back to the loving relationship between God and the person praying. God answers out of His infinite store of merciful love.

*Bible's Answer*
*Therefore confess your sins to each other and pray for each other so that you may be healed. The prayer of a righteous man is powerful and effective. Elijah was a man just like us. He prayed earnestly that it would not rain, and it did not rain on the land for three and a half years. Again he prayed, and the heavens gave rain, and the earth produced its crops* (James 5:16-18).

*Additional Answers*
1.  Those who wish to do good works in God's kingdom must learn to distinguish between doing works for God and doing the works

of God. To do the latter requires us to learn prayer, which pro-
duces ministries that have life. *Brad Long & Doug McMurry*
2. Hudson Taylor...prayed about things as if everything depended
on the praying... but worked also, as if everything depended on
the working. *Roger Steer*

*Your Answer*

## 23. What is the role of the Bible in prayer?

*My Answer*
   God works through His word to strengthen our faith. His Word
can also guide our prayer life. Try reading Scripture, and then pray
your own prayer for whatever person God brings to your mind concerning the topic of the Scripture read. It can and does become a
thrilling, stimulating, inspirational time.

*Bible's Answer*
(Pray this prayer of Paul's for someone you know. I have especially
prayed this prayer for our sons.)
*For this reason, since the day we heard about you, we have not
stopped praying for you and asking God to fill you with the knowledge of His will through all spiritual wisdom and understanding.
And we pray this in order that you may live a life worthy of the Lord
and may please Him in every way: bearing fruit in every good work,
growing in the knowledge of God, being strengthened with all
power according to His glorious might so that you may have great
endurance and patience, and joyfully giving thanks to the Father,
who has qualified you to share in the inheritance of the saints in
the kingdom of light. For He has rescued us from the dominion of
darkness and brought us into the kingdom of the Son He loves,
in whom we have redemption, the forgiveness of sins* (Colossians
1:9-14).

*Additional Answers*

1. If our prayers are not responses to Scripture—formed and shaped by Scripture—we will soon be drifting away in our own self-centered concerns and will find that our prayer lives are dry and empty. *A. L. Barry*

2. If we would feed the fire of our prayers with the fuel of God's Word, all our difficulties in prayer would disappear. *Cynthia Heald*

3. (Luther stresses the close connection between prayer and use of God's Word.) This is another good thing about prayer. If you use it and practice it and thus ponder the Word of His promise, your heart keeps getting stronger and firmer in its confidence, and finally gets much more than it would have otherwise. *Martin Luther* (LW 21, 233).

4. Prayer and the Word are inseparably linked together, for I can't pray intelligently about His plans unless I understand what His Word says. *John MacArthur*

5. If you can read the Word of God and not be driven to prayer, you're not listening to what you're reading. *John MacArthur*

6. The Word generates prayer, because when it speaks of God, we long to commune with Him. When it speaks of blessing, we long to praise Him. When it speaks of promise, we long to receive it. When it speaks of sin, it leads us to confess it. And when it speaks of hell, it leads us to pray for the lost. The Word of God causes prayer. *John MacArthur*

7. "To have prayed well is to have studied well" was a wise sentence of Luther's. *Lance Wubbles*

8. Here, let it be said, that no two things are more essential to a spirit-filled life than Bible-reading and secret prayer... The study of the Word and prayer go together, and where we find the one truly practiced, the other is sure to be seen in close alliance. *E.M. Bounds*

9. The Holy Spirit enables us to understand Scripture and turn it into proper prayer. Thus, prayer that is kingdom-focused will not be merely sentimental; it will be scriptural. *Archie Parrish*

*10.* A man may study because his brain is hungry for knowledge, even Bible knowledge. But he prays because his soul is hungry for God. *Leonard Ravenhill*

11. The mightier any is in the Word, the more mighty he will be in prayer. *William Gurnall*

*Your Answer*

### 24. When can we pray?

*My Answer*
Anytime! God doesn't have office hours.

*Bible's Answer*
*And pray in the Spirit on all occasions with all kinds of prayers and requests. With this in mind, be alert and always keep on praying for all the saints* (Ephesians 6:18).

*Additional Answers*
1. You can pray while you work. Work doesn't stop prayer and prayer doesn't stop work. It requires only that small raising of the mind to Him: I love you God. I trust you. I believe in you. I need you now. Small things like that. They are wonderful prayers. *Mother Teresa (Jaya Chaliha and Edward LeJoly)*

2. Love to pray. Feel often during the day the need for prayer and take the trouble to pray. *Mother Teresa (Jaya Chaliha and Edward LeJoly)*

3. It is well to let prayer be the first work in the early morning and the last work in the evening and to guard with care against the false, deceptive thoughts which say, wait a bit - after an hour I shall pray. First I must do this or that. For with such thoughts one gets from prayer into business matters, which then hold one captive. As a result, nothing comes of prayer on that day. *Martin Luther* (WA 38, 359)

4. You must learn to call. Do not sit by yourself or lie on a couch, hanging and shaking your head. Do not destroy yourself with

your own thoughts by worrying. Do not strive and struggle to free yourself, and do not brood on your wretchedness, suffering, and misery. Say to yourself: "Come on, you lazy bum; down on your knees and lift your eyes and hands toward heaven!" Read a Psalm or the Our Father, call on God, and tearfully lay your troubles before Him.... Here you learn that praying, reciting your troubles, and lifting up your hands are a sacrifice most pleasing to God. It is his desire and will that you lay your troubles before Him. He does not want you to multiply your troubles by burdening and torturing yourself. He wants youth to be too weak to bear and overcome such troubles; He wants you to grow strong in Him. By His strength He is glorified in you. *Martin Luther* (LW 14, 60-61)

5. If you really want to spend time praying, you give up something else, and just do it. *John Maxwell*

*Your Answer*


## 25. How long should prayers be?

*My Answer*

Any length is suitable that can be offered with a sincere heart and without vain repetition. Prayer is not an arithmetic process, not how eloquent, and not how logical. God wants a combination of fervency and sincerity with perseverance. One of the hardest lessons to learn is not to give up. The Bible does give us three time-guides for personal prayer. 1. "Pray without ceasing." 2. Daily quiet times similar to the life of David found in Psalm 5:31. 3. Extended times of prayer, like Jesus spending a whole night in prayer.

*Bible's Answer*
*And when you pray, do not keep on babbling like pagans, for they think they will be heard because of their many words* (Matthew 6:7).

*Additional Answers*

1. It's not the number of words you say or how eloquent you are that counts with God. As you speak, it is the sincerity of your words that matters to God. What is in your hearts gives your voices credibility. *John Maxwell*

2. A lack of endurance is one of the greatest causes of defeat, especially in prayer. *Dutch Sheets*

3. "How much time must I spend in prayer?" The thought that now possesses me is, "How much time may I spend in prayer without neglecting the other privileges and duties of life?" *R. A. Torrey*

4. A consensus among Christian leaders who have specialized in matters of prayer, devotional life, spirituality, and Christian discipleship is that there should be a time of prayer every day. *C. Peter Wagner*

5. Some brethren pray by the yard, but true prayer is measured by weight - not by length. A single groan before God may have more fullness of prayer in it than a fine oration of great length. *Lance Wubbles*

6. Korean pastors average 90 minutes a day in prayer. *C. Peter Wagner*

7. The time factor in prayer is very important. In the exercise of prayer God is not tied to our clocks... It takes time to know the mind of God, to shut out the material things of earth and to be wholly abandoned." *Hugh C. C. McCullough*

*Your Answer*


### 26. How often are you supposed to pray? How much praying should we actually do?

*My Answer*

Make prayer a regular daily habit. Never lose contact with God. The spirit of prayer is keeping so in tune with God so we can lift our hearts in request or praise anytime through the day.

*Bible's Answer*
*Be joyful always; pray continually; give thanks in all circumstances,*
*for this is God's will for you in Christ Jesus* (1 Thessalonians 5:17).

*Additional Answers*
1. Christian people are to develop a regular and faithful habit of prayer, a structured and ordered life of prayer, grounded in the Word. *A. L. Barry*
2. Everything starts with prayer. Love to pray - feel the need to pray often during the day, and take the trouble to pray. If you want to pray better, you must pray more. The more you pray the easier it becomes. Perfect prayer does not consist of many words but in the fervor of the desire which raises the heart to Jesus. *Mother Teresa (Jaya Chaliha and Edward LeJoly)*
3. In our finiteness there is one way of "multiplying" our time - prayer. *Edith Schaeffer*
4. God the Father wants to release the work of Jesus through your prayers. *Dutch Sheets*
5. This is what we need in prayer, an attitude of persistence. *Dutch Sheets*
6. I do not suppose that God has called many of us, if any of us, to spend seven or eight hours a day in prayer, but I am confident God has called most of us, if not everyone of us, to put more time into prayer than we now do. *R. A. Torrey*

*Your Answer*


### 27. How do you pray? Are there many different ways to pray?

*My Answer*
When Jesus taught His disciples to pray, He said, "Pray like this: 'Our Father....' Jesus told us to talk to our Father-God just as you talk to your human father, or the best example of a father that you know. When you start talking with God, you can say whatever you want to and say it in your own way. Ways to do it are almost endless. It is up to the creativity of the one who prays. God will listen.

*Bible's Answer*
*One day Jesus was praying in a certain place. When He finished, one of his disciples said to Him, "Lord, teach us to pray, just as John taught his disciples" (Luke 11:1).*

*Additional Answers*
1. Though all Christians believe in Jesus Christ, most of them do not know how to pray effectively. *David Yonggi Cho*
2. Free Style Prayer is like taking a walk freely without any planned place in mind to go. *David Yonggi Cho*
3. Topical Prayer...is like taking a walk with a certain destination in mind...has a specific goal for prayer. *David Yonggi Cho*
4. Positional Prayer...affirms our position with God as Creator... Redeemer ... Shepherd...Potter...Vine... Bridegroom... *David Yonggi Cho*
5. Ripple Prayer begins from the closest area - yourself first... those closest to you... your relatives and friends... goes on to another subject... your city or country... neighboring countries... world. *David Yonggi Cho*
6. The prayer of "Gethsemane"... is praying for more than one hour every day.... *David Yonggi Cho*
7. Trinity Lutheran Church of Lisle, Illinois, suggests the following three methods to be used by their members:

**The ACTS of Prayer**
- **A**doration - praising God for who He is and what He is.
- **C**onfession - agreeing with God about my inability to obey His commands.
- **T**hanksgiving - thanking God for what He has done in my life.
- **S**upplication - humbly asking God for his help in a specific area of my life.

**The Five Finger Prayer**
1. Thumb - Your thumb is closest to your heart. Pray for your family members.
2. Pointer - Your index finger is used for pointing. Pray for a friend or acquaintance who needs to be pointed to Jesus Christ.

3. Tall Man - Your third finger is the prayer for those in leadership positions.
4. Ring Finger - Your ring finger is the weakest. Pray for those who are weak: widows, orphans, the sick, the addicted.
5. Pinky - Your smallest finger is your pinky. Pray for yourself.

**Five steps to victory in Prayer**
1. *Praise* - Our Father who art in heaven, hallowed be Thy name. Praise God for who He is and what He has done.
2. *Cooperation* - Thy kingdom come, Thy will be done; on earth as it is in heaven. Pray for God's kingdom to come to your city, in your church, and in your family. Submit yourself to God's will for your life.
3. *Petition* - Give us this day our daily bread. Pray for specific concerns. Pray for the needs of other people. Pray for those who are ill.
4. *Forgiveness* - And forgive us our trespasses as we forgive those who trespass against us. Pray for God's forgiveness and cleansing in your life. Forgive those who have wronged you.
5. *Victory* - Lead us not into temptation; but deliver us from evil. For Thine is the kingdom and the power and the glory forever and ever. In Jesus' name claim victory over the attacks of Satan. Pray for God's continued protection from Satan's attacks. Ask that God be glorified in all you do.

*Your Answer*

## 28. What is the best way to ask God for something?

*My Answer*

A great fisherman will learn how to fish but even more he will know about the fish. He will know the right lures, the right time, the right places to fish. The same can be said for prayer. Learn all you can about prayer. Learn about God. Learn about God's conditions. Learn about God's desires for the world. Then you will begin to understand the best ways to ask God for something. I once read this: Begin your prayers with *humility* (helplessness). Continue your prayers with *trust* (faith). Conclude your prayers with *obedience* (righteousness).

*Bible's Answer*
*I write these things to you who believe in the name of the Son of God so that you may know that you have eternal life. This is the confidence we have in approaching God: that if we ask anything according to His will, He hears us. And if we know that He hears us—whatever we ask—we know that we have what we asked of Him* (1 John 5:13-15).

*Additional Answers*
1.  It is simple, yet so beautiful. Is this prayer fitting me? Can I say this prayer with an open heart, with a clean heart? Everything is there: God, myself, my neighbor. If I forgive them, I can pray. There are no complications, and yet we complicate our lives so much, by so many additions. *Mother Teresa (Jaya Chaliha and Edward LeJoly)*
2.  We learn to pray by praying, aided always by the Holy Spirit, who prays for us and with us and in us. *Ronald Klug*
3.  True intercessory prayer, then, is generated by God's Word, grounded in God's will, characterized by fervency, realized in self-denial, identified with God's people, and strengthened in confession. *John MacArthur*
4.  To be clothed with humility is to be clothed with a praying garment... If you would learn well the art of praying, then learn well the lesson of humility. *E.M. Bounds*
5.  So no one receives anything from God because of the quality of the prayer, but only because of God's goodness. *Charles Swindoll*

*Your Answer*

### 29. Is there actually a "formal prayer?"

*My Answer*
Jesus did give His disciples a pattern or formal prayer to follow. The "Lord's Prayer" is what we call it today. It is a model prayer to

show that an infinite variety of wants and requests can be compressed into a few humble words. It skips fancy words and asks directly for the things we need. Prayer does not just consist of form but of the Spirit.

*Bible's Answer*
*"And when you pray, do not be like the hypocrites, for they love to pray standing in the synagogues and on the street corners to be seen by men. I tell you the truth, they have received their reward in full. But when you pray, go into your room, close the door and pray to your Father, who is unseen. Then your Father, who sees what is done in secret, will reward you. And when you pray, do not keep on babbling like pagans, for they think they will be heard because of their many words. Do not be like them, for your Father knows what you need before you ask Him."*

*"'This, then, is how you should pray: 'Our Father in heaven, hallowed be your name, your kingdom come, your will be done on earth as it is in heaven. Give us today our daily bread. Forgive us our debts, as we also have forgiven our debtors. And lead us not into temptation, but deliver us from the evil one.'" (Matthew 6:5-13).*

*Additional Answers*
1. Another benefit is that as we use these great prayers, our own prayers are enriched and expanded. *Ronald Klug*
2. ... Written prayers can be helpful. The Lord's Prayer and the Psalms, for example, are good things to pray, and they help us think of ways to pray and things we can talk to God about. Some people memorize prayers and recite them at mealtimes or at bedtime. We just need to be careful that we really mean the words as we say them. If we say them over and over again, we may not pay attention to what we are saying. *Daryl J. Lucas*
3. The disciples went to our Lord and said, 'Lord, teach us to pray' (Luke 11:1). They did not ask Him how to pray; they weren't looking for lessons on technique or an outline for ritualistic prayer. They had obviously heard our Lord pray, and they wanted to learn how to pray on the same high level as He did.

This is a request many of us today need to make: "Lord, teach us to pray." *J. Vernon McGee*

*Your Answer*

### 30. Does a good prayer have any requirements?

*My Answer*
God listens to all prayers. The main requirement for answered prayer is still a relationship with Jesus. He asks for total allegiance (Deut. 6:4-5). The power of the Holy Spirit helps us to have good prayers (Rom. 8:26-27). Other qualifications for good prayers are the following: humility - Luke 18:13-14; boldness - 1 John 5:13-15; truthfulness - Ps. 145:18; persistence - Luke 18:7; and according to His will - 1 John 5:14.

*Bible's Answer*
*Hear, O Israel: The Lord our God, the Lord is one. Love the Lord your God with all your heart and with all your soul and with all your strength. (Deuteronomy 6:4-5)*

*The Lord is near to all who call on Him, to all who call on Him in truth* (Psalm 145:18).

*Additional Answers*
1. We might think of adoration and thanksgiving as songs in a major key and confession and supplication as in a minor key. *Ronald Klug*
2. It is more important to thank God for blessings received than to pray for them beforehand. *Ronald Klug*
3. In adoration we thank God for being God. In thanksgiving we thank Him for His gifts to us. *Ronald Klug*
4. A single thankful thought towards heaven is the most perfect of all prayers. *Ronald Klug*
5. Our prayers of thanksgiving can also flow over into concern for others. *Ronald Klug*

6. The heart of all true prayer is an awareness that we don't deserve to be in the presence of God. *John MacArthur*
7. Living in the Name of Christ is the secret of praying in the Name of Christ.... *Andrew Murray*
8. True prayers of confession are also prayers of repentance. *Andrew Steinmann*
9. Prayers of confession should be prayed because we trust God's promise of forgiveness.... But prayers for forgiveness can be confident that God will forgive because of who God is. *Andrew Steinmann*
10. We need to center our prayers on God's promises. *Andrew Steinmann*
11. After the Master had taught the lesson of prayer, He went out and became the lesson. *Walter Wangerin, Jr.*
12. Jesus' life and death deduce that it isn't words alone that make up a prayer. *Walter Wangerin, Jr.*
13. That is the highest learning, the most complete accomplishment of the fourth act of prayer. It is called obedience. Walter Wangerin, Jr.
14. When it comes to prayer, we do not want to feel duty bound. We want to pray as we feel drawn to it. *Richard J. Foster*

*Your Answer*


### 31. What are some major obstacles to a life of prayer? How do I know if I am praying correctly?

*My Answer*

The more you study God's will in Scripture the more you know. Also, one can use the self-examination items that can be obstacles, such as, unconfessed sin - Ps. 66:18; insincerity - Matt. 6:5; fleshly motive - James 4:3; unbelief - James 1:5-6; pride - Luke 18:10-14; refusing to forgive or to be forgiven - Matt. 5:23-24; refusing to submit to Biblical teaching Prov. 28:9; praying to be seen - Matt. 6:5,7.

*Bible's Answer*

*"Two men went up to the temple to pray, one a Pharisee and the other a tax collector. The Pharisee stood up and prayed about himself: 'God, I thank you that I am not like other men—robbers, evildoers, adulterers—or even like this tax collector. I fast twice a week and give a tenth of all I get.'*

*"But the tax collector stood at a distance. He would not even look up to heaven, but beat his breast and said, 'God, have mercy on me, a sinner.'*

*"I tell you that this man, rather than the other, went home justified before God. For everyone who exalts himself will be humbled, and he who humbles himself will be exalted"* (Luke 18:10-14).

*If I had cherished sin in my heart, the Lord would not have listened* (Psalm 66:18).

*"And when you pray, do not be like the hypocrites, for they love to pray standing in the synagogues and on the street corners to be seen by men. I tell you the truth; they have received their reward in full"* (Matthew 6:5).

*Dear friends, if our hearts do not condemn us, we have confidence before God and receive from Him anything we ask, because we obey His commands and do what pleases Him* (I John 3:21-22).

*Additional Answers*
1. Prayer is a difficult matter and hard work. It is far more difficult than preaching the Word or performing other official duties in the church. When we are preaching the Word, we are more passive than active; God is speaking through us, and our teaching is His work. But praying is very difficult work. This is the reason why it is also very rare. *Martin Luther* (WA 43, 381)
2. The prayer from a heart that is not right with God or with men will not succeed. *Andrew Murray*

3. For the veracity of what you say in prayer shall be revealed in how you live the prayer, and then your living and doing shall become a ceaseless praying unto the ultimate God, our Father. *Walter Wangerin, Jr.*
4. Nothing can set a barrier between a praying soul and its God. Lance Wubbles
5. One of Satan's chief objects is to get the believer to put away the weapon of all prayer. *Lance Wubbles*
6. If you have an earnest desire to pray well, you must learn how to obey well. If you have a desire to learn to pray, then you must have an earnest desire to learn how to do God's will. If you desire to pray to God, you must have a consuming desire to obey Him. *E.M. Bounds*

*Your Answer*


## 32. How can you tell if you shouldn't pray for something?

*My Answer*

Anything that Scripture reveals to be outside of God's will, should not be included in prayer. Prayers should conform to God's plan for this world and may clash with the desires of this world. We are to seek first the kingdom of God and His righteousness. What content is included in a prayer is a skill that can be learned by the person praying.

*Bible's Answer*

Not everyone who says to me, 'Lord, Lord,' will enter the kingdom of heaven, but only he who does the will of my Father who is in heaven (Matthew 7:21).

*Additional Answers*
1. In other words, it's a waste of time to ask God for anything that contradicts who He is or what He has said. *Leith Anderson*
2. To the man or woman who is acquainted with God and who knows how to pray, there is nothing remarkable in the answers

that come. They are sure of being heard, since they ask in accordance with what they know to be the mind and the will of God. *E.M. Bounds*

*Your Answer*


### 33. Where is a good place you can pray quietly?

*My Answer*
We may pray at any place, but naturally some places are better than others, as in a prayer chapel or church, out in nature, in the privacy of our bedroom (closet). In the Christian life, the place of prayer can be the "power room." We need a quiet place where we can be alone with God. Here is where we can gain our strength to face the challenges of the world.


*Bible's Answer*
*But when you pray, go into your room, close the door and pray to your Father, who is unseen. Then your Father, who sees what is done in secret, will reward you* (Matthew 6:6).


*Additional Answers*
1. One of their first lessons of our Lord in the school of prayer was: Not to be seen of men. *Cynthia Heald*
2. Nor is it a necessary part of this commandment that you have to go into a room and lock yourself in. Still, it is a good idea for a person to be alone when he intends to pray, so that he can pour out his prayer to God in a free and uninhibited manner, using words and gestures that he could not use if he were in human company. Although it is true that prayer can take place in the heart without any words or gestures, yet such things help in stirring up and enkindling the spirit even more; but in addition, the praying should continue in the heart without interruption. *Martin Luther* (WA 32, 415)

3. We cannot intercede fervently and very personally for people we do not know exist...prayer can be in secret, but we need to know people, personally or through others. *Edith Schaeffer*
4. John Dalrymple rightly observes, "The truth is that we only learn to pray all the time everywhere after we have resolutely set about praying some of the time somewhere." *Richard J. Foster*

*Your Answer*


## 34. What are some prayer topics we can pray about?

*My Answer*
Praising God - confession of sins - thanksgivings - our needs - intercession for others - needs of the world are just a few topics.

*Bible's Answer*
*But I tell you: Love your enemies and pray for those who persecute you* (Matthew 5:44).

*Additional Answers*
1. We are to pray not only for ourselves, but also for others, even including our enemies (Matt.5:44). *A. L. Barry*
1. I like Spurgeon's prayer, "Lord, if what I ask for does not please You, neither would it please me...." *Cynthia Heald*
2. ... pray for courage, direction, and willingness to be where He would have us be. *Edith Schaeffer*
3. The greatest need of foreign missions today is prayer. *R.A.Torrey*
4. All intercession is prayer, but not all prayer is intercession. *C. Peter Wagner*
5. "Intercession is the act of pleading by one who in God's sight has a right to do so in order to obtain mercy for one in need." *C. Peter Wagner*
6. My prayers for forgiveness, then, beg life for a drowning man and peace for his family. *Walter Wangerin, Jr.*

7. He invited you to ask of Him wisdom, and He says He will give it to you. Will you add to all your other sins the sin of thinking that God would lie? *Lance Wubbles*
8. C. S. Lewis counsels us to "lay before Him what is in us, not what ought to be in us." *Richard J. Foster*

*Your Answer*

## 35. How specific should one be in prayer?

*My Answer*

Bring all your problems big or small to the Lord in prayer. Leave the solutions up to Him.

*Bible's Answer*
Then he said, "Jesus, remember me when you come into your kingdom" (Luke 23:42).

*Additional Answers*
1. I challenge you to exceed in prayer the Master's bounty. *Lance Wubbles*
2. 8 Things to Pray For.

| | |
|---|---|
| 1. Ourselves | Gen. 24:12; Matt. 14:30; Luke 23:42 |
| 2. One another | James 5:16; Rom.1:9 |
| 3. Pastors | Eph. 6: 19-20; Col.4:3 |
| 4. Sick believers | James 5:14-15 |
| 5. Rulers | 1 Tim. 2:1-3 |
| 6. Our enemies | Matt. 5:44; Acts 7:59, 60 |
| 7. Israel | Ps. 122:6; Isa. 62:6 |
| 8. All men | 1 Tim. 2:1 |
| | H.L Willmington |

*Your Answer*

### 36. Is it necessary to pray for every little decision?

*My Answer*

No, but pray for wisdom to make wise choices with important decisions.

*Bible's Answer*

*Cast all your anxiety on Him because He cares for you* (1 Peter 5:7).

*So I say to you: Ask and it will be given to you; seek and you will find; knock and the door will be opened to you. For everyone who asks receives; he who seeks finds; and to him who knocks, the door will be opened* (Luke 11:9-10).

*Additional Answers*

1.  Yes, God listens to all prayers, no matter how big or small they are... That is what God wants us to do. The important question is what is on our mind? What do we care about? God will listen to any prayer if it is sincere. *Daryl J. Lucas*

*Your Answer*

### 37. How can I concentrate more on prayer?

*My Answer*

Set prayer as a priority in your life. Stop making excuses why you can't pray. Your attitude toward prayer is essential. If you still are having trouble, try speaking your prayer out loud. Try writing out your prayer or do prayer journaling. This has personally helped me.

*Bible's Answer*

*Delight yourself in the Lord and He will give you the desires of your heart* (Psalm 37:4).

*Additional Answers*
1. I learned and also took the proper stance of prayer before God himself— faithful trust and humility. Walter Wangerin, Jr.

*Your Answer*

### 38. Can you just picture the prayer, or do you have to be verbal?

*My Answer*
Yes, you can picture the prayer. The Holy Spirit will take it to the Lord.

*Bible's Answer*
*In the same way, the Spirit helps us in our weakness. We do not know what we ought to pray for, but the Spirit Himself intercedes for us with groans that words cannot express* (Romans 8:26).

*Additional Answers*
1. The Spirit comes to help us in weakness. For when we cannot choose words in order to pray properly, the Spirit expresses our plea in a way that could never be put into words, and God who knows everything in our hearts knows perfectly well what He means, and that the pleas of the saints expressed by the Spirit are according to the mind of God. Prayer is the work of the Holy Spirit. *Henri J. M. Nouwen*
2. Wondrously and mysteriously God moves from the periphery of our prayer experience to the center. *Richard J. Foster*
3. There are ideas in our hearts, there are wishes, there are aspirations, there are groanings, there are sighings that the world knows nothing about; but God knows them. So words are not always necessary. When we cannot express our feelings except in wordless groanings, God knows exactly what is happening."
- *D. Martyn Lloyd-Jones*

*Your Answer*

### 39. Is prayer in groups as important as praying individually?

*My Answer*
Both are important. It is good to come together and pray together as one body in Christ so we can support each other.

*Bible's Answer*
*They all joined together constantly in prayer, along with the women and Mary the mother of Jesus, and with his brothers* (Acts 1:14).

*They devoted themselves to the apostles' teaching and to the fellowship, to the breaking of bread and to prayer* (Acts 2:42).

*Again, I tell you that if two of you on earth agree about anything you ask for, it will be done for you by my Father in heaven. For where two or three come together in my name, there am I with them* (Matthew 18:19-20).

*Additional Answers*
1. The Bible calls Christians a "body." This means that they work best when they work together, like the different parts of a body. When believers pray together, they strengthen and encourage each other. They complement each other. And they can share prayer requests and pray for each other. It is powerful. *Daryl J. Luca*
2. Whatever the specific shape of our life together, it is of utmost importance that we pray in community. While prayer is often private and personal, it is never outside the reality of the worshiping, praying fellowship. In fact, we cannot sustain a life of prayer outside the community. Either we will give it up as futile, lacking the support and watchful care of others, or we will make it into a thing of our own. *Richard J. Foster*
3. If added power attends the united prayer of two or three, what mighty triumphs there will be when hundreds of thousands of consistent members of the Church are with one accord day by day making intercession for the extension of Christ's Kingdom. *John R. Mott*

4. According to my humble judgment, the greatest need of the present-day church is prayer. Prayer should be the vital breath of the church, but right now it is gasping for air. *J. Vernon McGee*

*Your Answer*


## 40. Is it true that God listens most if you pray for yourself, instead of another praying for you?

*My Answer*
He listens to all prayers of those who have a relationship with Him.

*Bible's Answer*
*My intercessor is my friend as my eyes pour out tears to God; on behalf of a man he pleads with God as a man pleads for his friend* (Job 16:20-21).

*I urge, then, first of all, that requests, prayers, intercession and thanksgiving be made for everyone* (1 Timothy 2:1).

*Your Answer*


## 41. Why do we pray in Jesus' name?

*My Answer*
Jesus himself taught His followers to pray in His name. This means praying with His approval, authority and His glory. We are asking God the Father to act upon our prayers because we come in the name of His Son, Jesus. It is only because He died for our sins that we can come to God. Praying in His name can also encourage me to pray according to Jesus' mission.

*Bible's Answer*
*And I will do whatever you ask in my name, so that the Son may bring glory to the Father. You may ask me for anything in my name, and I will do it* (John 14:13-14).

*In that day you will no longer ask me anything. I tell you the truth, my Father will give you whatever you ask in my name. Until now you have not asked for anything in my name. Ask and you will receive, and your joy will be complete* (John 16:23-24).

*Additional Answers*
1. Jesus isn't praying for us; He is interceding for us so we can pray. This is what is meant by asking "in His name." *Dutch Sheets*
2. To pray, then, in the name of Jesus Christ, means simply this: that we recognize that we have no claims whatever on God, that we have no merit whatsoever in His sight, and furthermore, that Jesus Christ has immeasurable claims on God, and has given us the right to draw near to God, not on the ground of our claims, but on the ground of His claims. *R. A. Torrey*
3. Prayer is the work of faith alone. No one, except a believer, can truly pray. Believers don't pray on their own merits, but in the name of the Son of God, in whom they were baptized. *Charles Swindoll*
4. Lord, help me to do great things as though they were little, since I do them with Your power; and little things as though they were great, since I do them in Your name. *Blaise Pascal*

*Your Answer*


### 42. Why do we end prayers with "Amen"?

*My Answer*
At the end of a prayer the "Amen" expresses the genuineness of the petition. The word amen means the same thing as "So let it be" or "It is true." It is a word that tells God we have said a prayer that we really meant. It shows that we believe God has heard our prayer

and will answer it in His perfect way. "Amen" reminds us that God always has everything under control, even the hard things.

*Bible's Answer*
*Praise be to the LORD, the God of Israel, from everlasting to ever-lasting. Let all the people say, "Amen!" Praise the LORD* (Psalm 106:48).

*He who testifies to these things says, "Yes, I am coming soon." Amen. Come, Lord Jesus.*
*The grace of the Lord Jesus be with God's people. Amen* (Revelation 22:20-21).

*Additional Answers*
1. Each time we pray the prayer Jesus taught, we can end with a strong, confident, and joy-filled "Amen." This is our statement of faith to our gracious heavenly Father who, because of Christ's work, accepts our prayers in spite of our sins. *Dean Hempelmann*
2. By not believing Him, we insult God's truthfulness, the same truthfulness we rely on when we pray. This is why we say the little word *Amen* at the end of our prayers. We use it to express our firm, heartfelt faith. It's like saying, "O God, I have no doubt that you will give me what I ask for in prayer." *Charles Swindoll*
3. For at the end of your prayers, you say Amen with heartfelt confidence and faith. When you say Amen, the prayer is sealed, and it will be certainly heard. Without this ending, neither the beginning nor the middle of the prayer will be of any benefit. *Charles Swindoll*

*Your Answer*

## 43. Is it true that God answers all prayers?

*My Answer*
   Yes, in one way or another God answers all of those with a relationship with Him. There are times when God chooses to answer

your prayers before you even pray them. There are times when He answers in a different way than you had prayed. There are times when He answers in such a way that goes far beyond what is expected. In other words, God thoroughly amazes us by giving more than we asked for! When God says YES, rejoice in Him. When God says WAIT, continue in Him. When God says NO, trust in Him.

Bible's Answer
*Before they call I will answer; while they are still speaking I will hear* (Isaiah 65:24).

*To keep me from becoming conceited because of these surpassingly great revelations, there was given me a thorn in my flesh, a messenger of Satan, to torment me. Three times I pleaded with the Lord to take it away from me. But He said to me, 'My grace is sufficient for you, for my power is made perfect in weakness.' Therefore I will boast all the more gladly about my weaknesses, so that Christ's power may rest on me* (2 Corinthians 12:7-9).

*'Call to me and I will answer you and tell you great and unsearchable things you do not know.'* (Jeremiah 33:3).

Additional Answers
1. God will answer our prayers in the way that He knows to be the best (Luke 18:1). *A. L. Barry*
2. God answers prayer any way He chooses. But we have seen four ways revealed in Scripture and personal experience: through nature, through angels, through the Holy Spirit, and through us. *Brad Long & Doug McMurry*
3. The Lord always answers, if we really pray through. This discovery really jolted me! It also straightened out some tangled thinking which, I found, came not from God's Word but from within myself by assuming and presuming. Answers! The Bible is loaded with them. It answers any need or problem we might have. If God is not answering, the problem is in our asking. *Armin Gesswein*

4. He usually answers yes. He accents the positive, because He is positive. God is not negative! His promises are not negative. Every word of His gives our faith the upward look! *Armin Gesswein*

*Your Answer*

## 44. How far in the future can I pray for an answer to my prayers?

*My answer*
The present day is ours, the future belongs to God. Prayer is the task and duty of each day. God tells us to leave tomorrow entirely with Him and not worry about it. This doesn't mean we can't pray for the future. Jesus did this in prayer for us in John 17:20. He included you and me in His prayer over two thousand years ago. I can pray for generations to come.

*Bible's Answer*
*My prayer is not for them* (disciples) *alone. I pray also for those who will believe in me through their message* (John 17:20).

*Additional Answers*
1. No amount of praying today will be enough to suffice for tomorrow's praying. *E.M. Bounds*

*Your Answer*

## 45. How come God sometimes doesn't answer prayer?

*My Answer*
No one person really knows why sometimes God doesn't answer prayers the way we think they should be. We have to trust that what He does is the best for us and for the rest of the world. Sometimes we just ask for the wrong thing. Sometimes our own

character would not give Him glory if we received what we asked to be given. Sometimes it is unconfessed sin hindering our prayer life.

*Bible's Answer*
*The Lord detests the sacrifice of the wicked, but the prayer of the upright pleases Him* (Proverbs 15:8).

*But your iniquities have separated you from your God; your sins have hidden His face from you, so that He will not hear* (Isaiah 59:2).

*Additional Answers*
1.  11 Hindrances to Prayer

| | |
|---|---|
| 1. Unconfessed sin | Ps. 66:18 |
| 2. Insincerity | Matt. 6:5 |
| 3. Carnal motives | James 4:3 |
| 4. Unbelief | James 1:5-6 |
| 5. Satanic activity | Dan. 10:10-13 |
| 6. Domestic problems | 1 Pet. 3:7 |
| 7. Pride | Luke 18: 10-14 |
| 8. Robbing God | Mal. 3:8-10 |
| 9. Refusing to submit to. Biblical teaching | Prov. 1:24-28; 28:9; Zech. 7: 11-14 |
| 10. Refusing to forgive or to be forgiven | Matt. 5:23-24; 6:12, 14 |
| 11. Refusing to help | Prov. 21:3; John 3:16-17 |
| | *H.L. Willmington* |

2.  He sorts and answers our prayers based on what is best for Him. What is best for God is in turn always best for us. *Leith Anderson*
3.  ... central issue of unanswered prayer - trusting God. *Leith Anderson*
4.  In everything He acts with a higher priority on achieving our good than on simply granting our prayers. *Leith Anderson*

5. If He's going to answer our prayers God wants to be even more than our partner. He expects to be the Chief Executive Officer of our lives. *Leith Anderson*

6. Remember - God is too wise to ever make a mistake and too kind to ever do anything cruel. *Leith Anderson*

7. He promises most plainly and positively to answer the prayers of those who believe on Jesus Christ, but never does He promise to answer the prayers of those who do not believe on Jesus Christ. *R. A. Torrey*

*Your Answer*

### 46. What do you do when it looks like none of your prayers are heard?

*My Answer*

Self-examination might be wise. If you can honestly say that what you find are not problems, then continue to persevere in your prayers.

*Bible's Answer*

*Then Jesus told His disciples a parable to show them that they should always pray and not give up. He said: "In a certain town there was a judge who neither feared God nor cared about men. And there was a widow in that town who kept coming to him with the plea, 'Grant me justice against my adversary.' For some time he refused. But finally he said to himself, 'Even though I don't fear God or care about men, yet because this widow keeps bothering me, I will see that she gets justice, so that she won't eventually wear me out with her coming!'And the Lord said, 'Listen to what the unjust judge says. And will not God bring about justice for His chosen ones, who cry out to Him day and night? Will He keep putting them off? I tell you, He will see that they get justice, and quickly. However, when the Son of Man comes, will He find faith on the earth? (Luke 18:1-8).*

*Additional Answers*
1. Sit and wait on the Lord... The key to receiving from God is learning to ask for the things that are already on His heart. *Fred A. Hartley III*
2. For me the greatest value in my lack of control was the intimate and ultimate awareness that I could not manage God. *Richard J. Foster*
3. Trust is how you put your spiritual life in neutral. Trust is confidence in the character of God. Firmly and deliberately you say, "I do not understand what God is doing or even where God is, but I know that He is out to do me good." This is trust. This is how to wait. *Richard J. Foster*

*Your Answer*


## 47. How long does it take to get a response from God?

*My Answer*
It may be a lifetime. The story is told that a man prayed all his life that a friend might become a believer. It didn't happen until the unbeliever came to the believer's funeral.

*Bible's Answer*
*Then He said to them, "suppose one of you has a friend, and he goes to him at midnight and says, 'Friend, lend me three loaves of bread, because a friend of mine on a journey has come to me, and I have nothing to set before him.'"*

*Then the one inside answers, "Don't bother me. The door is already locked, and my children are with me in bed. I can't get up and give you anything." I tell you, though he will not get up and give him the bread because he is his friend, yet because of the man's boldness he will get up and give him as much as he needs.*

*So I say to you: "Ask and it will be given to you; seek and you will find; knock and the door will be opened to you"* (Luke 11:5-9).

*Additional Answers*

1. Patience perseveres in prayer until the gift bestowed in heaven is seen on earth. *Andrew Murray*

2. A lack of endurance is one of the greatest causes of defeat, especially in prayer (Gal 6:9). *Dutch Sheets*

3. He often answers quickly! In almost every case in Scripture, whether it is the praying of a blind beggar, a leper, a Roman centurion, a woman in Syria, a close disciple or a far out prodigal — Jesus is ready to answer. There is no record of Jesus turning anyone down! *Armin Gesswein*

4. I myself have for twenty-nine years been waiting for an answer to prayer concerning a certain spiritual blessing...Thus, you see, dear reader, that while I have hundreds, yes, thousands of answers, year by year, I have also, like yourself and other believers, the trial of faith concerning certain matters. *George Mueller*

*Your Answer*

## 48. Can prayer really heal people?

*My Answer*

Prayer doesn't heal, but God does. He tells us to pray for the sick.

*Bible's Answer*

*Is any one of you sick? He should call the elders of the church to pray over him and anoint him with oil in the name of the Lord. And the prayer offered in faith will make the sick person well; the Lord will raise him up. If he has sinned, he will be forgiven (James 5:14-15).*

*Additional Answers*

1. Prayer could work as marvelous results today as it ever could, if the church would only betake itself to praying, real praying, prevailing prayer. *R. A. Torrey*

2. If we truly love people, we will desire for them far more than it is within our power to give them, and this will lead us to prayer. Intercession is a way of loving others... Normally the aid of prayer and the aid of medicine should be pursued at the same time and with equal vigor, for both are gifts from God. *Richard J. Foster*

3. The laying on of hands in itself does not heal the sick – it is Christ who heals the sick. The laying on of hands is a simple act of obedience that quickens our faith and gives God the opportunity to impart healing. *Richard J. Foster*

*Your Answer*

### 49. How can prayer help me to direct my life?

*My Answer*

God promises to answer prayer. He gives guidance for our lives in Scripture, through a vision and through other people that are consistent with Scripture. To know God's will for your life - KNOW THE BIBLE!

*Bible's Answer*
*Delight yourself in the Lord, and He will give you the desires of your heart* (Psalm 37:4).

*Additional Answers*
1. ...the power of prayer is not in the words I pray, the place I pray, the way I pray, how loud I pray or how long I pray, but in the One to Whom I pray." *Anne Murchison*

*Your Answer*

### 50. Can God really accomplish my prayer?

*My Answer*

God promises to answer prayer. It is not our words that give prayer power. The power is in God who listens. We have an awesome God that can accomplish anything consistent with His character and will.

*Bible's Answer*
*For no matter how many promises God has made, they are "Yes" in Christ. And so through Him the "Amen" is spoken by us to the glory of God* (2 Corinthians 1:20).

*Additional Answers*
1. To the faith that knows it gets what it asks for, prayer is not a work or a burden, but a joy and triumph. *Andrew Murray*
2. The greatest tragedy of life is not unanswered prayer, but unoffered prayer. I believe in definite prayer. Abraham prayed for Sodom. Moses interceded for the children of Israel. How often our prayers go all around the world, without real definite asking for anything! And often, when we do ask, we don't expect anything. Many people would be surprised if God did answer their prayers. *D.L. Moody*

*Your Answer*


**51. How do I know if God is talking to me?**

*My Answer*
It is God's nature to speak. Look at the creation story. He also tells us to listen. How do we do it? First of all we are to turn to Scripture and listen to the words that possess power and purpose. Then, when we think we have heard God talking somewhere else, we will return to the Bible and check it out. The Bible is the history book of how God spoke to people in the past. The more believers know the Bible thoroughly, the more we can hear the voice of God in all of creation. Does what is heard from God agree with Scripture, benefit others, and glorify Him?

*Bible's Answer*
*The watchman opens the gate for Him, and the sheep listen to His voice. He calls His own sheep by name and leads them out* (John 10:3).

*Additional Answers*
1. Hearing God makes sense only in the framework of living in the will of God. *Dallas Willard*
2. All who have much experience in the Way of Christ, however, will know that it is somehow right, when trying to hear what God is saying to an individual, to look to circumstances, the Bible, and inner impulses of the Spirit. And all will know that these three do somehow serve to correct each other. *Dallas Willard*

*Your Answer*

## 52. How do you know when your prayers are answered?

*My Answer*
    This answer comes from Rev. Bill Hybels: First, is the answer consistent with Scripture? Second, is it consistent with the gifts, talents and interest He has given me? Third, is it leading me into servanthood and not self-interests?

*Bible's Answer*
*'Call to me and I will answer you and tell you great and unsearchable things you do not know'* (Jeremiah 33:3).

*Additional Answers*
1. The Bible is the final and true dictionary by which we can accurately interpret God's speaking unto us. *Walter Wangerin, Jr.*

*Your Answer*

# Conclusion

Having answered these and many other questions about prayer, I have expanded my own understanding of prayer. This study has also clarified my beliefs about communicating with God.

What beliefs do I have about prayer? Here are a few of them in no particular order of preference.

**I believe...**
1. I can communicate directly with God.
2. I direct my prayers to the Triune God: Father, Son and Holy Spirit.
3. The Word of God causes me to pray.
4. Prayer does not earn me God's grace, Jesus has already earned it.
5. My prayers are a response to what God has done for me.
6. I can learn how to pray by studying God's word, praying, reading books on prayer, and by having personal Christian teachers or coaches.
7. When I don't feel like praying I can choose to pray anyway.
8. I do not have the gift of praying in tongues and that is okay.
9. Humility, trust, and obedience are important in receiving answers to prayer.
10. Jesus is the bridge to God the Father.
11. I should start everything with prayer.
12. God listens to my prayers.
13. I can communicate anytime and anywhere with God.

14. A person brings problems, concerns and desires to God, not the answers.
15. Perseverance is needed in prayer.
16. Prayer can be a regular daily habit.
17. I need a private place to pray.
18. I need a written prayer list to assist with my prayers.
19. Praising God and thanking God are different. Both are important.
20. Prayer may sometimes be hard work.
21. I should only pray for what is God's will.
22. I need the prayer support of other Christians.
23. Prayer is a privilege and not a problem.
24. My sin can hinder my prayer life.
25. God always answers my prayers.
26. Prayer changes me.
27. I pray to glorify God.
28. To pray is a joy.
29. I pray in and with the Holy Spirit.
30. I can pray anytime and anywhere.
31. I can have an ongoing conversation with God, my friend.
32. Prayer can be hard work.
33. Prayer is the most important thing I can do for others.
34. Praying by myself and with others are both important.
35. I want to pray in Jesus' name and say amen at the end of my prayers.

# SECTION III

# PRAYER INSIGHTS

# 1

# Pondering the Principles of Prayer

P rayer is a powerful resource for followers of the Lord Jesus Christ. Christ's payment for our sins empowers us with His righteousness in order to face the daily challenges in this evil world. As a Christian, I want to be aware of this; otherwise, I will never reach my God-given potential. My source of power lies in my relationship with God Himself.

The importance of God speaking to us through the means of His Word cannot be overstated: *"All Scripture is given by inspiration of God, and is profitable for doctrine, for reproof, for correction, for instruction in righteousness, that the man of God may be perfect, thoroughly furnished unto all good works"* (II Tim.3:l6-17). We want to get into the Word, and we want the Word to get into us.

Again, I would like to stress the importance of memorizing Scripture as I did in Section One - Chapter 9. I'm still trying to put verses to memory and relearn the ones I have forgotten even at this late stage of life. There is great value to memorization. I once heard a testimony of a Chinese pastor who memorized the book of Romans, not knowing that he would become a prisoner for the next 15 years by the Communist government. I am aware of people today who are putting God's Word to memory. I'll never forget the Reverend David Reed reciting from memory the whole book of

Philippians in a student chapel at Valley Lutheran High School in Saginaw, Michigan. I didn't understand what he was doing the first few minutes. I doubt that many of the students ever caught on to what was happening. He spoke it so smoothly.

God speaks to us through His Word and we speak to Him through prayer. As we study Scripture we see two kinds of prayer. One kind God accepts, and the other, He doesn't. Jesus illustrated this in a parable:

> "Two men went up into the temple to pray, the one a Pharisee, and the other a tax collector. The Pharisee stood up and prayed about himself: 'God, I thank you that I am not like other men – robbers, evildoers, adulterers – or even like this tax collector. I fast twice a week and give a tenth of all I get.' But the tax collector stood at a distance. He would not even look up to heaven, but beat his breast and said, 'God, have mercy on me, a sinner.' I tell you that this man, rather than the other, went home justified before God. For everyone who exalts himself will be humbled, and he who humbles himself will be exalted" (Luke 18:10-14).

The Pharisee's prayer was done only to impress others. The publican's prayer was a fervent prayer accepted by God. James also tells us that prayers offered by those who have God's approval are effective (James 5:16). Over the years I've watched Christians and non-Christians pray. They have represented many different cultural backgrounds, and I'm sure some prayers were effective fervent prayers and others were not. "Ripley's Believe It or Not!" provides two examples of the bizarre prayer extremes that people practice across the world:

- The people who worship themselves, Natives of Anjar, Bombay, pray only to their own reflection.
- Every YOGI of the Pagal sect repeats his prayers 5 times each day while standing on his head.

When all the considerations are weighed, I can't tell which Christian style is the most effective. Why? Prayer has to do with the heart. I can't judge that. From outward appearance, from the Christian people I am most familiar with, I would guess that generally the Korean Christians have the most sincerity. The African Christians have the most enthusiasm. The Indonesian Christians have the longest and most intense prayers. Other observers may have different opinions. We can talk a lot about prayer, but what counts is not the number of our prayers, nor the position, nor the volume, nor the content, but our intimacy with God. It is the character or relationship with Jesus, not what is said. Finally, only God knows the individual's relationship with Him. Each individual must examine where, how, and what to say, and above all, the motivation for coming to God's throne. Fortunately, Jesus intercedes for us in our feeble utterances, and the Holy Spirit gives us the right words to say when we falter.

We can all hone our skills with practice and grow in our understanding of how to improve our prayers. Periodically, I need to review and apply what I've learned on this topic. I ask myself some tough questions about how and why I'm praying. Am I closing the gap between what I say I believe and the way I act? Am I really praying for the people and situations I tell others that I am? The attempt here in these few closing pages is to present a format for self-evaluation of our individual prayer lives. It has helped me to take time to look at my past, examine what I believe about prayer, look where I want to be, and decide how to get there. It is important to live what we believe about prayer. Being true to who we are or being true to who God is may be difficult. My desire is to present some good questions to guide us into becoming Christians with strong prayer foundations. It now becomes an opportunity to formulate new goals for praying. I am certain you can meet this challenge! I am sure you will never, ever, regret looking at your prayer life from a new perspective.

What do you know for sure about prayer? What I believe about prayer was summarized at the end of Section Two. Prayer is powerful and empowering, as God and people say it is, therefore, I believe it is essential to learn everything possible about the subject. Being involved in sports all my entire life, I love to watch athletic skills and coaching strategy. Many sports fans I have known can tell every detail of games they played or about teams they have watched play. Now just how valuable are these statistics or stories? I have to admit they are enjoyable to recall, but they lack substance for real life. What if the Christian sports fan puts at least equal time and effort into learning about prayer as to reading the sports page of the local newspaper or the internet? There is no substitute for being well informed about prayer. What is the impact in conversing with God Almighty? What are the expectations and needs?

What questions do you still have about prayer? Author Jane Fryar shares this illustration about the Christian theologian Augustine who lived in the fifth century in her book called "I believe but I still have Questions:"

"...He was struggling to understand a stubborn doctrinal dilemma. As afternoon became evening, he still had not been able to untangle all the knots. So, he decided to take a walk along the beach.

"As he walked, he came upon a little boy. The boy had dug a hole in the sand and was running back and forth from the ocean to the hole with a cup.

"The theologian watched the boy return to the ocean again and again. Finally he asked, 'What are you doing, son?'

"Emptying the ocean into my hole, sir," the boy answered.

"Augustine chuckled, turned, and walked back up the beach. As he went, the truth began to dawn on him. He had spent his day doing the same thing – trying to contain an infinite God in his own finite mind."

Understanding what the Bible promises about prayer makes "emptying the ocean" look simple. We need an open mind as we look for answers to our questions on prayer.

# 2

# Self-Reflection on Prayer

E valuation of my prayer life began by trying to remember when I first started praying as a child. The prayer I hung on my wall was the first formal prayer I can remember. Your story will be different. Quickly recall some details and circumstances related to your early prayer life by answering the questions below. Go to Appendix B for a complete self-assessment.

- Were there particular people who helped you to learn to pray?
- Did you have any memorized prayer(s) that you prayed consistently when you were growing up?
- What role did prayer play in your family?
- Was prayer important in your family?
- On what occasions did you pray with a group?
- When did you start praying on a regular basis?
- What was your attitude towards praying?
- How has your attitude changed over your life?
- Where did you like to pray?
- Were there any special times you remember communicating with God?
- When did you lead a prayer in public for the first time?
- How did you feel about praying in public?

- Make a mental list of answers to prayers that you know for sure were very special experiences.
- What steps of growth have you taken in your prayer life?
- Do you see any pattern to your prayer life as you matured in your understanding of who Jesus is?
- Where do you currently rate yourself in your prayer life on a scale of one to ten, with one being poor and ten being superior?

Whenever I look at my present circumstance or level of praying, I consistently say to myself that I can do better than what I'm doing. However, I don't have to change my pattern. God will love me just the way I am, but how can I improve? I once read an old Chinese proverb that said that unless you change direction, you will arrive at where you are headed. What did you rate your current prayer life? 3? 5? 7? I'm still trying to reach a nine or ten. Where are you headed over the next years in your praying? Take a serious look and make a realistic appraisal of where you are and where you would like to be in the future. Think about these questions for forming a prayer plan for the future.

- On a scale of one to ten, where would you like to be in your prayer life?
- What are you doing presently that could be considered strengths in your prayer life?
- What are your weaknesses in your prayer life?

After thoroughly evaluating yourself begin to consider how to build on your strengths and improve on those areas where you believe you are weak. I find it helpful to share hopes and dreams with others. An accountability group can hold you to the vision that motivates your plans for praying.

# 3

# A Plan for Future Prayer

What do you wish to accomplish through your prayer life? How do you see God working in your life through prayer? I believe setting goals, objectives, or having a vision serves to inform and inspire. It clarifies purpose and gives direction. It helps to reflect the uniqueness of a person, to serve as a guide to strategy and action for improving your prayer life. I would hope that your vision for prayer is so powerful that it would shape your prayer life each day. For example, what prayer practices need to be improved and/or broadened? I collect possible practices that have a biblical basis from other authors and adapt them to my prayer life. Make your goals clear in time, space, method, and purpose. Answer these questions before writing your goals or objectives or vision:

- What are your most critical prayer concerns?
- What do you personally and passionately want to happen in your prayer life?
- What are your own needs and desires?
- Who will you pray for, and who will your prayer not include?
- What specific places or locations will I include in my prayers?
- How will you know if you have a successful prayer life? (example - journal)
- What are possible measures of success?

It is important to find the right direction for your unique prayer life. Answering questions helps me to formalize a direction. Identify future developments that may influence your life. What are your general plans and expectations for the future? All this information could guide your prayer life. Once a person has an understanding for the future, then a plan can be made, possible obstacles predicted, and prayer supporters recruited. A strong approach to praying can be achieved.

I believe the most valuable time I can spend for all people is to spend time in prayer for them. Therefore, writing a plan and how you will achieve it is of prime importance. There is a sense of urgency. Writing these statements is well within the capabilities of any average person. There is no correct form. Whatever fits a person is fine. No one else has to see it. Faithful Christians can be passive about their personal prayer lives, but they are missing immeasurable blessings. Someone said, "Never passively accept what is in your power to change." I want to improve my prayer life. I want to fit my vision to my needs. My middle name is "Flexible." Not really, but I'm open to new thoughts and risk taking without being foolish. I try to make a mental map for my future prayer life. It includes praise, confession, thanks, and supplications. However, I want to state it as clearly as possible and reach my potential as a man of God who prays. I believe I can improve my life of prayer. I want to make a plan for doing it.

Writing your approach to praying could be the biggest decision in your life - besides accepting Jesus as your Lord and Savior. Spending serious time in prayer can have global significance. The "enemy" is the devil. He is roaming around ready to devour every Christian. NOW is the time in your personal history when prayer is needed. It is at this point that prayer is critical. There is always a gap between what we know and what we do to carry out our plans to pray. Make the decision to transform your prayers to reach their potential in communicating with our great God. Write your answers to the questions in Appendix B with honesty. Summarize your current practices of prayer. Envision yourself praying in the future and God accomplishing a difference through you. Picture the impact! Be in tune with the power of God through prayer.

Prayer is one of the keys to living a faithful life to the glory of God. Changing prayer habits is not easy because the direction and outcomes are rarely clear when the journey starts. As a result we could spend time in endless analysis but never make progress. Nobody can steer a vehicle until it starts moving. In a similar way, God most often guides people who are moving, even slowly, tentatively, obediently, as best they know how. The finest way to know how to pray is to pray. If I could live my life over, I would have to say the same as my dying friend Louie Armbrecht said: "I would pray more." Does this just mean more time? No, I think Louie meant more time with additional quality, fervency, and without vain repetition.

This question keeps coming back to me: "How much praying time is enough?" Our God does not give us such a law as our Muslim friends. There are no requirements to pray a certain number of times a day to get into heaven. Instead, He gave us His Son who freed us from such laws. This gift from God has motivated me to keep in contact with God the Father, through His Son and by the power of the Holy Spirit. Does this mean I'll reach perfection in praying if I work hard enough? No, I'm just trying to improve my relationship with my Heavenly Father, the Master of the Universe. The joy of it all is the knowledge that God loves me regardless of the level of prayer my life has attained.

> Bless, Savior dear,
> Be always near.
> Keep me (and keep all)
> From evil, harm, and fear.
> Amen

# Memorizing Scripture On Prayer ABC...

**A**

*After He had sent the crowds away, He went up on the mountain by Himself to pray; and when it was evening, He was there alone.*
Matthew 14:23 New American Standard Bible (NASB)

**B**

*But I tell you: Love your enemies and pray for those who persecute you.*
Matthew 5:44 New International Version (NIV)

**C**

*Call to me and I will answer you, and I will tell you great and mighty things, which you do not know.*
Jeremiah 33:3 (NASB)

**D**

*Do not be anxious about anything, but in everything, by prayer and petition, with thanksgiving, present your requests to God.*
Philippians 4:6 (NIV)

**E**
*Enter His gates with a song of thanksgiving.*
*Come into His courtyards with a song of praise,*
*Give thanks to Him; praise His name.*
Psalms 100:4 God's Word (GW)

**F**
*First of all, then, I urge that entreaties and prayers, petitions and thanksgivings, be made on behalf of all men.*
1 Timothy 2:1 (NASB)

**G**
*GOD met me more than halfway; He freed me from my anxious fears.*
Psalm 34:4 The Message (MSG )

**H**
*Hear my prayer, O God; listen to the words of my mouth.*
Psalm 54:2 (NIV)

**I**
*I also tell you this: If two of you agree down here on earth concerning anything you ask, my Father in heaven will do it for you. For where two or three gather together because they are mine, I am there among them.*
Matthew 18:19-20 New Living Translation (NLT)

**J**
*Jabez cried out to the God of Israel, "Oh, that you would bless me and enlarge my territory! Let your hand be with me, and keep me from harm so that I will be free from pain." And God granted his request.*
1 Chronicles 4:10 (NIV)

**K**
*Keep on asking, and you will be given what you ask for. Keep on looking, and you will find. Keep on knocking, and the door will be*

*opened. For everyone who asks, receives. Everyone who seeks, finds. And the door is opened to everyone who knocks.*
Matthew 7:7-8 (NLT)

**L**
*Let your hope make you glad. Be patient in time of trouble and never stop praying.*
Romans 12:12 Contemporary English Version (CEV)

**M**
*Make this your common practice: Confess your sins to each other and pray for each other so that you can live together whole and healed. The prayer of a person living right with God is something powerful to be reckoned with.*
James 5:16 (MSG)

**N**
*Never give up praying. And when you pray, keep alert and be thankful.*
Colossians 4:2 (CEV)

**O**
*One who turns away his ear from hearing the law, even his prayer is an abomination.*
Proverbs 28:9 New King James Version (NKJV)

**P**
*Pray ye therefore to the Lord of the harvest, that He will send forth laborers into His harvest.* Matthew 9:38 King James Version (KJV)

**Q**
(Quiet Listening)
*About midnight Paul and Silas were praying and singing hymns to God, and the other prisoners were listening to them.*
Acts 16:25 (NIV)

**R**

*Rejoice always; pray without ceasing; give thanks in all circumstances for this is God's will in Christ Jesus.*
1 Thessalonians 5:16-18 (NASB)

**S**

*So let us come boldly to the throne of our gracious God. There we will receive His mercy, and we will find grace to help us when we need it.*
Hebrews 4:16 (NLT)

**T**

*Take delight in the Lord, and He will give you your heart's desires.*
Psalm 37:4 (NLT)

**U**

*Until now you have not asked for anything in my name. Ask and you will receive, and your joy will be complete.*
John 16:24 (NIV)

**V**

*Verily, verily I say unto you, whatsoever ye shall ask the Father in my name, He will give it to you.*
John 16:23b King James Version (KJV)

**W**

*When you pray, don't be like hypocrites. They like to stand in synagogues and on street corners to pray so that everyone can see them. I can guarantee this truth: That will be their only reward. When you pray, go to your room and close the door. Pray privately to your Father who is with you. Your Father sees what you do in private. He will reward you.*
Matthew 6:5-6 (GW)

**X**
**(Example of Jesus)**
*I have set you an example that you should do as I have done for you.*
John 13:15 (NIV)

**Y**
*You can ask for anything in my name, and I will do it, because the work of the Son brings glory to the Father. Yes, ask anything in my name, and I will do it!*
John 14:13-14 (NLT)

**Z**
**(This is the word of the Lord to Zerubbabel)**
*"Not by might nor by power, but by my Spirit," says the Lord Almighty.*
Zechariah 4:6 (NIV)

# Appendix B

# Self Guide to Better Praying

Note: Make these questions your questions. Answer whatever ones help you to improve your communications with God.

**Part I: What Have I Done In Prayer?**

1. Were there particular people who mentored me in how to pray?

2. Did I have any memorized prayer(s) that I prayed consistently when I was growing up?

3. What role did prayer play in my family? (Was it important? Meaningful? Neglected?)

4. On what occasions did I pray?

5. When did I start seriously praying?

6. What was my attitude towards praying?

7. How have my attitudes and actions towards praying changed during my life?

8. Where did I prefer to pray?

9. Were there any special times I remember talking with God?

10. When did I first lead a prayer in public?

11. How did I feel about praying in public?

12. Below is a list of answers to my prayers that I know were supernatural experiences.

13. What changes have I made in my prayer life?

14. Did any habits or patterns occur in my prayer life as I gained in understanding of who Jesus is?

## Part II: What Do I Believe About Prayer?

15. What Scripture passages guide my beliefs about prayer?

16. What are the major beliefs I hold about prayer?

## Part III: How Am I Presently Conducting My Prayer Life?

17. Where do I currently rate myself in my prayer life on a scale of one to ten, one being poor and ten being superior?

    1   2   3   4   5   6   7   8   9   10

18. Why do I rate myself at this level?

19. What am I doing presently that could be considered strengths in my prayer life?

20. What are weaknesses in my prayer life?

**Part IV: What Can I Include In My Vision?**

21. Where on the scale of one to ten would I like to be with my praying in one year?

    1    2    3    4    5    6    7    8    9    10

22. What do I personally and passionately want to happen in my prayer life?

23. What are my own needs and aspirations in prayer?

24. How can I make the most impact for God's kingdom through prayer?

25. Who are the most important people I want to include in my prayers?

26. What will specific groups of people will I include in my prayer life? (It is impossible to pray for everyone in the world every day.)

27. What specific places or locations will I include in my prayers? (It is impossible to pray for every place in the world.)

28. How far ahead should my prayer life focus? (today - weeks – months - years)

## Part V: What Plans Do I Have For My Prayer Life?

29. Try to write your ideal for praying in less than twenty-five words. Some people would call this a vision statement for personal prayer.

## Part VI: What Will Be The Strategy For My Prayer Life?

30. Try to write goals or objectives or a mission statement in less than twenty-five words. This would be how you plan to achieve your prayer vision,

## Part VII: How Can I Turn My Prayer Vision For My Life Into Action?

31. What is my plan of action to improve my prayer life?

32. How much of my financial income am I willing to invest in books and other possible resources?

33. Who can I ask to coach, train me and keep me accountable to working my plan?

34. When do I plan to begin my strategy?

## Part VIII: What Obstacles Do I Face?

35. What hinders my prayer life?

36. Who are the people on my prayer list making it difficult to pray for them?

37. What are the critical environmental problems affecting my praying?

38. What interruptions are keeping me from praying?

39. How do I overcome these problems?

## Part IX: How Will I Know When I'm Successful In Prayer?

40. How will I know if I have a successful prayer life?

41. What are possible measures of success?

## Part X: How Will I Celebrate When I'm Successful at Praying?

42. What will my response be when I know that God has answered my specific prayers?

# SCRIPTURE INDEX

## Old Testament

## New Testament

# Bibliography

- Alderfer, Kay Soder. *Adventures In Prayer.* Parish Life Press, 1977.
- Anderson, Leith. *When God Says No: Discovering the God of Hope behind the Answer We'd Rather Not Hear.* Minneapolis, Minnesota: Bethany House Publishers, 1996.
- Andrew, Brother and Al Janssen. *PRAYER: The Real Battle.* Plano, Texas: Dunham Books, 2009.
- Barry, A. L. *Let Us Pray: A Study of Prayer and the Devotional Life.* St. Louis: Concordia Publishing House, 1998.
- Bounds, E.M. *The Complete Works of E. M. Bounds on Prayer.* Grand Rapids, Michigan: Baker Books, 2005.
- Brooks, Keith L. *The Cream Book.* Chicago: Moody Press, 1938.
- Carmody, Denise & John. *Prayer in World Religions.* Maryknoll, New York: Orbis Books, 1990.
- Chaliha, Jaya and Edward LeJoly. *The Joy In Loving: A Guide to Daily Living With Mother Teresa.* New Delhi, India: Penguin Books Ltd., 1996.
- Christenson, Evelyn. *A Time to Pray God's Way.* Eugene, Oregon: Harvest House Publishers, 1996.
- Cho, David. *Patterns of Prayer.* Seoul, South Korea: Seoul Logos Co., Ltd., 1996.
- DeVries, John F. *Why Pray?* Grand Rapids, Michigan: Honor Books, 2005.
- Dunn, Ronald. *Don't just stand there... Pray Something!* Aylesbury, Bucks, England: Alpha, 1992.

- Foster, Richard J. *Prayer: Finding the Heart's True Home.* San Francisco, CA: Harper Collins Publishers, 1992.
- Friesen, Bob and Sandy. *Reach Around the World.* Wheaton: Victor Books, 1994.
- Gunter, Sylvia. *Prayer Portions.* Atlanta, GA: Sylvia Gunter, 1995.
- Hallesby, O. *Prayer.* Minneapolis MN: Augsburg Publishing House, 1959.
- Hartley, Fred A. III. *Prayer on Fire.* Colorado Springs, CO: Navpress, 2006.
- Hawthorne, Steve and Graham Kendrick. *Prayer-walking: Praying On-Site With Insight.* Orlando, FL: Creation House, 1993.
- Heald, Cynthia. *Becoming a Woman of Prayer.* Colorado Springs, CO: Navpress Publishing Group, 1996.
- Hinton, Jeanne. *A Year of Prayer.* Minneapolis, MN: Augsburg Fortess, 1995.
- Hoffmann, Oswald. *The Lord's Prayer.* San Francisco, CA: Harper & Row, Publishers, 1982.
- Hunt, Art. *Praying with The One You Love.* Sisters, Oregon: Multnomah Books, 1996.
- Jones, E. Stanley. *How to Pray.* Reston, VA: Intercessors for America. Reprint, 1945.
- Klug, Ronald. *My Prayer Journal.* St. Louis, MO: Concordia Publishing House, 1983.
- Long, Brad and Doug McMurry. *Prayer That Shapes the Future.* Grand Rapids, Michigan: Zondervan Publishing House, 1999.
- Lucas, Daryl; ed., Veerman, Dave; Galvin, Jim; Wilhoit, Jim; Osborne, Rick; Farrar, Jon; Crump, Lil. *107 Questions Children Ask about Prayer.* Wheaton, IL: Tyndale House Publishers, 1998.
- Luetje, Carolyn and Marcrander, Meg. *Face to Face with GOD in Your Home.* Minneapolis, MN: Augsberg Fortress, 1995.
- Luther, Martin. *What Luther says: an anthology.* Saint Louis, Mo: Concordia Publishing House, 1959.

- Luther, Martin. D. Martin Luthers *Werke: kritische Gesamtausgabe. Weimarer Ausgabe. Weimar*: H. Böhlaus Nachfolger, 1883.
- Luther, Martin. *Dr. Martin Luther Sämmtliche Schriften,* St. Louis, Mo: Concordia Publishing House, 1880-1910.
- MacArthur, John, J. *Elements of True Prayer.* Panorama City, CA: Word of Grace Communications, 1988.
- Maxwell, John. *Partners in Prayer.* Nashville, TN: Thomas Nelson, Inc., 1996.
- Moody Dwight L. *Prevailing Prayer.* Chicago, IL: Moody Press, N.D.
- Mueller, George, Answers To Prayer. Chicago, IL: Moody Press, N.D.
- Murray, Andrew. *Prayer Guide.* Springdale, PA: Whitaker House, 1995.
- Murray, Andrew. *With Christ in the School of Prayer.* Springdale, PA: Whisker House, 1981.
- Myers, Warren & Ruth. *31 Days of Prayer.* Sisters, Oregon: Multnomah Publishers, 1997.
- Nouwen, Henri J.M. *The Only Necessary Thing.* New York: the Crossroad Publishing Co., 1999.
- Osborne, Rick. *Teaching Your Child How to Pray.* Chicago, IL: Moody, 1997.
- Parrish, Archie. *Improve Your Prayer Life.* Atlanta, GA: Serve International, Inc., 2002.
- Pelikan, Jaroslav. Editor. *Luther, Martin. Works.* American ed. Saint Louis, Mo: Concordia Publishing House, 1955-1986.
- Prince, Derek. *Prayer and Fasting.* India: Derek Price Ministries, 1973.
- Raguse, Dan. *Prayer.* Loveland, Colorado: Group, 1990.
- Ripley Enterprises. *Ripley's Believe It or Not! The World of Religion.* Westwood, New Jersey: Fleming H. Revell Co., 1967.
- Rupp, Joyce. *Praying Our Goodbyes.* New York: Ivy Books, 1988.
- Savage, Robert C. *Pocket Prayers.* Wheaton, IL: Tyndale House Publishers, Inc., 1989.

- Schaeffer, Edith. *The Life of Prayer.* Wheaton, IL: Crossway Books, 1992.
- Schuller, Robert H. *Prayer: My Soul's Adventure with God.* Nashville, Tennessee: Thomas Nelson, Inc., 1995.
- Steer, Roger. *Hudson Taylor Lessons in Discipleship.* Crowborough, England: Monarch Publications, 1995.
- Stedman, Ray C. *Talking with My Father: Jesus teaches on prayer.* Grand Rapids, MI: Discovery House Publishers, 1997.
- Steinmann, Andrew. *Are My Prayers Falling on Deaf Ears?* Grand Rapids, MI: World Publishing, Inc., 1995.
- Swindoll, Charles R. *Growing Strong in the Seasons of Life.* Portland, Oregon: Multnomah Press, 1983.
- Tirabassi, Becky. *Let Prayer Change Your Life.* Nashville: Thomas Nelson Publishers, 1992.
- Torrey, R. A. *The Power of Prayer.* Grand Rapids, MI: Zondervan Publishing House, 1971.
- Vander Griend, Alvin J., Edith Bajema, John F. DeVries and David J. Deters. *Developing a PRAYER – CARE – SHARE Lifestyle.* Grand Rapids, MI: HOPE Ministries, 1999.
- Wagner, C. Peter. *Intercessory Prayer: How God Can Use Your Prayer To Move Heaven And Earth.* Ventura, California: Regal Books, 1996.
- Wangerin, Walter Jr. *Whole Prayer: Speaking and Listening to God.* Grand Rapids, MI: Zondervan Publishing House, 1998.
- Warden, Michael. *Teaching Teenagers to Pray.* Loveland, Colorado: Group, 1994.
- Water, Mark. *Prayer Made Easy.* Peabody, MS: Hendrickson Publishers, Inc., 1999.
- White, Tom. *City-Wide Prayer Movements: One Church, Many Congregations. Ann Arbor, Michigan: Vine Books, 2001.*
- Willard, Dallas. *Hearing God.* Downers Grove, Illinois: InterVarsity Press, 1999.
- Wilkins, John. *How I Pray.* Bandra, Mumbai: St. Pauls, 1993.
- Wilkinson, Bruce. *The Prayer of Jabez.* Sisters, Oregon: Multnomah Publishers, 2000.
- Willmington, H.L. Willmington's *Book of BIBLE LISTS.* Wheaton, Illinois: Tyndale House Publishers Inc., 1987.

- Winsor, James P. *The Privilege of Prayer.* St. Louis: Concordia Publishing House, 1994.
- Wubbels, Lance. Ed. *Charles Spurgeon on PRAYER.* Llynnwood, WA: Emerald Books, 1998.

# Author
## Rev. Robert W. Smith

B ob Smith is retired and living in Frankenmuth, Michigan. In the summer of 2006 he and his wife, Alice, returned from serving as educational missionaries located in Lippo Karawaci, Indonesia. They have also lived and worked in the United States, Hong Kong, Nigeria and South Korea. The Smiths have led mission trips to Russia, Hong Kong, Guatemala, the Philippines, India (Calcutta), and within Indonesia. In 2002 Bob was a member of a three-person team which surveyed Afghanistan for humanitarian reconstruction projects.

While teaching at St. Lorenz Lutheran School in Frankenmuth, Michigan Bob was honored as the director of the first non-public demonstration center by the USA's President's Council on Physical Fitness and Sports. In 1988 Concordia University, Chicago, Illinois, recognized his contributions to Christian education by selecting him as Alumnus of the Year. Bob was awarded a Servant Leader award by Seoul Foreign School in 2001. He has written articles for several publications and has authored a previous book on prayer (*Keep Me From Evil, Harm and Fear*, 2004). From 1991 to 1996 he served as Chaplain of Valley Lutheran High School in Saginaw, Michigan. Alice closed her teaching career with the honor of being selected as the Lutheran Education Association Distinguished International Lutheran Teacher in 2006.

Author's email: rwsmith316@yahoo.com